Fox Island Stories

Susan D. Roebuck

PAISLEY PUBLISHING

First edition. First printing June 2003. Printed and bound in
Anchorage, Alaska, United States of America on recycled paper.

Grateful acknowledgement is made to the following for granting
permission to reprint previously published and/or copyrighted
material:

Plattsburgh State Art Museum, Rockwell Kent Gallery and
Collection for excerpts from *Wilderness-A Journal of Quiet
Adventure in Alaska* by Rockwell Kent copyright © 1996.

Nor'westing, Inc. for an excerpt from *How To Cruise to
Alaska Without Rocking the Boat Too Much!*
by Walt Woodward copyright © 1985.

Although the author and publisher have made every effort to
ensure appropriate usage of ideas and quotations borrowed from
other authors and printed works, we assume no responsibility for
errors, inaccuracies, omissions or any inconsistency herein. Any
slights of people, places or organizations are unintentional.

ISBN: 0-922127-06-9
Library of Congress Control Number: 2002115696

Cover art © Dora Mae Holen
Illustrated by Susan D. Roebuck

For Mama and Daddy

CONTENTS

Preface

My father-in-law has a small farm in Oregon. He lives by a creek in the mountains, and raises pigs, cows, chickens, garlic and tomatoes. It's fairly idyllic. When Michael, my husband, and I learned that Dad's grandson and his grandson's new wife had come to live with him on the farm, I said, "So, it's like The Unbearable Lightness of Being." Michael said, "Yeah, the unedited version." I had to laugh.

Like any memoir, this story has been edited. I've changed almost everyone's name, including my own. Many people who are important to me are left out. There are some slight adjustments to the order of some events. Other events—like the five-week sailboat excursion Fletch and I made to the Carribean—are not included. And of course, many of the complications of daily life and life in general just didn't seem to move the story along. Everything that I left in, though, did happen, and it's all true.

Throughout this book, I refer to Native Americans as Indians. That's because it didn't feel authentic to change to a term that was different from the way I spoke during the time that this book covers.

Naturally, the guests who stayed at our lodge, my friends, and others in this book would tell the stories a different way. This writing comes from my own memories, and from my own perspective.

Writing is like hard-rock mining. When you're that kind of miner, you're often alone. You spend the morning drilling into the rock face, and setting your charge. By lunchtime you walk a respectable distance away and let it blow. Afterward, there might be enough of the day left to clear out the rubble and see if there's a silver vein. You make about six to eight feet of progress a day on your drift. But all the time you're enjoying yourself. This is *your* mine: you staked the claim, you hauled the timbers up the long rutted road, you know your mine's air, its every drift and stope. Then too, you're working hard at something you enjoy. And you're in the mountains, giant ponderosa pines waving in the breeze, their scent in the air, ravens in the blue sky above. But it's not just that. Being a miner is a good life, and the treasures you find are far more, and more varied, than precious metal.

My lake adores my mountain — well I know,
For I have watched it from its dawn-dream start,
Stilling its mirror to her splendid snow,
Framing her image in its trembling heart.

ROBERT SERVICE

~1~

From Desert to Sub-Arctic

Kevin's World

I watched him stride across my dirt yard in the evening sunlight to see Kyra. I stood beside the window in shadows, shifting the curtain to spy on him. His shadow whipped over me as he passed by and I watched him and his shadow glide over the dirt to Kyra's shady-dark portal. He knocked on her door and I saw her door open and him go in.

Kyra was blond, and bucktoothed just enough to make her naturally pink lips very full. She was German. And now, a widow. She always wore dresses or skirts and blouses. I remember a white embroidered one with a low-gathered peasant neck. Her difficulty with English made her seem to me both heroic and vulnerable. Maybe because just a month before, her husband, Kevin's brother, had shot himself in the head out on the West Mesa, beyond the outskirts of Albuquerque. Afterward, Kyra moved out of her in-laws' home and into an apartment across the yard from me near the University of New Mexico, in a part of town called the "student ghetto." Now Kevin was with her, believing it was his obligation.

Deuteronomy 25:5-10 says the duty of the dead husband's brother is to go unto his childless sister-in-law and bed her, take her as his wife, and bring up an heir named for his dead brother. Except for schoolbooks and the phone directory, the Bible was the single other book in his parents' ranch-style house, for all of Kevin's 21 years.

In spite of all this religion and being raised in a limited world, Kevin came across to me as a dark-eyed gypsy boy, tricky, perhaps. And playful. I believed then that he possessed some kind of extraordinary knowledge. He was innocent, not sophisticated. I loved this and much more about him. We had met in the fall when aspen groves on the Sandias just east of Albuquerque rimmed the mountain's blue crest with bright yellow; when at any time it might snow up there. It could be warm during the day and frosty in the night for a few weeks of glorious Indian summer. He delivered blueprints to my mother's office downtown and had seen me there one day, and asked her for my number. She told me later that she wouldn't give it to him for weeks — she saw him and his qualities like she knew I would, and knew once we met, that'd be that. But he was appealing and earnest and she finally gave in. We had our first date at Manny's Restaurant on Central Avenue and with that, he drove his old white pick-up truck into my college world, with his black hair, dark eyes, and an exuberant curiosity about life. His neighborhood on the West Mesa lay on the edge of Albuquerque, with seventy miles of empty high desert between his house and my own childhood home in Grants. I learned that he'd had a horse named Honcho and he played guitar.

Kevin had chosen work instead of college and did welding on the side. In our maroon booth across from each other at Manny's, awkward, breathless with attraction, we talked until the waitress began vacuuming. We stepped outside, leaving the noise of the vacuum for the quieter whoosh of traffic on Central Avenue. Kevin told me that he still lived at home with his parents, and out of respect for them he always tried to be home by midnight. He drove me home and outside my door he kissed me, running late for his self-imposed curfew.

Just before sunrise he came to my door. We spent that day together, pushing aside plans, unwilling to be apart. And then he stayed the night. When he didn't return home until mid-morning the following day, his Baptist mother, her gray hair pulled back at the temples and long down her back, her hands in yellow dishwashing gloves, warned him in her kitchen: "You're playing with fire, Kevin, you're playing with FIRE! I don't know *what* kind of girl would let a boy she just met spend the night with her. Kevin, you should *stay away from that girl!*" Kevin, in faded jeans, boots, and a black shirt, sat at the table while she washed dishes. Their parakeet made a racket in its cage. He comforted her with a soft voice.

"We just slept together, Mom. I only slept with her—that's all," and he reminded her about two people in a certain verse and line in the Bible who slept together without sex.

"And Mom, please don't call her 'that girl.' Her name is Susannah."

He told the truth—we didn't make love that first night, nor for weeks after this conversation with his mom. He had powerful self-control and deep devotion to his beliefs. The strength of Kevin's religious devotion made me love him all the more. When we did finally make love, it intensified our lives unbearably, put us together in our own private world and set us apart from all others. It created for us a bond we believed no others could experience. For Kevin, there was a euphoric conviction that somehow, God must surely approve; this was God's plan for him. When he felt this way he was playful, full of light, at ease, like a child. This alternated, though, with abject feelings of guilt, of being a sinner, of needing to repent.

I witnessed Kevin's sways into extremes of thought with unsettling concern.

Kevin and I were a lot alike—except for the religion. I could hardly understand all the new viewpoints he brought into my life, because I was only 21, and raised without religious influence. Well, that can't be quite true, because religion influences everyone. When I was 12 and living in Wyoming, my friend Kimberly and I got on the Baptist bus that came down our road one summer morning, just for something to do. We bumped along in the little white bus on the dirt road to the little white church. Inside, the preacher talked a long time, and then after a certain amount of talking he said a prayer. I tried to grasp what he was talking about, but found it impossible. Then he looked out at us and intoned, first quietly, and then with increasing volume, "If anyone here today, young or old, rich or poor, wants Jesus—oh, dear Jesus—in their heart, today, come up now! His arms are open to you! Come and be SAVED! *Praise* the Lord."

We looked at each other, two scrawny bareback riders, and Kimberly whispered, "Do you want to?" So we shuffled forward and the congregation quietly called out, "Thank you, Lord. Thank you, Jesus." It felt sort of strange the way everyone smiled at us and gave us hugs and shook our hands afterward. After the church bus brought us home we headed straight for the corral and spent the rest of that day like most other summer days—on horseback, out along the river and into the hills. We both had sorrel cowponies. Hers was named Sharlo and mine Trinket. Sharlo and Trinket both loved to gallop flat-out, every chance they got. Kimberly and I sometimes raced each other, and occasionally challenged neighborhood kids and their horses.

Anyway, it took a lot of deep thinking on my part, once I met Kevin, to try to understand his religious perspective. I never did really get it. He thought in this way: "The world" was one place, and there was somehow another place, or realm, too, and this realm had a whole different set of natural laws, a different structure, a different way of speaking our own familiar language, even, from the world I was used to. I asked him if "the world" was the earth, and the other place was the rest of the universe, and he said he didn't think so. He said he thought the rest of the universe was probably "of the world," as well. To me everything was in the universe. It was infinite, wonderful and mysterious, and I was glad to be in it. How could there be more? But I did see that he wasn't prepared to flourish easily here in the world. It was going to be a struggle. "The world" made him feel guilt, caused confusion, and sometimes anguish. Though we had many days in the sun, his recurring difficulties adjusting to life outside his parents' home created many a storm for us.

Once, he told me he had been called to "go West." He spent that bright day while I was at school giving away everything he owned. His old white truck. His acetylene tanks and welding helmet and gloves. Started walking. He threw the watch I'd given him for his birthday into the Rio Grande. Probably as he walked along he had thought about keeping it, and the thought shamed him for being a worldly thought and by that time he was nearing the river. So into the river went the watch in an arc of sunlight-on-metal and he felt lifted up. He walked up from the river to Interstate 40, which had replaced Old 66 a few years before, and started hitchhiking. When I came home from school and he was gone (gone for good, for all I knew), I drove into the mountains north of Placitas. I tried to have enough courage to drive off a cliff. But I merely parked near the edge for a while, cold gusts of night air shuddering the car, blasting through the open windows, and then went home to my apartment in Albuquerque. Before dawn, Kevin slipped into bed with me, cold-limbed, and as lost as ever. I held him to me. He was my inspiration, tormentor, and child in need all in one. I stared into the darkness hating to think what L.A. would have done to him. But no one had stopped to pick him up. He *had* done a lot of thinking and, I guess, talking to God out there under the stars on

Interstate 40 with the semi trucks roaring by.

Kevin started bringing homeless people to my apartment next, cooking them meals, giving them clothing and books. And on the city bus or in a neighborhood park he would meet strangers who held church meetings in their homes. One time I went with him, into someone's living room in the South Valley, and the people spoke in tongues— "SHIM in a ma kye, Oh! SHIM in a ma kye!" — and waved their arms, rolled their eyes.

Just over a month after Kevin's calling to go west, his brother died. Kevin and his father had been the ones to find him in a sandy arroyo a mile or two from their home. Kevin felt not only grief within himself, but he absorbed through empathy what his sister-in-law Kyra endured. We visited her often. My boisterous friend Katy moved to Albuquerque from Grants and we all went places together, four twenty-one-year-olds. Katy moved into a single-wide in the South Valley, which Kyra helped her fix up with white lace curtains and a German coo-coo clock on the dark paneling. Over the weeksKyra seemed to be recovering. She was managing. But Kevin's confusion worsened.

He sat down heavily on my couch, put his head in his hands, his black hair falling between his fingers, his dark eyelashes wet with tears. I sat beside him. He said, "Susannah, poor Kyra! She's so lonely. She's all alone here, without even her own mom and dad!"

"I know. But I think she's gonna be all right, Kevin. It just takes time. And she's not alone, she's got us, and Katy, and your parents. She's just like a real daughter to your mom and dad."

"She needs a man, Susannah. Don't you think she needs a man, do you think that would help her?" This took me by surprise, which I tried not to show.

"Oh, she will in time. But she needs time. I don't think I'd want another relationship so soon. She mentioned going back to Germany for a visit," I said. "That might be good for her—to be away from here."

"I don't know. Susannah, the Bible says a brother is responsible for his brother's widow. It says I'm *responsible* for her. Do you know, it says a brother should become his brother's widow's husband?"

"It does?"

He looked up toward the ceiling, sighed deeply, pausing, then looked back at me, directly. "I think Kyra needs me. I don't know what to do!" I didn't know what to say, exactly. But then he stood up. "I'm going to see her."

I peeked out behind my curtain and watched his feet puff up clouds of dust on his way to her. He came back before long and told me she had cried and he just held her. But his line of thought could not be altered through either reason or emotion on my part. He was kept on high alert by the role of salvation he imagined he could play in Kyra's life. This is not to say that I didn't think, in my uncharitable moments, or my less optimistic moments, that all this was because he wanted to get into bed with Kyra, to put his hands on her smooth warm skin and kiss her mouth and neck. Two mornings later, I walked along Harvard Street to my classes, knowing that as soon as I left, he would go to her. It was too much. I kicked a rock. It hit a dirt bike parked on someone's weedy yard. A cat ran around a bush and disappeared. A small flock of birds flew away as I approached. I crossed Central Avenue onto the campus. The morning sun shown off the windows of the Student Center. The Sandia Mountains made a pretty blue backdrop to the east of the city. I walked into my first class of the day, but couldn't pay attention and left after ten minutes. Outside the classroom door I felt lost for a few moments, but then I saw the blue Sandias, and knew where I needed to be.

Forty-five minutes later, in Placitas at my parents' house, my mother said, "What are you doing at home, Susie, don't you have school today?"

"Yeah, but I couldn't concentrate. I just want to go for a ride." "Go for a ride" was in my dogs' vocabulary. They leapt to their feet, capering, an excessive counterpoint to my own feelings.

"What's wrong?"

I sighed, struggling for control. "Kevin—" and then just looked out the window, my eyes filling, embarrassing me.

"What's wrong, honey?"

"I just need to go for a ride." I could see Trinket in her corral out there. "Is there some food I could take?"

All day I rode, to my favorite places—the wide, sandy arroyo where the dogs chased jackrabbits up side arroyos, the tiny spring far up the mountain in a steep canyon. I tied Trinket and let her graze on the mountain grass while I sat by the water on a boulder, looking first at the reflection on the surface of the water, then through the reflection, into the amber-clear pool with its secret life.

There was nothing else to do but get as far away as possible. I decided to fly to Alaska the day following my last final exam. I could stay with my sister who had lived there since '76.

Final exams approached. His mouth next to my ear, Kevin whispered, "Please stay, please don't go, Susannah, please stay…" But to afford a plane ticket, I had already sold Gemini, my ornery young gray horse. Nothing would ever make me desperate enough to sell Trinket. The anticipation of adventure gave me strength. Kevin alternated between me and Kyra, taking comfort when he could. I barely managed to repel surges of hope for us. If I had not already set the whole plan in motion, Kevin and I could have stayed in some kind of heartbroken limbo for who knows how long. My mother said, "I had a feeling about that boy…"

Alaska

The big spruce log in Anne and Neal's front yard lay soggy and cushioned with moss. I sat on it playing with their tabby kitten and looking around. What a strange place I had come to! Unlike New Mexico's vibrancy, Alaska was cool shades of green, white, and blue. Here in the woods, suspended moisture softened contours. Anne and Neal lived on "the Hillside" in Anchorage, on the foothills of the Chugach Mountains at an altitude just below the scrub spruce zone, which is just below the treeless alpine tundra. Tree level that far north is low—only about fifteen hundred feet. Not just the Chugach, but even some of their *foothills* are above tree level, and people live in neighborhoods up there above the trees. In New Mexico, tree level was at an alpine region not often visited by humans. It was disorienting to see city suburbs above tree level.

At that time of year in Alaska, the earth's rotation brings dawn, day, twilight—and then dawn again. No darkness or stars, but a pale and delicate crescent moon that hangs low to the horizon. During the midnight hours, not just the sky, but the light itself is velvety blue, like a blue light bulb shining in the mist. Little brown

hermit thrushes sing, invisible on mossy branches, deep in shaggy spruce trees. The Chugach, icy and hard, like stone-age spear-tips, axe-heads, and other weapon-ends piled up against the sky, hold the city of Anchorage between themselves and the cold, dreary sea on a great sloped plane. If the mountains tipped up more, Anchorage would slip into muddy Cook Inlet with its treacherous gray tides. In fact some of Anchorage did just that during the Good Friday Earthquake of 1964.

I sat on the log and dragged a twig along it for the kitten to chase. It pounced, over-estimating its velocity, and flipped off the log, and just that quick, clawed its way back up. I laughed. I breathed a deep sigh of relief and pleasure and spruce-tree scent. I was free.

The house my sister and her husband rented belonged to an old-time Alaska couple who had moved to Anaktuvuk Pass. Strange, unfamiliar Northland showed up in any window I passed. Spruce forest and snowy crags, pale northern sky. Inside, artifacts: dog sleds, bear skins, kayaks, caribou antlers, ceremonial masks, oosiks and ulus. Anne said oosiks are walrus penises (which are bone) and ulus are Eskimo women's knives with a curved, rocking blade, good for separating whale blubber from whale skin. Outside, a big, orange, inflated float, the type that is used for crabbing, shrimping, long-lining and such, hung on a rope from the bough of a spruce tree. It made the best swing! Swinging was another thing I could do well, besides riding. Whoosh! That free feeling.

I got re-acquainted with Anne, who like her husband, had become a high school teacher. I hadn't seen much of her in the past few years. Some people say they see a resemblance between us. We both have brown hair, but hers is brunette brown and mine goldish brown. We both have brown eyes, but mine are regular sized, and hers are big and darker. I am on the tall side whereas Anne is petite. In my conversations with her, I discovered an older sister who was also a friend, who listened and gave good advice, and was happy to have me around. She was excited on my behalf for the adventures that awaited me in Alaska.

Anne and Neal had been married about a year. Neal was small like Anne, with an athletic build. He had short dark hair, a slightly wide nose, and eyes like an elf, adding up to an open, friendly-looking face. A springiness to his body and movements matched his playful nature.

As Anne and Neal prepared supper my first evening in Alaska, Neal opened the double porch doors to the blue light and the forest, the song of the hermit thrush, and me on the swing. He clicked a cassette into the stereo and sent the guitar and harmonica of Bob Dylan's "Pat Garrett and Billy the Kid" outdoors to blend with birdsong. I swung and listened, enthralled by being in Alaska and yet listening to this music, this story that took place in *haciendas* and dusty settlements in the mountains of southern New Mexico.

The distance between Kevin and me helped a lot. And not long after I arrived, I met another dark-haired, dark-eyed man, who taught history to seventh graders. Instead of being just a boy, this man out-aged me by 16 years. He had gray in his beard. He had a career, and was even beginning to think about taking early retirement. He looked like a sea captain from Nova Scotia in a heather-blue wool sweater and old, worn leather boat shoes, and he had just bought a new boat and was set to start a fishing charter business in Kachemak Bay, near the town of Homer, Alaska.

Neal and Anne hosted the end-of-school party the night Fletcher and I met. When he arrived at the door Neal said, "Hey, Hatfield! Come in! Meet Susannah, Anne's sister. Want a beer?"

"Hi!" said Fletch, in a friendly way.

Someone's dog jumped on Neal, who was holding a potato chip. The owner yelled over the party noise, "When he does that, just tell him to 'get down!'" Neal struck a disco pose and shouted, "Get *down!*" He was playful and fun and, along with Anne, had listened to my heartbreak story with a thoughtful, attentive manner that I found comforting. He and Fletch had known each other for years, and with my sister they often made a threesome spending weekends skiing, hiking, or boating.

In the crowded kitchen sometime in the wee hours, everyone sang Willie Nelson's "Crazy" and outside some old custodian or art teacher pushed me on the swing, so high I could touch spruce boughs twenty feet off the ground. I didn't need to be inside, surrounded on all sides, trying to socialize. I swished through the cool evening air and listened to the drunken rendition of "Crazy", slowed down to less than half its normal speed, and complete with several harmonies and disharmonies. Fletcher came to the doorway, leaned there and smiled at me. Before he left, just as the sun lit the horizon bright again, he said, "Susannah, would you like to help me run fishing charters this summer?"

I looked him right in the eye. I wasn't a bit disturbed that I knew nothing about boats, or the sea, or how to fish in the ocean. I was thirsty to learn, thirsty for adventure, and I liked this man. I could just see myself sailing Alaskan waters with him. I said yes.

But I had better back way up and introduce myself. My name is Susannah. Description: loves outdoor adventures, rides horses really well, and wonders about things. "Why are some dogs so dumb?" "How come the Australian aborigines' word for wife is 'best friend' and there is no word for 'wife?'" (Could it be that "best friend" is as good as it can get?) "How did the Western saddle develop?" "If a huge oak tree grew very fast—like in a minute—wouldn't it look a lot like an explosion?" "Can you listen to the radio if you're going faster than the speed of sound?" I wondered about things all day, every day, starting when my eyes popped open in the mornings. I spent a lot of time outdoors, often alone, hiking or riding my horse—activities in which my lack of confidence was never an issue.

Unfortunately, I had no social graces. I could say "please" and "thank you," but I tripped over my feet and had no idea how to make small talk. I could be playful as well as participate in deep conversations, but I suffered from under-confidence. One time in Santa Fe a boyfriend's mother gave me some of her old clothes and since I was much too honest, I said, "I think these shoes are too *old* for me." The words stung, I could see that, but I had no idea how to fix my mistake. I was inept socially, and just as innocent, in many ways, as Kevin, only without the religion. So maybe more innocent.

My father is a geologist, my mother an artist. I am the youngest of three girls; Betsy's the oldest, then Anne, then me. Betsy could draw so well at age five it scared people. Then Anne came skipping along perpetually praised for her perfect grades, and she never, *ever* got in trouble. I could neither draw well nor was I that smart, and I often got in trouble. I was always respectful toward adults because that's how I was raised. I did get in trouble, but not on purpose. Punishment always came as a surprise. I was sent to sit in the hall outside the classroom, or for more serious infractions, my teacher put me in a small, dark room near the principal's office. In my third grade year on a weekend hike with our dog, Smoky, my sisters and I found a cow skeleton. It fascinated me lying there white, scattered some, but still partly articulated. At school the next day I guess I could wait no longer with the cow skeleton event kept inside. I drew it onto a piece of my notebook paper and wrote the story of our finding it, how Smoky had been ahead of us herding some cows into a bunch, how we'd come across it, stood staring down. Betsy had explained it to us, carried home a long rib. I'd taken a tooth. We left the skull. But I created this detailed memory during math, or maybe spelling, oblivious to anything but getting the scene across. The teacher was very angry, I remember. She pulled it from my hand. I went to the darkened room by the principal's office. There happened to be a spiral notebook in there. I took out a page and recreated the drawing and the story, even better.

Another time my teacher read Laura Ingalls Wilder, which I loved. Laura's eyes had gotten "big as saucers" when she saw the orange and the penny in her Christmas stocking. Certainly that scene struck me because I sat up with such glee, outlining my eyes with my fingers like big saucers, looking as surprised and delighted as I could, and causing my classmates to giggle. The worst of that punishment was missing the rest of that day's reading. But out in the hallway, banished, I could see the double door that was at the end of the long hall. That door intrigued me not just because we were let out of it at recess, but also because just a hundred feet from that door, beyond the chain link fence, was empty desert and boundless, exhilarating freedom.

Somehow the bad experiences never changed my basic nature, which, as a child, was to be curious and carefree, to seek adventure, and to daydream. Then again, I suppose my school troubles and other experiences ultimately did erode my self-confidence; that over time I reacted to the way unpleasant turns of event (punishment) seemed to come suddenly out of the blue, and probably concluded this trouble was caused by my own unique collection of flaws. Perhaps this in turn made me more observant, less of a participant in the usual human circles.

I belonged to a far-flung family. My father's large family stayed all together where Grandpa and Grandma had settled when they came from Norway: in Wisconsin. But Daddy left for Idaho after graduating from the University of Wisconsin with his geology degree in hand, for a job at the Homestake Mine in Wallace. My parents met there, and then Daddy took a job with the Atomic Energy Commission. Betsy was born in Utah, Anne in Michigan, I in Spokane, Washington, and then we settled in Grants—"Uranium Capital of the World"—long enough for me to grow to thirteen years with a passion for the high desert. Then on to Wyoming for a three year stay, and then back to New Mexico. I realized many years later that my many Midwest cousins had what we three girls didn't: extended family with all its support and guidance, role models within the family, a taken-for-granted sense of belonging to a group, stability.

My mother's mother came from a Montana ranching family. Grandma's upbringing had been in a place aptly named Pleasant Valley. When Grandma and Grandpa married, her fortune was tied to his, and Grandpa had staked a homestead claim in "dry farming" country. This was the promoters' dubious language for a way homesteaders could make a go of it once the railroad extended as far as Montana. Mama's family, along with most others who homesteaded that country, *couldn't* make a go of it. And then too, the depression started early in Montana. Mama and her two brothers were raised in poverty. But they lived on, dirt poor, and my mother loved to ride horses and draw.

Our family in Grants existed apart from both my parents' roots. We were a remote outpost from family on both sides. Even within our own family we did not counsel or guide. Not much. With my artist mother who disdained membership in bridge clubs and other ladies' groups such as the Wives of Miners, we were separate even from Grants's mainstream. I have been grateful for this all my life. My life has been extraordinary in the ways I've gone, the people I've known, the places I've lived. Yet I realize, once again, that a sense of village life, or a sense of extended family, could surely have made life easier. As a mere girl, I was very young to realize that I would have to be self made. I had but a hazy, inaccurate sense of such a journey, and not the faintest idea how to begin. Yet self making was the only choice.

Daddy had a stable government job that fit him pretty well, allowing him to travel by jeep and on foot in remote country quite a bit and having to be involved in bureaucracy only part of the time. Mama and Daddy, Betsy and Anne and I had our happiest family times outdoors, hiking, fishing, camping, tramping all over Mt. Taylor each December in the snow, looking for a perfect Christmas tree. In any season my sisters and I might leave the house early on a Saturday, our water, food, and matches in canvas knapsacks, to explore the countryside until suppertime. We would be likely to do the same thing the following morning, choosing Lobo Canyon or the distant stock-pond or some familiar spot on the mesa beyond, for our destination. The stock-pond was special to us because it was water, with a rim of green willows. Its water was clay-red. Sometimes the pond dried up and we loved to peel up the flat, crispy-dry blocks that formed on the surface of the bottom. Sometimes in the sun and silence of a big New Mexico day we'd walk back and forth across the pond bottom, treading on the cakes of cracked clay, making a symphony of crunching sounds.

My first best friend at age four was a boy named Mark Forest. He lived across the backyard cinder-block fence and climbed over it each day to play. Mama wouldn't let Mark and me inside because she was painting in her studio and didn't want to be disturbed. I once climbed the cinder block fence to Mark's house, but his yard was foreign—flat dirt and dog poop and weeds. His mean little dog dashed up and bit me. I felt betrayed because her name was Susie. How could a dog with my name bite me? I still have the scar on my palm. Anyway, our yard, thanks to my parents, was a deep, cushy green, bordered in brilliant flower gardens. Mark and I make-believed a whole world of adventure there, but when we were six, he moved away to Sparks, Nevada. He and his mama sent a postcard showing an aerial view of Hoover Dam. I held the postcard and thought that's where Mark lived, on the edge of Hoover Dam, a mile-high of concrete in a barren canyon, with unfathomable green water on one side, monstrous turbulence erupting at its base on the other side. I thought it horrible that he lived on the edge of a cliff above such deep water with no shoreline.

Throughout my school years I had girlfriends who liked to ride and fish and cook over a fire. With me as leader we found and named secret hideouts on the mesa, played wild horse roundup, swam in the pond. In Wyoming we rode across the Platte River, made horse obstacle courses in alfalfa fields. We had dirt under our nails, suntans, tangled hair and fun, always thinking up something unusual to do. Girls who weren't like me—the clean, tidy ones with curiously vacant eyes—were mysterious to me. They could offer only a limited amount of entertainment, and were unavailable for any sort of camaraderie as far as I could tell. Eventually, though, in junior high and high school, I wondered how in the world they could always be so *confident*. It confounded me then, but the answer was simple: school and society was their milieu. I couldn't see that it was just a difference of where we felt comfortable, and sometimes I was sure I was defective. There was no one to tell me any different. I also discovered with disappointment that good old friendships never developed with the boys I eventually dated. I still missed Mark Forest and all the fun we had, I guess. But after a certain age boys seemed practically unable to relate to girls as people. When they could, it was great but it hardly ever happened. So by my senior year in high school, I discovered older men.

We had moved from Wyoming back to New Mexico, to what was then a small village on the north end of the Sandias, called Placitas. My high school was down the mountain, in a town called Bernalillo. My first evening in our new house, I rode Trinket bareback up a dirt road, new country for us, destination unknown. A heavy rain had just blown through, leaving the dripping forest of *piñon* and juniper to give off a soul-gladdening scent. The way rose gradually, looking as if it would eventually enter a cleft in the mountain. A sense of exciting potential always came over me as I set off on horseback. After a mile or so I pulled Trinket up to look behind for a minute. Great clouds sailed over the valley and distant buttes far below, dropping hazes of sun-lit rain. Sunlight made the Rio Grande and Jemez rivers into gold threads. Trinket and I continued along the road. After a couple of miles, we topped a hill, descended through a tunnel of cool deciduous trees, rounded a bend, and beheld a very long, very ancient adobe house, like a horizontal pueblo, tucked up against the mountain. Out came a friendly-looking bearded man wearing blue jeans and that's all. He flashed a friendly smile and stood there looking at us. After a brief pause during which he seemed to be waiting for something funny to happen, I said, "What is this place?"

He said, "This is the Land of Oz! And I'm a munchkin!"

"Do you *live* here?" I asked.

"I sure do! Tie your horse and have a cup of tea with me!"

So I did. He was Dave, age 26. He was a Viet Nam vet, a carpenter by trade, a gardener, a dancer, and a student at UNM. Dave turned out to be a perfect new friend that summer, running to get books on art and philosophy and ancient history when I came to visit, brewing up pots of herbal tea, introducing me to music, modern dance and theatre, teaching me chants, putting flowers in my hair, telling me about vegetable gardening as we stood among the tomato plants, he with hose in hand, me looking for pottery shards in the cultivated soil.

By the time I was twenty, and a college student myself, along came tall, dark-eyed Kevin. Kevin, as eager as a puppy, as magical as a gypsy, who was my age, and who, like me, had a long ways to go. I was with a *boy* again. Like I said, he used to drive me nuts!

Because of his angst, confusion, and immaturity, it was necessary for me to the "reasonable" one, which was practically impossible. Still, we had had a mystical connection. That had made it excruciating to leave, but I couldn't have stayed.

After meeting Fletch at Anne and Neal's end-of-school party, I promptly moved with him to Homer, on the coast of the Kenai Peninsula. When we weren't in Kachemak Bay running charters or in the harbor cleaning fish and mopping up the boat, we were at his cabin. The little A-frame with the red door clung to the edge of Olsen Mountain on a bluff high above town. Up there, wind blew constantly, wild creatures scurried about in the head-high grass and *pushkies*, a wild parsnip named by the early Russians, whose descendants, called the Old Believers, still populate the Kenai Peninsula. Wildflowers shot up everywhere. The place reminded me of those scenes in the old Star Trek series when Captain Kirk beamed down to a strange planet. Heavy clouds dropped fine rain from just a few feet above our heads. When the clouds parted, the view from our perch opened up on the fishing hamlet of Homer, far below us, on the blue-gray waters of Kachemak Bay. Beyond the bay stood lofty mountains heavy with glaciers, and beyond them were more mountains and glaciers. Early each morning we climbed into Fletcher's red VW pick-up and drove down the dirt track from the cabin to the harbor on the Homer Spit.

Tutka

Fletcher had a big black dog named Tutka, with brown-and-navy-blue eyes. He was the best. A true boat dog, he'd ridden in everything from a canoe to the big blue Alaska ferry, the Tustumena. More like a bear in size, he could jump into any boat, big or little, including a canoe, without tipping it. He'd ride where he could keep his center of gravity appropriate to the boat. All I had to do was look at him for him to wag his tail, lay his head in my lap, tell me how much he adored me.

Fletcher, Tutka, and I were always together. I learned how to fish for halibut, set shrimp pots, and drive the boat. I already knew how to help people fish, having taught the little kids who lived near me when I lived in Wyoming. But back then we fished for trout on the shores of the Platte River, not for giant flat fish with both eyes on one side, out in the ocean. I learned how to rig the heavy monofilament line with a three-inch hook and eight or ten ounce weight the size of a golf ball, instead of six-pound test line with a small hook and little bitty weight. And I knew how to teach people to bait hooks, drop their line in 'til it hit bottom, set the hook when they got a bite, reel in, and not get tangled up. I knew how to set the drag, when to encourage and when to give suggestions, and when to sit back and watch the fun. This was my first summer in Alaska, and I was helping to provide great fun and adventure for people. I took to this role with something like ecstasy. Tutka was right there with me.

Fletcher

It rattled the brains in his head like seeds in a pod to think where he was here, in Saskatchewan, not merely on the way to the great lone land, or on its edge, but in it, and going deeper. He had lived a dream in which everything went right.

−Wallace Stegner, *Wolf Willow*

At age eighteen, Fletcher had joined the Army and come to Alaska from Vermont. At that time, in the early '60s, a person could stake a land claim in Alaska just by going to see it and filling out some papers. On a dismal, rainy day, he and a friend took a skiff and went out and staked land on Fox Island, fourteen miles out in Resurrection Bay from what was then the raggedy town of Seward. His claim covered about a third of a beach in Northwest Cove on Fox Island. Years had passed, and now Fletcher got the idea half-way through that summer with me, to turn his claim property into a wilderness lodge where people could come and stay in cabins and go fishing and sightseeing. Maybe he had the idea before. Maybe now he felt the time was right. He said, "What would you think of helping me build a lodge there? Ours will be the only place around. It's very remote. No electricity, no running water, no phones. The nearest road is 14 miles away, in Seward. Would you like that?"

"Yes!"

"I thought you would," he said, smiling.

We loaded the boat onto its trailer one morning and left Homer behind, driving up one side of the Kenai Peninsula and down the other, arriving in Seward late that afternoon. On the way, Fletch said Resurrection Bay was narrower than Kachemak, that it was really more of a fjord, and that because the landscape was more rugged, it seemed like more of a wilderness to him than Kachemak Bay. Seward existed at the head of it, he said, because the bay was ice-free in winter. Seward was settled in 1903 when a shipload of men arrived from Seattle to begin a railway that would reach to Anchorage and on into the interior of Alaska. Now it's a lovely little town, clean and charming and welcoming, smack up against Mount Marathon, right on the beach, with a thriving tourism business. But at that time it was still a rough place. As we pulled in I noticed its dusty buildings and banged-up assortment of cars and trucks, lawns decorated with fishing floats and wooden boat hulls full of flowers, loose dogs and children and men everywhere, working mostly in the marine industry, in some capacity. There wasn't much tourism. The people of Seward were then, as they are now, uncommonly unpretentious and friendly. We slipped the boat off the trailer into the harbor, tied it up, and headed back into town for dinner.

In Seward, Alaska, we dined in the closest thing to a five-star restaurant I had yet to experience, despite having lived in Albuquerque and Wyoming. The Van Gilder Hotel is gone now. It was in a building that I suppose had been built when the railroad link was complete, when hopes and ambitions were at their height. The Van Gilder's restaurant was dark inside, cushiony red, ornamented with deep polished wood, gilded wallpapering, velvet drapery, and crystal chandeliers. I had filet mignon and Fletch ordered lobster. We slept on the boat in the harbor and the next morning we were on our way to my new home, Fox Island.

Fox Island

Another A-frame, as tiny as Fletcher's cabin in Homer, sat all alone on the beach. Its weathered gray was a shade darker than the many dead trees on the beach, which had succumbed to the '64 earthquake. For years the cabin had stood alone, and few had passed its way. Local folks said a fisherman built it, others said it was the work of a wandering hippie. Instead of the door being on the front, like the cabin in Homer, the door was on the back, facing the bulk of the island, which rose up almost vertical a few yards away.

Resurrection Bay, all the Kenai Fjords and beyond in either

direction, all the many miles to Prince William Sound in one direction and to Cook Inlet the other, were mostly deserted then. A few long-liners (commercial fishermen) plied the waters and the occasional adventurer came through. A small number of boat captains ran fishing charters on weekends. Those with recreational boats ventured from the harbors on weekends. A family-owned sightseeing tour company had just started up out of Seward. But thriving populations of animals filled the fjords, intermingling and coexisting in all their various habitats: several kinds of whales, harbor seals, Steller's sea lions, Dall's porpoise, and sea otters, along with countless species of fish; eagles, songbirds, numerous varieties of sea birds by the hundred-thousands; land otters, porcupines, bears, mountain goats, mountain sheep, moose, foxes, wolverines, and more.

We set up home in the cabin and Fletcher stated the obvious: We needed more cabins if we were going to have paying guests. He went to Anchorage and came back with a one-ton truck. Tutka and I stayed on the boat in the Seward Harbor while he was gone. When he returned we visited a one-man lumber mill deep in the damp woods just north of Seward. The man lived next to his mill in a truck camper that was nearly completely buried in sawdust. In fact it looked rather like a huge pile of sawdust until I looked closely and saw a door. I thought that was probably good insulation. Fletch bought the rough-cut lumber, we tied it in a huge bundle, hauled it to the harbor, slipped it off the truck into the water by stopping the truck suddenly on the boat ramp, and towed it out to the island. It took three hours to tow enough lumber for the new twelve by fourteen cabin.

Already I had learned an awful lot from Fletcher. He knew how to find what he needed and get the help he needed. He could figure things out and make arrangements. He was respected and tactful and diplomatic, and a good storyteller. People just loved him. I did, too. In several ways, he reminded me of my father: kind, decent, and steady and he always treated me well. He had a wonderful, eye-twinkling chuckle. Though I did not forget Kevin, I was happy to forsake the intensity and confusion I'd experienced with him. Fletcher was good-looking, too. He had almost black hair, like I said, with good, dark eyes and a thick beard, a mustache that curled upward on the ends, making him look amiable at all times, and a strong, relaxed body. For a 38-year-old, his flexibility surprised me. He often sat casually with his legs crossed "Indian style."

John Tuttle

Fletcher knew we needed extra help, and contacted a friend of his named John Tuttle. John taught seventh-grade woodshop in Astoria, Oregon. He liked to spend his summers in Alaska, he was a working fiend, and he was just who we needed to help build our lodge. He showed up in Seward one day, and came back to Fox Island with us, and now we were three—or four, with Tutka, though John wouldn't have counted Tutka. He didn't seem to like dogs. John was in his fifties, short and strong with a tan, bald head fringed with curly iron-gray hair and a curly iron-gray beard. He had big blue eyes and a big nose. He was always happy and nearly always loud about it. I would soon learn that he never minced a single word in his life and often got in trouble for that. He could be preposterously contemptuous and tactless. He could not accept in anyone what he perceived as laziness or an unwillingness to pitch in. He could treat people like a drill sergeant. He often angered me.

The three of us got busy right away and built the new guest cabin. One warm day on top of the new cabin, gluing sheets of roofing paper down with tar from a sticky black bucket, I paused to take in the view of toothy mountains across the sparkling water. I figured all the land I could see—the long, mountainous peninsulas to the west and east, which enclosed our bay—were the peaks of mountain ranges mostly under water. Snow and ice covered most of them except for the bottom third, which grew dark blue spruce forests down to the water. On the dark blue part, waterfalls fell from snow level above, some cascading wide, wispy and veil-like, some forming ever-so-thin lines. I had seen that after a day or two of rain, they leapt off the mountainsides breaking in powerful gushes that you could even sometimes hear from far away, over rocky outcroppings, down to the sea. To the southeast, a rounded, bulky-

looking mountain on the mainland stood framed in the deep U-shaped valley between two of Fox Island's peaks. The image of this bold mountain reflected into a lake, which lay nestled into Fox Island behind the beach. I named the mountain an Indian word, "Mamamowatum," which means, "Oh-Be-Joyful." It might not be a real word. I had read it in a book called *Mrs. Mike* by Benedict and Nancy Freedman.

I went back to work on the roof, slapping on the tar, fantasizing about what I would see if I could fly to the top of Mamamowatum. I imagined I saw all kinds of things: in a forest, a hunter sitting on a dead moose. The hunter was crying. I wondered why. Was he lost? Had he not meant to kill the moose? Was he injured? Did his wife leave him? I flew on and saw four wolves chasing a caribou across a shallow, braided river, and then a man and woman building a log cabin. They had two dogs that slept in the sawdust. I worked on that fantasy and worked on the roof, gluing and nailing, 'til the sun sank (but didn't set) and it was time for supper.

A series of Fletch's friends came out while we built the new cabin. We all took shelter in the old cabin, finding sleeping space in an assortment of sleeping bags wherever we could. Without the old cabin's shelter we would have been pitiful, wet creatures. It was the island's sole refuge from the weather, for humans. It was good to have a place to come inside and be warm, with the wood stove crackling, the rain loud on the roof, the surf loud on the beach. After dinner we listened to Jimmy Buffet turned up over these sounds and sometimes we sang, louder yet, and drank rum. Someone fed the stove. There's always someone who is Person in Charge of the Fire. We read magazines by the light of kerosene lanterns, talked, played gin and poker, and laughed. When the tide was at its highest the sea would reach up with cold, foamy fingers, then draw back, tumbling beach stones with a clatter just a few feet from the cabin's plywood wall.

But when the sun came out, *Glory*! It seemed to me that while the rain had fallen over a period of days and nights, we had been leprechauns in a fuzzy, mossy, dark under-world. Once the sky cleared we became gods and goddesses striding about the marbled

architecture among columns and fountains, olive trees, and sunlight, with views of the sparkling ocean! The old cabin was not our refuge in sunny weather. It was a moldy vacant rotting hull, its interior dark, full of broken parts of starfish, rusted lures and hooks, and wooden crates of old magazines. *Cruising World*, *National Fisherman* and *Woodenboat* mildewed and curled up together. The cabin was crowded with canned goods and rain gear and living spiders. Drifts of nearly weightless dead bug shells, which had collected in corners, flew briefly when disturbed by air currents. With the sun out, steam rose off the beach, but we were dry.

We spent those days outside and only went indoors at night to cuddle up in sleep.

And then, it was just John, Fletch and me again. At the end of the day when our last visitors had returned to Anchorage, Fletcher and I paddled the canoe across the lake to replenish our fresh water supply at a small spring. Tutka rode in the middle between us. In the twilight we stood on a tiny beach where the spring emptied into the lake, hearing its gurgle as it flowed over pebbles, filling an assortment of pails and jugs with fresh water. We loaded them into the canoe, hauled them back across the lake, and set them all in a row on the rough plank counter-top. While we were gone, John had put up a canvas wall tent down the beach among some trees. Now we had a new living arrangement. We three ate dinner together while Fletch and John discussed the plans for the next day, and then John went to his tent, and Fletch and I climbed the ladder to the loft.

The new cabin wasn't fancy, but simple and pleasant; good for keeping out the elements. On our next trip to Seward I had Mr. Brown at Brown and Hawkins mix a color for the cabin that blended in with the forest so well, that anyone traveling by had to come close to the beach before they noticed it. This was important to me because of my love of wild places. I had no desire to play too big a role in taming or altering them. Fletcher came back from another trip to town with a wood stove, a two-burner propane cook stove, a 50-gallon propane tank, a sink, and faucet. Thinking about the one-ton truck, the load of lumber, and this most recent purchase, I guessed Fletcher made pretty good money as a teacher and with the fishing charters we'd done in Homer, but in truth, I knew little of the actual finances involved in running our lodge. Next he bought about a half-mile of black PVC pipe, which we laid from a point high up in the spring to provide water to the cabins. Up to then we had hauled many gallons in a variety of containers, and it was a novelty to turn a handle and have water running into the cabin. But in a way, it seemed too convenient. It made me nervous. How easy was life going to get? Too easy? Were we going to get more conveniences? What kind? As things continued to get underway, and the date we'd have our first paying guests came closer, I began to wonder what was going to be expected of me at our lodge. Maybe mostly indoor-type jobs? Cooking and cleaning and such? Aside from an underdeveloped interest in interior decorating, I had yet to form any interest in such things. I made up my mind to make myself indispensable outdoors. Fletcher and John dug a deep hole and built an outhouse, and now we were ready for guests.

Through those first weeks of preparation, John kept right on with his passion for teaching and was an excellent teacher for me. When it came to sharing his knowledge, he was patient. He took me on as an apprentice. He taught me how to build a cabin from foundation to roof. John explained things clearly, shared many useful tricks of the trade, and showed me the right way to do things. He never held back teaching me how to use anything: power tools, chain saws, and generators. But watch out if you didn't work hard! I liked to work, and could put in a full day of physical labor, so I usually didn't have too much trouble with this quality of John's. But I sometimes got embarrassed for guests. Particularly if the guest was a boy in his teens. For some reason, this age of boy, if he wasn't a gung-ho help-out type, really got John's goat.

John also didn't seem to care for sensitivity or creativity, which are major aspects of my being. He gave me a hard time when I painted. If I sang, he mocked me in a loud, squally voice as he tramped past with a load of two-by-fours.

A few times John got to be too much. I'd think, either he goes, or I go. One afternoon Fletch and I shared a rare moment alone. Window-shaped sunlight lit the floor of the cabin, Tutka lay in one block of it, the sun warm on his black coat. I finished sweeping and then lifted a deer hide to the wall and asked Fletch what he thought of it in that spot. It was a hide I had found fresh in the mountains in New Mexico, still attached to a deer head. I had cut off the head, thrown the hide in the pick-up, and driven straight to the library where I got a book on tanning. At home I tanned it and then spent many evenings beading onto it a goat standing on a rock. I liked it a lot. John came tromping up to the cabin door, pulled the latch string with his usual unnecessary force, and came inside to tell Fletch something. He spied me. He said derisively, "What're you doing with that stinky old buffalo robe?" I stared at him, unable to react.

How could he be so cruel? Didn't I try to be nice to him? Didn't I go more than half way to get along with him? By insulting my artwork I felt he was insulting me. Fletcher stood up. "John, you're too harsh with her. Joking around is one thing, but there's a limit. If you're not more careful, I'm afraid Susannah will leave." John could drop his thoughtless behavior in a second, and did, when Fletcher said that. When challenged, he would reflect on what he'd said and how it might affect someone. He had a sweet side, in his own way. Sometimes, but not usually, I'd feel sorry for him for being such a jerk and then having to realize it. I loved Fletcher for sticking up for me and not wanting me to leave.

From Fletcher I learned how to drive the skiff with an outboard motor. I loved to watch how he would get into a skiff, placing his foot on the gunwale, stepping in and righting the boat in one smooth movement. He sat so relaxed in the stern, sitting on an overturned bucket usually, hand draped casually on the outboard's steering shaft and looking ahead to the waves, or the destination, talking, laughing. It fascinated me, these things that people did well. As Fletcher was with boats, so John was with building. I watched and learned. I sometimes felt out of my element and missed being in wild desert country and around horses, where I felt as skilled as John and Fletch. But as our first guests arrived and kept coming, the hardest thing of all to learn was how to be a good host, not just when I felt sociable, but *all* the time.

Running a lodge was exhausting. Guests arrived to stay and go fishing or sightseeing on board the boat, which Fletch had named the *Fox Islander*. Every few days we took them back to Seward, and picked up a new group of eager people. Much to my dismay, my social confidence came and went without predictability. When I was on, I was on, but when I was off, I wanted to be where I didn't have to interact with people. They seemed to seek me out.

My skittishness sometimes took an edge. I didn't like it when some well-meaning man began helping me at some task, and then took over, when I didn't need, want, or ask for help. Women wore me out with light conversation, bringing up subjects in which I had no interest or background, telling me long, involved recipes which I instantly forgot while I washed the dishes, while I fidgeted to be out of the kitchen, out of the cabin, out of range. I found myself unable to summon any knack for small talk. Sometimes such a crisis in confidence built and led to despair. I climbed the ladder to the cabin loft, sat on the floor, and cried. I longed to go off by myself. I couldn't go off for a hike in the woods or a paddle on the lake because now there were people around. Some curious person would ask where I was going, or Fletcher would need me to do something, or John would think I was lazy. *Then* that's how I saw it. *Now*, I would know to take the time to go off, for a half hour or an hour, with sketch book and pencils, camera, or journal.

In spite of those episodes, most of the time I knew I was having the time of my life. Many moments within days, and even whole days on Fox Island, were just pure glee. Guests left their everyday lives and became relaxed and vibrant when out with us. I loved seeing the happiness in their eyes and gestures, and, through them, experiencing anew the wonder of finding oneself in such a place. I recalled a Navajo song I'd learned at Mt. Taylor Elementary. It starts,

> I walk with beauty
> With beauty before me, I walk
> With beauty behind me, I walk
> With beauty above me, I walk
> With beauty around me, I walk

My heaven as host of Fox Island Lodge was complete whenever our departing guests thanked me, telling me that they felt toward me as if I were their daughter, or sister, or friend, and asking John to take photos of Fletch and me with their family. Most of the guests, at some point, expressed admiration for the life I led, and I understood this. I had the exquisite awareness that I was having a never-to-be-forgotten good time, a grand adventure, in a spectacular setting. Fletch loved the outdoor life as much as I. And I was in a place that I had come to love with all my heart.

Summer eased along at my island home among the wild things, berries plumped and ripened on the bushes, the sky darkened more each night, until one night in August a star shown and only a week of summer remained. I knew at summer's end I would return to

Albuquerque and school. The more I thought about leaving, the more I hated to. I began wondering if I was going to make some kind of major change in my life. I had never thought of leaving New Mexico for good. Now the thought of leaving either place threw me into mourning.

This dread made me think of Geronimo, the tough little Apache Indian whose territory later came to be called southern New Mexico and Arizona. He didn't want to see his people's land and way of life taken over by newcomers, and he and others fought like hell. Geronimo caused a lot of bad trouble for prospectors, miners, stockmen, and other settlers into the late 1800's. After he was finally captured in Skeleton Canyon in Arizona, on September 3, 1886, the U.S. Government took him to live in captivity near Fort Sill, Oklahoma. Over those years, defeated, sometimes on display for curiosity-seekers, he asked many times to be allowed to return to his desert home. When he was an old, old man, he asked once more. He said, "The acorns and *piñon* nuts, the quail and the wild turkey, the giant cactus and the [pines]—they all miss me." I sat with my legs dangling off the deck of the cabin we'd built, in a posture of sorrow and confusion, gazing at the gray flat stones of the beach. I thought how Fox Island's clear lake, the spruce trees, the trails through the forest, and the otters and porcupines would miss me, and possibly how Fletch might miss me. Fletch had shown himself to be kind, yet not demonstrative, and sometimes distant in a way that puzzled me. He had told me that he himself wasn't an artistic type at all, but that he had always found himself drawn to creative people. His former wife had been artistic, like me. Maybe that break-up had hurt too much, I thought, and he's just very, very careful. His taciturn nature often charmed me, but sometimes, this holding back of his filtered through my thought processes as a possible lack of interest. There had been no question of the feelings former boyfriends had had toward me. But with Fletch I just couldn't be sure that he was in love with me.

2

Being in a Rainbow

Albuquerque in the Fall

> *There was a new song in the blue air that had never*
> *been sung before. It was hard to tell about it, for it had nothing to*
> *do with words; it was like the light of the desert at noon, or the smell*
> *of the sagebrush after rain; intangible but powerful.*

> –Willa Cather, *Song of the Lark*

Fletcher took me to Seward where I would catch a ride to Anchorage. It was a chilly day with rain in the clouds. I knew it might look like that for days after I left, without raining. New Mexico weather was different. If heavy, wet-looking clouds blew in, it would likely rain hard for a while, and then the clouds would blow on out, casting shadows on the bright desert below. It was exhilarating to be in one of those racing shadows—it got so dark and cool and then suddenly you stood in sunlight again watching the cloud-shadow bump away over the mesas and canyons. In New Mexico you could usually see whole clouds, separate from others, with distinct edges. Here on the south-central coast of Alaska, the mountains stayed shrouded for days without anything moving. The clouds merged together into a great, pale mass. They drifted in low and settled downward, sagging through the mountain passes and down the valleys until they formed a low ceiling only fifty feet or less above our heads. It might rain, or not. Once rain fell, it might go on for weeks. If it got sunny, it might just as well cloud up again within a few hours.

We splashed through the chop on the way to Seward, holding mugs of hot coffee, trying not to spill it. Tutka lay on the rumbling floor beside us. Fletch sat in the captain's seat, and I stood beside him. He put his arm around me, pulling me close. He said, "Susannah, will you come back next summer?" I had been wondering and wondering if he would ask that. Did I hear some intensity in his voice? Yet he didn't look at me. I said I would come back, and felt tears of relief. He turned and smiled at me then, a brief, big smile, but other than an arm-squeeze around my shoulder, he showed no other emotion. The *Minot* came in sight ahead of us, traveling slowly alongside Caines Head. Fletch picked up the radio. "*Minot*, this is the *Fox Islander*, come in *Minot*, over—"

I stood watching him laugh and talk to Rick on the *Minot*, feeling relieved, puzzled, and much more light-hearted about leaving Fox Island, since I would be coming back. I thought again what an even-keel sort of man Fletch was and how possibly what I viewed as his lack of intensity could just be his maturity.

In Anchorage I said goodbye to Anne and Neal, telling them the news that I would be back in a year. "That doesn't surprise me," Anne said. She handed me my mail. Kevin had written several times, two long, intense letters, others that sounded more casual and well-adjusted, even a couple cheery postcards. Well-adjusted or not, I told myself, I won't go back with Kevin. A voice deep inside wondered how I could possibly avoid it, once I laid eyes on him again. I called my parents, instructing them not to tell Kevin when I'd be back.

In two days I was home again in New Mexico. I was more home than I'd been in years, for I moved back in with my parents. I'd moved out at age 17, and I was almost 22 now. Whether consciously or not, I reasoned that living with them in Placitas, as opposed to having my own place in Albuquerque, would give me a hedge against re-involvement with Kevin. Suddenly I had my old bedroom back, my mom and dad to live with, and my horse right out there in the corral to go for a ride on any time I wanted, just like the old days. Life was good. Soon I was happy, too, to be back in school in Albuquerque. I had discovered a passion for learning. My courses consisted of classes I signed up for only because they sounded interesting, like Ancient History of the Southwest and the Study of Language.

My new schedule came with an interesting professor. His name was Mark, and he had just moved to Albuquerque from Boston. Mark was a young, petite man, with brown hair and blue eyes. He wore wire-rim glasses, he was very, very smart, and he was a poet. Though his name was the same, he didn't look at all like Mark Forest, my best friend at age four. I imagined Mark Forest to look like an explorer now, tall, tan, sandy blond, with a slightly narrow head and masculine jaw and weathered skin. My professor had a round face and a bookish look.

I didn't realize how interesting he was at first. But he required his students to keep a journal, and he would write back on our pages after he read what we wrote. He wrote at length in my journal, sometimes many pages, and so well, that the pleasure of reading him brought a grin to my face. This was partly due to the fact that he complimented my writing. I turned Mark's compliments, written in his curly, backhand printing, over and over, enjoying them from every angle like a hard-rock miner with a just-found nugget of gold.

Mark required his students to take an "excursion" each week, and then write about it. Although I was now studying to be a teacher—for I'd just been told I was required to claim a major out of the disparate variety of classes I'd taken up to that point—my excursions weren't to museums or schools or libraries. I wrote instead about riding up on the side of the Sandias. Along the trail I dismounted for a rest and found at my feet a fossilized seashell. I picked it up and held it in my palm. It was dark pink in color, a bivalve shell, with every fine ridge and scallop preserved. I stood there looking out at land thousands of feet lower than where I stood on the mountain, and wondered about a seashell being up so high.

That evening, after supper with my parents, I wrote: "*I stood still and listened. I heard only wind-whispers. I could not hear the sound of surf.*"

I wrote about why I hadn't come to school one day. Instead, I'd taken another turn and driven up to Barley Creek in my dad's pick-up, for a day of fishing. Barley Creek is small—maybe five feet across and less than two feet deep—and runs through willows and meadow. It's not always easy to fish in a little creek like that, but long ago a friend of Daddy's had shown me how the trout like to rest under the edge of the bank, waiting for bugs and other food to drift by. If I put a tiny split-shot weight on, and just a fragment of a worm, dropped it about six inches into the water, and let the current twirl it along just an inch or so from the bank, I'd catch fish. I could bring home supper of fresh trout for dinner that night.

I carefully dangled my worm, and thought. I didn't have any direction. I didn't know what I was going to do with my life. I didn't know where I was going to live. Two cowboys, a father and his son, came by on horseback looking for their cows. They tipped their hats and said howdy and rode on, with a job to do. I envied the son, a bit younger than me, growing up secure in the knowledge that he would be a rancher, too, not having to wonder what he would become or where he would live.

In my journal I wrote about walking with my friends Katy and Raúl, from Katy's trailer to the Albuquerque zoo. We decided that whoever found the most interesting object along the way would get his or her admission paid. I found a doll head, a key and a fake grape. Katy found a blue rock and a yellow barrette. Raúl found a mule shoe. I thought the mule shoe was the best. I'd certainly never seen a mule in that part of Albuquerque. We asked the lady in the zoo booth to choose, and she picked the mule shoe, too, but it was 4:30 and we didn't think a half-hour until closing would be worth nine dollars. It had been a four-mile walk. So we played for a while in the playground by the zoo. I headed for the swings and Katy and Raúl went for the group of springy animals sticking up out of the dirt. They looked ridiculous with their knees poked up, hunched over the tiny reins. Raúl rocked wildly. Then he scowled and said, "Ah need another *hoss*, Festus, this'uns gettin' winded! We're losin' *ground* on them rustlers!" Katy said, "Ah do too! Look! There's a couple rat there!" And they switched to new animals, intent on the game, laughing like children.

Meanwhile I went to classes, criss-crossing UNM's adobe campus. I studied hard, worked hard, rode my horse, and made excursions. I turned in my journal each Thursday to Mark, and waited all weekend to get it back on Monday. Then I would go away after class and sit under a tree and relish every word of whatever he wrote.

That's when I saw Kevin—while walking to the duck pond after Mark's class, backpack of books slung over my shoulder, journal in hand. Seeing him, his tallness, his dark hair gleaming in the sun, my heart constricted into a thrilling little ball. It made me angry with myself. I tried to feign indifference, I tried to feel contempt. I felt some, too, but it was mixed in with that old, helpless attraction.

He came up to me. He looked into my eyes. I could feel his heat, smell his scent. I felt momentarily pulled toward him. I managed a half step back. "Susannah, I *missed* you."

I thought I would say something. I smiled a dumb friendly smile, tilting my head to the side, got serious, looked down, looked away; several emotions inside competed for expression. I'd make a lousy actress. My feelings are always right there on my sleeve, meaning whatever's on my mind is always what comes to mind to say, without any judgement of the consequences. I didn't think I needed to give Kevin *any* of what was on my mind. At least I knew that much. And if he wanted to get together, I'd say no. He said, "How have you been? When did you get back?"

"Oh, good! I've been great. Alaska was great. How are you? How's Kyra?"

"Well, I missed you a lot, Susannah. But I'm doing fine. It was a good summer. Kinda hot, though. Guess what! I'm a student. They're working my ass off so far!"

"How's Kyra?"

"Oh, Kyra's fine. I guess you know she moved in with Katy."

"Yeah, Katy said. That's good. So, she's doing all right?"

"Yep, yep," he said, nodding his head like a toy dog in the back window of a low-rider.

I said, "So…what classes are you taking?"

"Oh, let's see. Philosophy, American Literature, Psychology, Spanish, Judo."

"That's great, Kevin!" I said, feeling genuine pleasure on his behalf and hopeful about his widening horizons. "Sounds like a tough schedule, though. How do you like philosophy?"

"*Love* it. It's right-on, man. We can talk about it sometime if you want. Do you want to? I understand if you don't."

"You do?" Using expressions from the sixties was one of Kevin's particular verbal traits. I found it charming, if strange. He'd also say, "dig it," "sock-it-to-me" and "far out." I didn't know how I felt about him saying he 'understood.' That could mean he was seeing Kyra, or it could mean he understood that I'd been hurt possibly too much to want to see him, or it could mean that he was trying to protect himself in case I didn't want to see him. I said, "I'd like to sometime. Maybe we can have coffee at the Hippo. I gotta go—" I looked at my watch. "I'm late!"

"Oh, you do? Okay, see you! I'll call!"

"Yep! Bye!" *Damn. I just said the opposite of what I said I'd say.*

I got a job as cashier at the Frontier Restaurant, on Central across from campus. The Frontier served endless cups of tin-tasting coffee and the usual array of greasy food. All day and night, it teemed with students and vagabonds of all ages. The owner, a short, beige man, looked like a feedlot manager from West Texas. His towering wife put me in mind of Mrs. Munster with tall black hair and a gray streak. So there I was working, and Kevin went and got a job at the Frontier, too. We'd seen each other just once before that, at the Hippo. I'd told him I had a boyfriend in Alaska. With this, we were both able to keep our approach casual—lighthearted, even. We'd had an interesting conversation with plenty to think about afterward. But working around him was another thing. He was so good-looking, tall and healthy, and had such eyes. Such a child, such a man. He said he knew me before this life. We were shepherds together, he said, like Heidi and Peter in alpine meadows. Maybe we were.

"My purpose in *this* life," I said, "was to help you stay on an even keel. And it was hard. It isn't like I'm all that serene or steady myself."

Nevertheless, I had responded to his need by devoting countless hours trying to set his mind at ease about all the variety and complexity in the world. Raised in a close family, a close community, a close church, raised to believe that there was only one reality, he had launched into wider society, quickly becoming bewildered that everyone didn't agree and follow. Then he had begun to consider the possible validity of *every* belief. His lack of general knowledge—of an education, I guess—was astonishing. Maybe my dad was the son of immigrants, maybe my mom was raised dirt poor, but we had books in our house, lots of them. I had attempted to reassure Kevin that he wasn't wrong or mistaken, or had to change. He sometimes feared he had been misinformed, by his parents, by his church. It seemed important to me that he didn't feel that. "There's just a lot of variety, that's all." I'd said. He was lost and paranoid at times. At other times he made great, confident strides in his effort to integrate his daily onslaught of new and startling information. He'd be his happy self and off we'd go, back then. Other times he would hold his head, close his eyes, disappear for a few days. His mother must have shuddered when she finally let him out of her house. She must have prayed and prayed and prayed. I think I knew how she felt.

I left the Frontier to get away from Kevin—again—and got a job as a waitress at the Hiway House farther up Central Avenue. I *hated* waitressing. I couldn't keep track of so much food and condiments and dinner-ware, and who wanted what in what order. The new owners of the Hiway House (situated on Highway 66, which is Central Avenue in Albuquerque) had moved from Ohio and were just lost in New Mexico. Especially the poor wife. The husband had a restaurant to run, but his wife was just his helper and had left her life and all her friends, her covered bridges, her farm country, and cultured cities for a sprawling, tacky city in the desert. This was her husband's deal, not hers. I felt sorry for her. When business slowed and we had time to talk, I tried to make her feel better about the barren landscape she found herself in. It must have looked like the moon to her. I talked to her about sudden fields of delicate wildflowers and native grasses after a rain, and quail families running zig-zag through the stems, making grass tassels and colorful blossoms nod and bobble. I told her about hidden canyons with little clear pools of water, teeny ponds with watercress like miniature lilies, that you could pinch off and taste.

Jack Snow

He wants to crawl out at the first break in the weather,
with that same old burro with the split ear.

–Willa Cather, *Song of the Lark*

An old, crippled man came every day to the Hiway House to sit at the counter along with other regulars. His name was Jack Snow. His hands and face were palsied, he had no teeth, he could barely be understood, and then only if you paid close attention. Each day, he juggled the coffee creamers my way and asked me to open them. Whenever it was slow, we'd talk. I came to love Jack. He was fierce. He was a kindred spirit. He told me he had hired himself out as a photographer on archaeological digs in Arizona in the 1920s. When he wasn't working as a photographer, he'd been a prospector, with a burro, a gold pan, a shovel, and a pick-ax. He didn't know how old he was, but he guessed late-eighties. His love for the desert burned bright. Back in his days as a young desert rat, he'd had a horse named Peppersauce, no schooling, and no obligations but to "eat, sleep, shit, and try not to die." But now Jack lived on the corner of Lomas Avenue, and he hated it. He called Lomas a "river of concrete and steel." And perhaps due in part to a bit of old-age paranoia, he loathed the people next-door because they were Christians. He said the only reason his neighbors treated him nice was because they were obligated to. They sought favors from God, he said. When they brought donuts and pamphlets over he told them to get off his property. The man had said, "Jesus loves you!" Jack shouted back, "Yeah, Jesus loves you too! But everyone else thinks you're an asshole!" I laughed when he told me this but felt bad for the neighbor. Anyway, I don't suppose the man could tell what Jack said.

It's what I loved about Jack—his passion for life, his ever-present humor, his memories, his love for horses and for wandering the desert. If he didn't come in for a few days and I asked him where he'd been, he'd say, "I've been to *hell!* Me and the devil had a card game. And I won!"

One time Kevin came by the Hiway House on his motorcycle.

Jack said, "Give me a ride home!" There they went—the old, white-haired, crippled Christian-hater with his cane and Kevin, on a black motorcycle, right down Central Avenue.

Spring came again. I attended my final exams, school ended, and I didn't have to be a waitress anymore. I didn't have to watch Kevin come into the Hiway House and flirt with the other waitresses. Best of all, I had money saved up for a plane ticket to Alaska. I said goodbye to my parents, my dogs Sara and Gustoff, and Trinket. I promised Mark I'd do some writing over the summer. I visited Jack Snow at his house, to say goodbye. His house smelled of dust and age. He beckoned me into the kitchen. In the living room I passed by his neatly made bed with its nightstand

and piles of books. His living quarters had shrunk to just the two rooms. The rest of the house was dark, full of old photographs stacked against walls, photography equipment, woolen Indian blankets and horse tack. He offered me coffee and a glazed donut from a box. In a back room he showed me paintings an Indian friend had done long ago in the Navajo style, colorful horses and clouds. When it was time to leave, Jack hugged me hard, and gave me a quick kiss on the lips. He shouted, "You look like a flower!" He gave me a worn photograph of himself on his horse, and in his big, shaky handwriting he wrote on the back:

PEPPERSAUCE
ORACLE CAMP NEAR THE SAN PEDRO RIVER
ARIZONA
THE BEST SORREL BROOMTAIL THAT EVER LIVED

—3—

Feeling Right Where You Are

Reunion

Fletch met me at the airport with a whiskery, wooly embrace. I had imagined how good it would feel to see his smile and hear his laugh, but I'd underestimated, and it took me by surprise. He took my carry-on saying, "Boy, is Tutka going to be glad to see *you!* He's in the truck. Are you hungry? Anne and Neal want to meet us at Simon's if you're up for it." At his home later, he left my luggage in the truck and took my hand, leading me upstairs.

We hit the ground running the next day, spending the morning at a warehouse store buying food and provisions for the summer. Fletch had said, "We need to pick up a few groceries." I'd learned that understatement was another of his qualities. He'd say things like, "The road out to their place is a little rough," when the road, in fact, was a nerve-wracking gauntlet of vertical-sided, ice-water potholes in cement-hard earth, chopped into a cliff side with surf pounding below. He'd called that winter and related a story, saying, "The bay was sloppy," and then went on to tell me a hair-raising tale about a sail boater he'd rescued off a beach, abandoning the sail boat to its fate. I'd provided my own mental picture of calamitous surf and howling wind.

After stocking up, we loaded the truck, drove to Seward, took the boat off the trailer and loaded it, and chugged out to Fox Island on glossy waves of mauve and green. I was clothed again in wool sweaters, jeans and rubber boots. Sea gulls flew about, breezes blew over my face and hands, and I breathed in the smell of the sea and salt air. I could see Fox Island in the distance, and I so looked forward to arriving. For me that evening, I couldn't imagine being in a better place, or with a better person than Fletch.

Fletch asked, "Are you glad to be back, Susannah?" To my yes he said, "I booked charters all winter—we're almost full for the season!"

"That's *good!*" I replied. I wasn't surprised. The summer before, many of Fletch's friends had brought out their relatives who had come up to visit from the lower 48. Fletch had many friends, he knew a lot of teachers, and everyone liked him. When their relatives visited, they thought of Fox Island. Fletch also had a solid reputation as a sea-captain and general all around top-notch guide, and for these reasons, Fox Island Lodge was being recommended to tourists in Seward and elsewhere. "It's going to be tough at first building another cabin and running charters at the same time. But I left some time off for us in June—I thought you might like to explore some new country."

John soon returned to Alaska from his winter life as well, just in time for all the work we had to do. Fletcher bought more lumber from the Seward mill, and this time he hired a friend with a bigger boat to tow it to Fox Island. Carl Schuman, 60-ish, in tan overalls, owned the 36-foot *Sea Chicken*—a wooden fishing boat he'd made in his garage. The previous summer it had been only thirty-two feet long, with a short deck and a big, tall cabin that made it look out of proportion. Carl was like John in some ways: another self-made man. A boat too short? No problem! Over the winter he had sawed the deck off, added six feet more, and reattached the end. Now the boat had perfect proportions. The splice had to have been strong, because towing the giant load of lumber to Fox Island didn't pull the *Sea Chicken* in half.

This time we built a much bigger cabin, while running back-to-

back charters at the same time. John and whatever crew he could wrangle up—friends from Astoria and Anchorage—did most of the work. If I didn't go out on the day's charter with Fletch and the guests, I'd stay and help build. As crew boss, John kept everyone working, all the time, and I liked that. I was never idle. My skills grew.

The new cabin would become home for Fletcher and me, plus it had a kitchen and a dining room so that we could serve meals. It was so nice that, as with the advent of getting running water, it bothered me. I suspected it might be thought of as my *domain*. I had come on the scene a summer ago, knowing little about northern coastal living and boats. I had learned much, still had boundless curiosity, and craved to know more. It was the outdoor work I loved.

The new cabin was what is called an "open plan." Downstairs was a kitchen complete with Formica counters, cupboards, drawers, and a pantry. Downstairs also had a nice dining area, and a living room area with a wood stove. Compared to the old gray A-frame and the shed-roofed cabin we'd built the summer before, which we now called the Middle cabin, the new cabin was spacious and civilized. The upstairs held rows of shelving for storing provisions and gear, with a sleeping area toward the front. Steep stairs came up through the floor at the back. There was a window there on the back wall, where I could stop and gaze out at the lake and Mamanowatum, and check on the duck families, as I came up or down the stairs. Windows took up nearly the entire front wall of the cabin, both upstairs and down. And downstairs rows of windows ran along both sides, like a church. Our bed was right up against the front upstairs windows, just like in the old A-frame. I opened my eyes each morning to the waves slapping the beach, my sleepy gaze taking in our cove, the sea, the mountains beyond, the weather.

After our cabin was done, John moved out of his wall tent and into the old A-frame.

The summer got into full swing, and permitted Fletch and me no leisure time. We worked together often, which I enjoyed, especially out on the boat. On shore we usually had our own jobs to do. When he wasn't cleaning and stowing gear, cutting bait, rigging poles, maintaining the boat, en route to or from Seward, running charters or doing other work, Fletch could be found with our guests, sitting on logs on the beach in the evenings. Most of the time, I'd be with him, listening to his and others' stories, telling a few of my own. I wished he and I had more time alone.

One August night as we sat with wine glasses in our cabin, enjoying a rare evening alone, we heard John's footsteps on the path and moments later his knock and shout outside our door: "Ding-dong, it's the Avon Lady!" He then hauled up on the latch-string with exaggerated force and let himself in, knowing that since we'd heard him walk this way from a long ways off, we would be prepared for company. I stayed a while listening to them talk, pushing away my disappointment at yet another interruption from John. It was a beautiful evening of blue, gold, and white. Long green wavelets swept into the cove one after another. I decided to take a walk with Tutka. He bounded to his feet as soon as I lifted the latch-bar. We stepped down off the deck under the boughs of a large spruce that grew there, and onto the cobbles. We passed the Middle cabin, passed John's, and angled downward to the water's edge, heading toward the eastern end of our cove. An otter suddenly appeared in the water just five feet away. Tutka and the otter had a game. Tutka sort of liked the game and sort of didn't. It was called "Pop and Bark." Tutka stood at the water's edge, the otter swam under water, unseen, and then suddenly popped up right in front of him. With a low growl that erupted into a bark—"R-RUFF!"—Tutka leapt at the otter, and with just a wee splash—hardly a drop displaced—the otter slipped under, disappeared, and popped up three feet away. But *which* way, Tutka could never know. So his body was on springs, his head swiveling. Pop! "R-RUFF!" Tutka jumped *into* the water, then back on the beach shaking off. Pop! "R-RUFF!" Tutka eventually wore out from wading in circles and leaping off the beach at the otter. He gave up after a while, and we continued our walk. I'd had a good laugh and had wished Fletch had been there with me. It was a lovely, clear evening.

Within a day Mamamowatum was invisible in heavy rain clouds and fog. I turned the marine radio to the weather: "Southwest winds at 15 miles per hour with gusts to 25 miles per hour. Rain. Seas to five feet. Small craft advisory, REPEAT: *small craft advisory...*" It wasn't a gale or even a bad storm, it wasn't an unusual weather forecast. It was just cold and wet and miserable. And it would probably last for days, possibly many days. The sullen sky hung only a few feet above the treetops. We had a group of six coming out who had reserved three days on Fox Island.

I felt sorry for the guests who came out when the weather was like that. They had made reservations months before and just had bad luck. But we did all we could to make the trip one to remember fondly. Hundred-pound halibut could still be caught when the weather was bad, crab pots could still be brought up from the depths and a feast of fresh tanner crab could still be served in the evening. In the big cabin, cozy with a fire in the stove and steam on the windows, friends could still laugh and tell stories and play games far into the night while the wind blew the rain sideways. It was wonderful even when it was horrible.

Most guests were either families or groups of friends. They wanted to go out in *Fox Islander* to fish for halibut and other deep-water fish, such as lingcod, black bass, or red snapper. Later in the summer they wanted to fish for salmon as the salmon came through the bay on the way to their spawning streams. Some guests wanted to go about in the boat to see glaciers and ice fields, fjords and mountains, whales and other wildlife, and sea birds by the thousands, surrounded by majestic scenery.

Fletcher took the group of six back to Seward, their coolers filled with fresh halibut, their cameras full of pictures. He cleaned the boat, did the shopping, picked up the mail, and met the next guest on the dock. She was an older woman by herself, the kind who wears tweed skirts and knit scarves, and carries several shoulder bags. She would be staying only one day.

As always, Fletcher called me on the marine radio when he was about 15 minutes from the island. I took my raincoat off the peg by the door, making sure to zip it up and pull the hood over my head. I walked the path to the guest cabin and built a fire in the wood stove. On this day I set a bouquet of wildflowers on the table to add some cheer. Fletcher invited the woman, Barbara, to dinner in the big cabin that evening. She reminded me of Mary Poppins —adventurous, but sensible. We learned that she was from Kansas and on her first trip to Alaska. She wanted to see wildlife, but she especially wanted to see puffins. She had been to Scotland and photographed the puffins there, and she coveted a photograph of an Alaskan puffin for her collection. Indeed, she had come all the way from Kansas to Alaska to photograph a puffin.

The next day the bad weather was worse. The rain blew horizontal, first this way, then that. Fletcher, Tutka, and I, and Barbara with her big camera and bags of equipment, climbed aboard the boat. I unhooked the boat from the mooring and we motored out of the cove. Fletcher hoped he could take the *Fox Islander* out to Rugged Island where sea lions by the hundreds hauled out on rocky shelves, but it was too rough. It was far too rough to make it to Barwell Island where auklets, murres, and puffins by the thousands floated in great rafts on the water, and nested on the cliff sides. For an hour we had to content ourselves with poking along with the heater on in the boat's cabin, sipping hot cider and peering through the fog and clouds. I wondered where the sea otters could be and wished for a whale. A big humpback or a pod of killer whales would make up for a lot. We watched ravens playing high above in the wind. Ravens like to be blown about in the stronger winds up high and were having a lot of fun that day, not just by blowing around, but also by making sounds. "RONK!" "CLOINK!" "RAAAA!" They reminded me of trash in a desert dust devil. As a child, I stood by and watched paper bags and small tumbleweeds spiral higher and higher until they became invisible. The ravens looked like wild black rags. Down on our level, a few seagulls floated near a tiny beach that nestled into the rocky shore. Up, down, up, down, went the boat.

Puffins aren't puffy or even fluffy. They're sleek. They're not fat, but they *are* heavy. They live on cliffs and when they jump off to fly, they fall fifty feet or more before they get enough lift to fly. They just have short, narrow wings, so they have to live on high cliffs. When they take off from water, they run and run to get up enough speed. They do the fifty-yard dash, their little legs kicking and thrashing the surface of the water. Sometimes they just give up and dive under the water, where they are expert swimmers. Sleek, with wings like propellers and feet like rudders, they swim deep and fast, and dart about like crazy torpedoes. Then they pop up like corks with a mouth full of silvery minnows.

My thoughts returned to Barbara, peering with dignity from the back deck, awash in wind and rain, her scarf tucked into her collar. I began to think that our guest from Kansas would be disappointed. But then Fletcher thought he saw something through the fog. In the next moment we all saw it: a lone, wee puffin bobbing on the waves, bright and colorful as a toy. The puffin stayed while Barbara, beaming, took picture after picture.

John decided to go with Fletch on the next day's charter, and I had a day to myself. I rejoiced to see John leave. I'd about had it with his constant stream of insults. He'd shouted, after I'd showered one day on the back deck of the Middle cabin, "Here she comes, Miss Beauty Queen!" making light, I supposed, of my usual carefree approach to grooming, or pretending that my taking a shower was an attempt, which failed, at making myself presentable. At any rate, I was beginning to weary of the game of deflecting his jabs.

Undoubtedly this was nothing other than his habitual jabbering, essentially meaningless. I couldn't abide it. John's rudeness got to me.

So I was alone on Fox Island on a big new day, free! And Tutka begged for a walk. We could travel in two directions, either down the beach, or up the beach. These are two very different destinations. "Down the beach" is protected in the arms of the island, sheltered from wind, peaceful. Ravens squawked about like black chickens on the gray cobbles. On the green water of the cove, a few black cormorants and white seagulls floated. A couple of Steller's jays followed us, flew ahead, stopped to perch on spruce boughs, then waited for us to catch up before flying ahead again.

After visiting the far end of the beach in the calm direction, we turned and walked the long, curving distance back past the cabins, on the way up the beach, to see what we could see. Just past the old cabin the solid granite of the island forms a cliff right down to the beach, beaten by waves at high tide. The trees here are the scrubby roots-in-crevasses kinds, alder and stunted spruce, hanging on in the wind. The stones underfoot are bigger and irregularly shaped, making the walking more difficult. Tutka walked with me, his paws clack-clacking on the slippery rocks. Along the base of the cliff, past a cave in which icicles still hang in the early spring, we came at last to the Point. There, standing atop fallen boulders, I looked around the edge of Fox Island, south to the open Gulf of Alaska. Big waves surged among the boulders on which we stood.

Long strands of green/black kelp swirled with the waves, signifying a kelp forest below in the deep. Three sea otters floated among the strands, watching us with calm curiosity. I looked up to see where the boulders had fallen off the mountainside. An eagle sat up there on a ledge, watching us with one eye, white head tilted. We couldn't stay long. The tide would come in and we'd be caught.

John's Ways

A few days later, Fletcher and our guests left for Seward in the morning. This meant the peacefulness of Fox Island without visitors would be the day's pleasure for John and me. It was nowhere near as peaceful with him here, though.

He was like Paul Bunyan. Every day he woke up happy, and loud. He'd burst out of his cabin, stand on the beach and yell, "WHAT A GREAT DAY!" After coffee and one of his brick-like cinnamon buns, he'd commence working. He'd work most of the day, quite often whistling a tune, and it was unbelievable what he could accomplish. When he stopped, he enjoyed his resting just as much. He would nap and come out of his cabin an hour later and yell, "THE COUCH MONSTER GOT ME!" But mostly John worked. Nothing stopped him. No job was too big, and he never saw a reason for putting anything off until later. Jobs could be started *now*, he knew, and be done in no time. He could figure out how to do anything. If something broke, John didn't adjust to a new way of doing things—he fixed whatever broke. He saw potential improvements everywhere, and made them with gusto.

His cabin, the old A-frame, perched on the narrowest part of the beach, closest to the steep side of the island and closest to the water. Long before Fletcher owned the land, an earthquake shook loose several large boulders, which had crashed down the mountain and into the "backyard" of John's cabin just outside his door. As we stood together watching the jay eat up a day-old sourdough pancake off one of the boulders, John said, "This backyard would be better without the boulders." He'd have more room to split wood. I didn't give it much thought, because, after all, they were really big boulders, and what could be done about them? John wasn't a big man, but he was strong. He strode away to the shop, and came back whistling and bristling with sledgehammers. Although John and I often worked together on labor-intensive jobs, today I stayed a safe distance away until the big boulders were in pieces. KaBAM! The pieces flew. Afterward, I helped John position the largest of them under his cabin to fortify the foundation. The remaining rubble was so small it just became part of the gravel of his yard. By the end of the day John had built a lean-to addition on his wood shed, creating a large outdoor room where he could sit splicing rope or tinkering with his radios outside out of the rain. And he had set up an efficient—and really quite attractive—wood splitting yard. Often after that I'd see him sitting under his lean-to early in the morning, sipping coffee while feeding pancakes to the jays.

John worked so fast and hard, he didn't take the time to set the tools down. He threw them instead. He'd throw the hammer—THUNK!—and pick up the hand saw, toss the saw—WHANG!—to grab the square, whip a pencil line down—TWANK! The square is gone, the pencil's in his teeth getting teeth marks in it. He'd cut up a big log with the chain saw, fling the chain saw down onto the beach—CRUMP! Position the log for the next cut. Male guests unaccustomed to John reacted in different ways. They would either try to match him in effort and effectiveness, which I recognized as a tremendous advantage because so much got done, or they would back up a few steps and wait until it was safe to participate.

John had wild ways, but once you got used to him, if you ever did, and if you could take his bluntness, you could see him as a fine and patient teacher. He taught *everyone*. He even taught guests who didn't necessarily *want* to do work, for he felt that to not work was to be lazy, and to be lazy was *detestable* unless you had worked really hard for a good long while already, and accomplished a lot for the greater good of all. Fletcher did the same thing, judiciously, and for different reasons. He never turned down a guest's offer to help, no matter how rhetorical the offer. There was always so much to do, and I think Fletch felt that working added to the guests' wilderness experience. It was rough, tough, homesteading-type work.

In the dark of winter Fletch had scheduled a week of the summer off for us. This gave us time for an "explore" to a remote bay that had recently become part of the nation's newest official treasure—Kenai Fjords National Park. There in the bay was a cabin owned by the Park Service. We unloaded our gear onto the beach, pulled the skiff up above high-tide line, and, loaded with gear, entered the dark forest along a path that led back to the cabin. It sat deep in a grove of wet alder trees. Being there gave a closed-in feeling. Inside, the well-built structure was even darker. The problem was easy to recognize: too many alder trees. John commented with disgust that the Park Service must be lazy. "Those damn alders need cut back." And he looked around inside with wild eyes and said, "There's not enough firewood here." Fletcher and I saw the look and stayed out of the way and didn't say anything while John fired up the chain saw and cut a quarter-acre meadow around the cabin. Without stopping he then turned the chain saw to the curvy trunks and branches that lay in a leafy pile all around him, cutting them into stove-length pieces. At last the awful noise of the saw abated. The blue exhaust smoke drifted away, we were in a commodious green meadow carpeted with grass, mangled twigs and leaves.

John was stacking several months' worth of firewood under the cabin porch, and I heard the sound of the surf again. Peace had come to the valley where the cabin stood. I felt like sitting in a rocker on the porch and playing a fiddle tune.

With generous hours of daylight yet ahead of us, we went off exploring across the bay to a lake we knew about, hoping we'd arrived at the same time the salmon were coming in. Just off shore from the entrance to the lake, using a light spinning rod with only two-pound test line, I hooked into a good-sized salmon. With such light line, it was going to be a long battle. Fletch sat back and relaxed, finessing the movements of the skiff, and together we closed the distance between the fish and us. "Where there's one, there's many!" John shouted. Fletch began to laugh and joke and I thought, *so, there's going to be fish!* I was happy not just because it was going to be fun, but because Fletch had been speaking for weeks about wanting to smoke and can enough salmon to last the winter. Now I looked over at him and smiled. He grinned and said, "You'll be in the Fox Island Hall of Fame if you don't lose it." John said, "We'll have enough for salmon all winter, Shit o' dear! Don't get too much tension on that line! Check your drag!"

After John netted my fish, we entered the lake and beached the skiff. Fletch got out the sturdiest poles with the heaviest line, intent on keeping any fish hooked. For the first time in weeks he wasn't worrying whether the guests were having the best possible time, he wasn't looking ahead to what needed done, he wasn't preoccupied about the boat, or the weather, he wasn't tired. John walked a ways down the beach from us, maybe out of a sort of kindness he occasionally had. Tutka ran back and forth between John and us, barking as each thrashing, flipping fish was dragged ashore.

"Ho ho, look at him go," Fletch chuckled.

Hours later we packed our catch of fat fish on ice and headed back to the Park Service cabin. There was a note on the door:

Hello—

We stopped to say hi and see how things were going. We'll motor over later today. In the meantime it would be appreciated if you would not cut any

more alders. Maintenance work is the job of Park
Service employees.

Mark Meyer
Eric Gorkin
Aialik Bay Rangers

P.S. Please contact the Park Service immediately upon
your return to Seward.

"A couple *college kids*," John said, but with a hint of false
bravado. He was in hot water, and he knew it. It wasn't the
first time, and it sure wouldn't be the last. But it was months before
he returned to Seward. He probably decided by then that it
was okay to let the matter drop.

John had another bad day a few weeks later. Anne and Neal
came for a visit and we met them on the beach to help pull the skiff
up and unload their gear. John started his series of astonishing

actions by throwing Anne's pack into the water. He meant, of course, to throw it onto the beach, but we hadn't quite pulled the skiff far enough up yet and he'd mistimed his gusto on the job of unloading.

Later that evening he took the skiff down to the quiet end of the beach on an errand to tell Anne and Neal that he'd be frying up some halibut for dinner in about an hour, and that they could bring some wine if they had any and a salad. Anne and Neal sat on the beach enjoying the sunshine and solitude. John's approach to beaching a boat differed from Fletch's. It was simpler. He went about it like this: gun the engine enough to run the boat quite a ways up onto and *into* the beach, which he figured would hold the boat—wave action notwithstanding—until he got back, as long as he didn't tarry. When John got back to the skiff, he gave it a hard shove out of the beach, jumped in, clambered toward the stern, lowered the outboard, and yanked the starter rope. He found to his dismay that he had left the engine on full throttle and in reverse, so that now he blasted off backward, carving a big circle, and throwing up a huge white wake. His legs flew up and he fell out but managed to hang on to the back corner of the skiff and reach over the side and kill the engine before the skiff made its circle and met up with the beach again. Anne and Neal witnessed the whole thing from their beach blanket. Fletcher had only the day before admonished John to be more safety conscious. Fletch thought the incident was funny as hell on the one hand. On the other hand, he was angry. He said that when he confronted him, John had acted sheepish, but I didn't actually see him act sheepish, although I thought his eyes seemed either bigger or bluer than usual. With those eyes, his big nose, and those gray and white curls floating around his bald head, he could look like the picture of innocence.

I had a good dream about John a few nights later. I guess you can't help it if you're around someone of the opposite sex a lot, even if you hate him part of the time. Nonetheless—despite my frequent recoiling at his affronts to me and to our guests (interestingly, never to Fletch)—I usually tried to excuse John as much as possible. This is how I was able to live and work in such close quarters for such long periods with him.

I admired John's love of knowledge and was grateful for his willingness to share it. Between what I had garnered from my father and now John, I had become a carpenter of sorts, sometimes suddenly deciding I needed a piece of furniture—a bench, a stool, a bookshelf—and then making it up out of my head. Some of them were downright rickety, but occasionally John complimented me: "You did a damn good job of that! *Damn* good!" He'd shake his head and shout, "*Shit o' dear!*" And later, he'd even tell others about it. When something impressed John, he became repetitive. To be honest, I never minded hearing a story of what a good job I'd done.

When we had our own jobs to do, I listened to his singing while he worked, and he listened to mine. Being secondary operators and not carrying Fletch's burden of concerns in this island endeavor, John and I had more relaxed time together than Fletch and I ever had. He saw me paint pictures on rocks and make kelp candles or seashell necklaces with children. I saw him carry out a lot of manly accomplishments and make a radio out of copper wire and share his fresh-baked cinnamon buns with the guests. If we two ever had what could be called deep conversations, they'd been about Fletcher's plan to build Fox Island Lodge into some kind of upscale destination or about Fletcher's drive, as I saw it, to civilize the place, and to increase the size of groups we could accommodate. As it was, if we had more than ten or twelve people out, I felt overwhelmed, as if people were barging into my sanctuary. All I can say is, it just didn't feel right. If our lodge had been anywhere other than in a perfect wilderness spot, if it had been reachable by road along a waterfront, say, or on a side street in a place such as Seward or Homer, I doubt I would have felt this way. But I cringed at any thought of developing Fox Island much beyond what we had already done. I worried over Fletcher's mention of constructing a permanent dock or sprinkling the cove with mooring buoys or of someday running a restaurant here. I loved the cove the way it was and for things to be rustic and wild. And I thought folks who came out ought to too, and by gosh, I think they all did, even if that wasn't what they'd had in mind to begin with. Because it was so wild and primitive, it was more of an adventure for some people than they bargained for, and I'll bet they still sit around and talk about it, like it's one of their most interesting stories.

However, I knew little of Fletcher's motives other than how they affected me. I was in it for love and for adventure, and as in the rest of my life, I had no ambitions. We couldn't be there at all maybe, if not for Fletch's ambitions. He was a businessman trying to make an income at something he loved and he had to make smart decisions. I didn't always feel good about those decisions, but what did I know? I thought, and I guess John thought too, why couldn't Fox Island Lodge just continue being what it was? John and I were allies in this way.

In my dream John and I had had a romantic interlude. It was night, moonlit. A log raft on which we stood pulled away from the shore, pushed by a sudden wind across a pond and into a grove of reeds, where it came to a standstill. We began to pole our way out. Someone was counting on me. I had to find a certain boy and deliver him to Tibet. He was to become a great leader. The quest seemed all but impossible. I'd been given instructions to find a winged horse. John took this information without surprise and only redoubled his efforts to get us out of the reeds and then finally to where the white horse stood in the wind. I ran to it, grabbed a handful of its mane, and began climbing on its back when John said from behind me, "Let me hold you before you go."

In that moment, there was nothing I wanted more than the comfort of that masculine embrace.

As the horse carried me upward, the shoreline slipped away, and the ocean lay black as night below. I flew through the cloud cover and then leveled out for our long journey above luminous, billowy clouds lit by the moon and stars. It was fabulous.

The dream was so vivid that I still felt inclined toward John when I awoke, an hour or so after Fletch had left for a day of fishing with our guests. I came out of the cabin feeling good about John for a change and he acted the same way toward me—real sweet. It was strange—had he had a dream about *me*? I watched him cleverly saw away a quarter of a short log, lengthwise, to make a beach couch and together we positioned it just so under a spruce tree facing the cove. He chatted about the young jay that had flown into his cabin while he was washing up that morning. It had perched on the plank shelf over his sink and he'd fed it a piece of sourdough, tearing off bits which the bird took one by one in its beak.

Well, things didn't stay like that. By early afternoon he'd made some insulting remark, I'd called him a shit-head under my breath, and we were back on solid footing. I was much relieved and was left to ponder the mystery of dreams. That evening while John and Fletch stood on the deck of our cabin, discussing the pros and cons of propane freezers, I sat on the new beach couch mesmerized by the water. The silky ocean touched the shoreline with barely a movement, as if it were a quiet lake in a forest. I thought that while I dreamt, Fletch may have gotten up to start his day, and I just might have heard him say, "Let me hold you before I go." Maybe this was why I'd had the dream. And maybe it was John in the dream instead of Fletch because in reality, John and I spent much more time together.

Before long it was time to return to school in Albuquerque again. I came away from Fox Island that second summer with a satisfying array of skills, feeling enlivened and fortunate. It hadn't all been easy. I had wrestled with John's insensitivity and what I perceived as Fletch's aloofness at times. And I had not stopped struggling with having to be around people all the time, and with the related feeling, at certain times, that people came gawking roughshod and heedless onto this island that had my heart in its soul. Fletcher and John and I had taken just a few days off that summer, when we made the trip to Aialik Bay to find salmon. The rest of the time we worked without let-up. As a person who finds equilibrium in solitude, I'd had only a few days alone, when John went on one of the charters or into Seward with Fletcher, instead of me. Other than that, I was with people every day, all day, for long hours.

Fletcher and I hadn't been alone together the entire summer. This made me uncertain whether he wanted to *be* together. Most mornings he'd get up at five, and never very romantically, because it just wasn't his nature, say something like, "Make two thermoses of coffee today. They want turkey sandwiches. Do we have any more of those pilot crackers?" And off he'd go. When I'd asked right-out, he'd assure me with a brief hug that he cared very much for me. But otherwise his motto seemed to be "It goes without saying."

I would attempt to convince myself that I wasn't being mature. If I were *mature*, I told myself, I wouldn't feel these *needs*. I didn't like to think that I was like Kevin, always needing some proof of love, constantly seeking reassurance. I allowed that maybe I did need someone to talk to. I had sat outside on the log couch one morning for more than an hour with Carl Schuman's wife, Sue, a pleasant woman in her early sixties. We sat there shooting the breeze, talking about this and that, and it had felt wonderful, companionable. I never thought I could enjoy aimless conversation so much.

I had spent two summers on Fox Island with no spoken intentions of moving north, I guessed because it was a given that I would finish school in Albuquerque. I suppose we both wondered if I was going to give up New Mexico. I made lame attempts, but put off trying to divine the future; it was just too hard to know what would be best. I was careless about the whole deal: What a lark I was on! I needed a sign from Fletch, and I decided to wait and see if he would bring up his own desires and then see how those influenced mine.

I got my answer after we had closed up the cabins, hauled away from the island all that needed hauling away for the winter, and tied up the boat in its place in the harbor. Fletch drove the pickup to the top of the ramp. He opened the hatch on the camper shell, lowered the tailgate, and we stowed our gear and let Tutka jump in. It felt strange to be in a wheeled vehicle. As we drove back to Anchorage, through Turnagain Pass between fall-colored, snow-tipped mountains, Fletch said, "Susannah, scoot over and sit beside me." So I did. He said, "You were wonderful this summer, a great help."

"Thanks!"

He said, "Aren't we lucky? When I get back to work I always feel so good about what I did all summer."

I said, "That's how I feel. I kind of hate to ask my friends what *they* did."

"I'm sure going to miss you this fall. Maybe you should think about taking a semester off sometime and spending it up here. Do you think you'd like that?" These windows into his feelings were a revelation to me. I listened carefully.

"Would *you* like that?" I said.

"Yes, I told you. I'll miss you. I hate to think of you going. If you took next year's fall semester off, we could come out to Fox Island after the season and have it all to ourselves. Just relax, do some projects. I'd like to see what being there in winter would be like. And we could take some ski trips up north."

"I'd really like that!"

"Will you come back in the spring, Susannah?"

I said yes. I felt a wonderful closeness to Fletch, and released from thoughts of my future any more serious than wondering what I would do for fun next summer. I knew Fletch felt the same.

One's Place

But then, I felt as if I'd left one love for another when I returned home. As the plane flew over the Sandias, I could see distant ranges to the south, their peaks obscured in massed thunderheads. I thought of the smell of mountain meadow grass and pine and rain. Miles and miles of sunlit country, tawny and warm like the hide of a cougar asleep in the sun, separated these mountain ranges and their rainstorms. On horseback it would take days to ride from one to another. In the mountains it would be cold, the creeks noisy and spirited. The usually dry arroyos in the low country would soon run deep with muddy water.

My Alaska and my New Mexico were two very different loves, and I could meld my spirit into either. I didn't sit there in my airplane seat thinking these two places on earth were capable of love, and yet I did feel loved by them. They were *so good* to me. "There's something there that loves you back," I said to myself.

My connection with New Mexico encompassed a lifetime of camping trips with my family, weekend hikes with my sisters, and day-long horseback rides. I could see myself exploring every square mile of it for the rest of my life. That evening, sitting with my parents on their brick patio, with the sunset glaring out of a crack between the earth and storm clouds, and my horse munching sweet alfalfa in her corral, I had a sudden clear memory. I remembered that as a child, never having seen the ocean, never having seen water larger than the local reservoir, I used to gaze in dismay at paintings in books of sailing ships being tossed on monstrous waves, and shiver at the coldness, the power, the vastness of the ocean. A part of me feared the ocean, yet there I was, drawn to a life on an island and on boats, with a man whose single direction in life was to spend as much time as possible on the water.

Susannah,

Well, I am back in town. School starts tomorrow. John and Tutka still out on Fox I. Think that John was glad to see Tutka stay.

Sure wish you could have been there last weekend. Van Wetzels had the nicest kids of the summer while we had the worst weather—storming with a record rain— more rain Sat. than in all of June, July and Aug. Kids played games, parents tried to keep them from getting too bored. We fished for several hours in front of the cabin with no bites. Sat. night was wild with anchors dragging and a boat sinking in Thumbs Cove. 10 people rescued and a 35 footer going high and dry in Sunny Cove. Decided to troll a little on the way in with the Van Wetzels—good thing. We landed a nice silver and two pinks along with a "shit load" of bass along Hive I.

Monday with improved weather I went to Fault Pt. With Schuman, John, Jay. In three hours we landed two 150 pounders. Jay got a 72 pounder.

I think a lot about you off and on but don't like writing down these thoughts too much as you probably know which doesn't mean I am not thinking.

Love, Fletch

I read and re-read Fletch's letters, and wrote and re-wrote long letters back, working hard to express myself without sounding dramatic. He called once a week or so and, back in my own territory, I spoke of my love for New Mexico and the dreams I'd had of raising horses, just in case he might find himself drawn to a complete change of direction in life. In response he called to ask if enough snow fell in the mountains of New Mexico to run a cross-country ski lodge. Another time a letter arrived from him with a cassette tape in it. He and Tutka had journeyed out to Fox Island, now virtually off-limits in the winter weather. A stiff wind blew in from the north as they'd taken a walk on the beach, and Fletch had recorded the sounds of the surf and of their footsteps in the cobbles. Over the pounding of the surf, he described what he saw—the mountain which I called Mamamowatum now covered in deep snow, the lake now frozen—and he spoke of how beautiful it was and how lonely he and Tutka felt to be there without me.

Galluping

The best thing about that winter was my friend Ned and a horse called Gallup. I lived with my parents and they lived right in some of the best riding country anywhere around Albuquerque. I never liked any other kind of riding more than trail riding. I could count the times on two fingers that I'd gotten dressed up and gotten in an English saddle on some long type of horse to circle around inside an arena. I didn't jump, not on a jumping horse, anyway. My style was jumping sagebrush at a flat-out gallop. When I was younger, I rodeoed some, just for fun. I mean, I liked *all* riding, but my favorite kind was trail riding and my favorite kind of horse was a horse that knew how to be on the trail. A horse that has only been in an arena might walk right off the trail, might even walk straight into a tree. A horse like that doesn't watch where she's going on the rough or steep spots. She waits for your cue. A trail horse picks her own way, with some guidance from you if you think you need to give it. A lot of the time it's better to loosen the reins some and let the horse have her head. A good trail horse is usually smaller, without anything too long, like back, or legs, or head, or neck. She is alert, calm, doesn't   panic easily, and enjoys the ride as much as you do. If the horse steps in wire, she carefully steps out or stops right there. If there's a dead thing nearby, she'll look at it real hard—but usually won't panic.

Sometimes the horse might need your reassurance, but she's so smart on the trail, so experienced, that you know you can count on her. Some horses plod along in a good-natured lazy state, but the best trail horse has personality and spirit and prefers to be in front if there's more than one horse on the trail. She keeps her ears up—they don't flop. But on a warm day, if you're on a long ride and you're both really relaxed and the trail is wide and easy, she might make an exception. Her ears might flop and you might relax so much that you turn around and ride backward for a while just to see where you've been. I used to ride bareback a lot. If you're riding bareback backward, you can lie down, fold your arms under your face on the horse's rump, and hook your feet over the horse's neck. It's real comfortable.

I had met Ned when I had an Irish roommate a few semesters back, before I got my own apartment and before Kevin came into my life. He was my Irish roommate's boyfriend. Ned was Irish, too, and wore a beard that went down the side, underneath his chin and back up the other side—one long strip, not that wide. He had curly hair and was tall and lanky. I hadn't seen him for a couple years, but he showed up again in my life and was now studying to be a doctor. I was still studying education and was now doing my student teaching at a junior high school in downtown Albuquerque. I was doing fine in education, because I was still taking classes I liked on campus. Off campus, I worked with small groups of five to seven kids in the school. Many were from underprivileged homes, which might mean they lived with a mom who was only 29 years old, and uncles who worked on big, low cars in their dirt yard. Being underprivileged might mean they didn't wear braces or take violin lessons. But these were great kids, and we had good times together. In many ways, they were hungry for education, especially if the lessons were creative and presented with imagination. I loved the way they asked so many questions.

My bad teaching experience came later, when I was responsible for a whole classroom of first graders. I'll get to that further along.

Dear Fletch,

Did you know I have been back for a month and four

days now? It seems as if I have been back longer, because school is so engrossing! I am at work right now and as usual there isn;t much to do. This morning Julie and I and our professor, Mark, went on a field trip with our six students: Francisco, Samantha, Cora, Theodore, Nick, and Tina. We went out to Indian Lakes where the people who bought Gemini from me used to keep him after I sold him. Yesterday it was warm, but today a storm moved in. Within a few hours it rained, snowed, got cold, got warm and sunny, and blew up to 50 mph. Incredibly enough, our field trip was a success. The kids didn;t want to go back!! We had a good time, but I am tired and I am so glad it;s Friday. This typewriter has a Spanish ball on it. Where the exclamation point is, is this Ñ. And where the question mark is, is this ". Where the apostrophe is is this ; . I have to search for the right symbols. I had a dream about you last night. I dreamed that I was fishing and you were watching. It sure was nice seeing you again. It is less than seven and a half months away, But it seems too long a time. I hope you don;t get tired of waiting. I have so much to keep me busy the time seems to fly by. I miss you so much. Guess what I'm going to do this weekend" ? "NothingÑ! I am so tired I am going to sleep in and take it easy all weekend. Wow I can;t wait.!

Did you get a dog bed for Tutka"!? I have been telling everybody about the four feet of snow there. I showed Mark the Anchorage Daily News articles about Anne because I was wondering if anyone else thought it was O.K. for high school students to write about issues pertinent to them. He didn;t comment on it, because he has this idea that I think my sisters are wonderful, talented and intelligent, and that I think I am not. He even seemed a little angry! He seems to have this idea that I am a :brilliant writer: (we have to keep journals and we write in them every day). I mean, he thinks I have a real talent, honest to God. I know you can't tell by the way this letter is put together! It really did amaze me when he said that, so I told him about Betsy getting an F on a paper once at Mt. Taylor because it was so good the teacher could not believe she wrote it. He told me he doesn;t *CARE* about other talent in the family, but that he would like to see something else I have written. He has some degree in Language Arts. I still can;t really believe it.

As usual there are so many distractions here that I don't know if I am making sense. Anyway, I get off on these tangents. I got off on a tangent in my journal and wrote the complete story of our trip to Aialik.

On our field trip today, we saw a red tailed hawk. We had two pairs of binoculars along and the kids just went crazy. I don;t know if these kids have a whole lot of experiences in general. I am enjoying myself. !

Love, Susannah

On Saturdays when Ned came out to Placitas, I'd borrow Gallup from the neighbors and we'd ride all day. Gallup was a big horse, but he was a good trail horse. He was so nicely built and smart and had so much trail sense, and such a heart, I didn't think I'd ever meet a horse like him again. He was a bright sorrel color, like sun on a polished fiddle. My horse Trinket was older by then—I'd had her since I was 11—and I didn't usually take her on the longer rides. Ned rode Gallup, and I borrowed a buckskin mare called Rae from another neighbor. She had a pretty face and head, a white blaze, and big, intelligent eyes. She looked and moved like a good cowpony.

On our rides that fall, through bright yellow scrub-oak forests, down into canyons, and along red dirt roads, Ned and I would talk. It was pure pleasure having someone to ride with, and especially having someone to get into interesting conversations with again.

One time we had what started out to be an argument about the destiny of I.V. bottles. His friend Beth had an organic farm in the Rio Grande valley south of Albuquerque. Beth raised honeybees and had asked Ned to keep his eye out for good containers for honey. He had brought her "these really great—beautiful!" I.V. bottles: sturdy, useful, and sterile. She refused them. She had raised the bees herself and harvested the golden honey that they had each processed from the flowers of the field. She didn't like the idea of putting this honey in a plastic bottle that came from a hospital because she felt that hospitals de-humanized people and exploited their misfortune. Ned felt she should have accepted the bottles because they were good quality and "stack up real nice."

I said, "There's something to that 'you are what you eat' that the Indians believed. They ate a deer and they could run and listen like a deer. Well, Beth thinks if you put good honey in institutional containers, you're just not keeping the whole thing spiritual from beginning to end."

Ned said, with rather too much feeling, I thought, "I.V. bottles are *useful* and it's a good thing to prevent them from going to waste!" I could see he'd felt personally rejected by Beth. After all, he had embarked on a journey to become a doctor, a journey that would place him in the inner circle of hospital life. I didn't like seeing him feel like that and so I tried to look at the whole issue from another angle.

"Well, maybe she could have left them out in the sunshine for a few days, get them used to farm life, and *then* go ahead and put honey in them." That didn't perk him up as much as I'd hoped. He still rode stiff and defensive.

"*I* work at a hospital, and hospitals are mostly good in spite of some of the stuff that goes on. She doesn't know about it like I do." He had the long end of the reins in his other hand. Gallup made hop-steps, like he was ready to feel a slap on the rump.

I said, "It *is* a shame to let the bottles go to waste. Maybe she should have accepted them."

"That's right. Because my hospital tosses them out by the truck-full."

"Yes, that's wasteful, and honey would make them become honey bottles," I said. "I'm surprised that Beth would want to be wasteful."

"And those bottles last forever, they're *great* bottles," Ned said.

"Yes," I said, "Beth should have put them to use." He slouched like an old cow-hand and let the long end of the reins loose. Gallup swished his tail and tossed his head, once, and settled into a relaxed walk again.

"Thank you, Susannah."

It was all about the romance of life versus being sensible, an intermingling that was too familiar to me, and with which I struggled.

Just the week before I had told Ned all about Fox Island and how I loved working in the outdoors, and of my desire to learn as much as I could. He said I enjoyed "accruing know-how" about "practicalities" in the outdoors. I didn't think he understood. That morning when we met at my house I tore a page from my journal and handed it to him.

> At dawn, a furry bee crawls its way into a big closed flower whose petals are gently twisted together. Its petals, so soft and fragrant, yield, and caress the bee. It must feel good to the bee to come and get what it wants. It must feel good to the flower, to give what it has.
> Much later in the morning, and the bee has left. The sun is high, the day will be hot. Dawn's coolness has departed. The flower has opened fully.

A bee comes to the flower, stays briefly, and leaves.
But at pink dawn when the flower was closed, forming a
soft tunnel to its very center, and the furry bee crawled into
it, clear in to the center, that bee must have felt happy.

"Susannah, what does this have to do with anything?"

"Well, Ned, last week you said I liked 'practicalities' in the outdoors. I am showing you that working and living in the outdoors is as romantic as it gets."

Ned was a natural on horseback. He hadn't had that much time on horses, but he was comfortable. I would say he learned quickly, except that he just seemed to *know* already. I wondered: *What is it about knowledge?* Things you don't know and maybe never will, things you seem to have been born knowing that others don't…things you need to know. I was drawn off into daydreams by the spaciousness of the day, the pleasant warmth, the occasional bee in a bush, the rhythmic sound of the horses' hoofs clattering against the ground. Ned and I were silent, lost in our own thoughts. I began to think of "Teachers" who came into and out of one's life, some obvious, some not so obvious, the significance of some missed altogether until years later. I decided to consider the people in my life and determine if they were Teachers and if so, in what way.

I thought first of my horse Trinket, who wasn't a person, but who had a personality separate and different from any others'. At a young age on long rides I began to discover her, and she'd discovered me, and we had formed a true companionship. She taught me about inter-species compassion and forgiveness.

Dave, the Viet Nam vet, brought philosophy, pan-pipe music, tea and intimacy into my life for the first time. Kevin was a Teacher, I was sure, but I hadn't figured out quite how yet, and anyway, I didn't want to think about Kevin. Jack Snow taught me about lifelong humor, and passion, and that when you're older than 80 you're as alive as ever. Mark, my professor, looked me in the eye and told me I could write. No one else could have told me that and brought me as close to believing it as Mark, because I admired him so much. A thing Mark said that I knew could be significant to me someday, if I ever did presume to write, if I ever did somehow form such a concept of myself, was about the existence and function of editors. "I don't think I know grammar good enough to be a *writer*," I said, sure that writers were some of the people with the highest I.Q.s. Mark said, "That's what editors are for! You just *write!*"

John taught me about how to build things and about exuberance. Fletch taught me about business and putting deals together, planning big endeavors, providing "experiences" for others, and being tactful and diplomatic.

Clippity-clop, clackity-clack, I rode along behind Ned, a mouse ran across the trail, under a root and disappeared, leaving a tiny two-inch-high trail of dust. Life itself is a Teacher, I decided. Lessons from life are the hardest because we're so stubborn to them. We're too afraid to rearrange everything we think we know, and to dispense with our illusions.

I marveled at the idea that learning was something you could do your entire life: there would never be any boundaries to it, even if you lost half your brain or got amnesia or lost the use of your body. With what remained, you could learn.

I wondered about the great curiosity of humans; how we want to solve the mysteries of life so much that we make things up; how all that's been learned has been added to and changed as we learn ever more; and how we are so curious about one another.

A teacher at Mt. Taylor Elementary, Mrs. DeSmet, had made my life as a third grader miserable. Back then, horn-rimmed glasses were in style. Horn-rimmed is when the rims make an upward sweep with a point on the outer edges, with diamond-shaped ornaments in the point. She wore them. Hers were black. I can't fathom what quality they were supposed to enhance or emulate, but they were a little scary, back then, on her face which was so often angry at me. It had been Mrs. DeSmet who sent me into the hall for expressing Laura Ingalls Wilder's joy and surprise at finding an orange and a penny in her Christmas stocking. It was also Mrs. DeSmet who had taken away my first illustrated story, about the cow skeleton, and sent me to the dark room. But Mrs. DeSmet read all nine volumes of Laura's books to us, her classroom of little students. The learning I absorbed from those books each school day after lunch, with my arms folded upon my desktop, my head cradled in them, was valuable just in terms of the pleasure it gave.

I felt a surge of gladness for my mom and dad. Daddy, a field geologist, had explained the formation of countless rocks I'd bring to him as a child. He let me "help" him in his wood shop. And he not only taught me how to fish, but had sometimes allowed me—albeit with some begging on my part—to come along on fishing trips with him and his friends from the time I was little.

Mama had taught me to *see*. With characteristic rapture she'd say, "Susie, look at the way that grassy hill looks almost lavender right now in this light, see that? And the blue shadows the trees are casting. Oh, I just *love* that! That hillside is in shadow, but look how the sagebrush in the foreground is in sun and grows in *up*ward strokes" —she'd gesture the upward sweep of the sage with her arms, fingers spread, like a conductor—"and those thunderheads behind the hill—look how they're forming with the *same upward movement*! Look how they're all lit up!"

Up ahead Ned said, "You're awfully quiet, Susannah, what are you thinking about?"

"I'm thinking about why you're riding so crooked."

"The saddle got loose and I'm too lazy to get off. It's kind of comfortable like this."

"Just hope he doesn't spook at anything," I said.

"Let's stop here and have a snack for a while. Are you hungry?"

"Yep."

Susannah,

Good to hear from you. Your letter and pictures really gave me a lift. Have had the blahs this week. Be sure to keep track of the negatives for reprints for the album.

There is more snow falling on the mountains and it won't be long before it's down here. I envy you being down south and am a little jealous even if you aren't romantic with your riding partner. If there isn't any more attraction than there is with Rhonda, my former student, who stops by weekly to get me to jog with her,

I won't worry too much.

Sure missed you this weekend. Hinckly's, Anne and Neal, Zolton, Mona Cronk went out to Fox Island Friday afternoon. Tutka and Katie (Mona's dog). Nice trip out in drizzle. Saw porpoise and sea otters. Sat. it rained like crazy all morning. By afternoon we decided to go over to Sunny Cove to beachcomb and pick up some firewood. Got a batch of good logs—the driving rain turned into a driving snow storm. Flakes were the size of silver dollars—never seen them so huge. Called Neal who had stayed behind and had him fire up the sauna while we towed the logs back. Sauna was great. Took a dip in the cove during snow storm—a first for me—then a good nap (not a first). Scott and Ann put on a great K-bob dinner. The cove was really pretty with the snow coming down. Scott cooked with charcoal out front.

Sunday was crystal clear and cool. Water line had frozen up because I had forgotten to let it run. We took a tour out around Rugged I. on our way back in. Zolton took a lot of pictures. Several hundred sea lions in Mary's Bay. Stopped in Thumbs Cove for lunch and then back to Seward. Only one thing missing—you.

Love, Fletch

In addition to school and riding with Ned, on occasional Sundays I'd pick Jack Snow up at his house and we'd go for a drive. He'd have a tour in mind. He was a direct source of historical information because he remembered things that had been gone a very long time. As he talked, I found myself swept up in the drama of history in a way I never had been before. I was fascinated with history's connections to the present, and to me. He had been all around Albuquerque in the early 1900s, and he even remembered the stagecoach route along Old 85, along the Rio Grande. Jack pointed out the stage stops, recognizing remnants of those and other places that still existed in the clutter of aged buildings, hay fields, and modern commercial development. And he told stories. I gazed out of the car window and taught myself to see the past, erasing each element of the present with my imagination. I got so good at it that I sometimes had the eerie sensation of *being* in the past.

A ways out of Albuquerque, Old 85 passes by the Sandia Indian Pueblo. Jack had a friend there, whom we visited, an Indian man around his own age. Sandia is situated around a central dirt plaza. With my coffee cup in hand, I sat by the open door and listened to Jack and the old man talk and laugh about old times. I looked out the door onto the plaza and was struck not just by the peacefulness, but also by the beauty and orderliness of the ancient community. I loved the simple, homemade look of everything. The pueblo was made of sun-dried *adobe*, from the earth on which it stood and was the same soft tan color as the plaza. I saw no clutter, or straight lines, or sharp corners, or excessive decoration.

The pueblo's doorways face east to the morning sun and to the sacred Sandia Mountains, which rise up against the deep blue dome of the sky. Looking to the west I could see treetops in the cottonwood *bosque* forest crowded with ancient trees along the Rio Grande. The cottonwoods are brightest with their new spring leaves, and I've never seen trees that seem to pulsate in a breeze like cottonwoods. The air is so clear that the edges of things seem to have a thin, vibrating aura, if you look hard enough. With the cottonwoods pulsating, and the colors so true and bright, and the clouds so stark white they can hurt your eyes, well, there can seem to be a lot of subtle vibration everywhere.

Although there are pueblos near Grants, where I grew up, I'd never visited one. Later, when I learned to drive, I still didn't visit. People live in the pueblos, and I felt that it was an imposition to come through, no matter how curious or interested I was. At Sandia I felt privileged to be invited in and to sit by the door and listen to the two old friends.

Susannah,

Just finished a four day weekend. Teachers' conference

which we were not required to attend. Neal and I went down to Homer—cabin was fine but had settled 6 to 12 inches which surprised me—must be pretty high water table there.

Grogan and I went to Seward to bring back the 1-ton. Then Neal and I returned with 17' Gregor aluminum boat and Merc 25 I broke down and purchased. Went out to the island and found all OK—lake partially thawed, avalanches down but no damage—lots of rain. Seaweed stuck on the windows of the Middle cabin— must have been some high winds. They were coated with salt. Stayed the night—went over to the spit to check things out and hit a bonanza. This time Neptune delivered some beautiful finished 4 x 6's in a nice assortment of lengths (6-18 feet) along with 4 x 8 marine plywood—about 8 sheets. Bundled 4 x 6's—20 pieces—and towed back to cabins. Had to leave 6 sheets of plywood. Wonder what is at Bulldog, Porcupine, and Bear Glacier. Merc is good on gas. 1/2 tank total out and back (about 1-1/2 gallons each way).

Sure did rain though—and still pretty cold out there. So now to get the Fox Islander in shape and in the water. Though it was raining it sure was beautiful. We got real close to an eagle and saw lots of other wildlife— seals, sea otters, sea lions.

The new cabin seemed nicer than I had remembered. Your ideas are going to work perfectly. Hope and imagine that you are enjoying your vacation.

Miss you and think of you more than you probably realize.

Well that's about it for now. Hope to hear from you soon.

Love, Fletch

Kevin's Friend

I'd met up with Kevin and a girl on campus, so when he called one night, I asked him if he had a new girlfriend.

"Who, Missy? Naw, she's just a friend," he said. "Isn't she a cutie? You'd *really* like her."

He used to be jealous of my male friends. He had said about two months after we had gotten together, "How would you feel if I had friends that were *girls?*"

"Well, *don't* you?" I had asked.

"Just *Kyra,*" he'd said, "and she's my *sister*-in-law."

"I wouldn't care," I said. " 'Friend' is something different than 'lover.' If you had friends as wonderful as my friends, I'd be *glad* to know them! They'd be *my* friends, too!"

So now Kevin had a friend. But she wasn't one I'd be glad to know. She looked like an off-brand Barbie doll from a discount store, and her name was Missy. She lived in the dorms, she wore little clothes, she had the longest, fluffiest, blondest hair and a very dark tan. I couldn't stand the sight of her. *So, have I misjudged Kevin all this time?* I had so much admiration for Kevin's basic nature that this was like seeing the young Dali Lama in Las Vegas, wearing snake-skin boots and tossing back Jack Daniels. Although Kevin had a way of causing me pain, at least I had been able to go on caring about his welfare. I'd gone on being interested in his mind and his sensibilities and believing in him. He had still seemed like a fascinating person to me, with a great gift to give to the world, someday. Now I wasn't so sure. Maybe he was really someone I couldn't relate to. I questioned my judgement for ever having loved him. Because of Missy I wrote Kevin out of my life. I was sure of it.

Marina and Deb

No matter how carefree and independent I thought I was, the truth was that I had bonded with Fletch and Alaska. I didn't know the extent of it. I had spent two summers with him there and I wanted to do it again…and that was all I knew. Maybe I'd move there someday. If Fletch asked me to, then maybe I would. On the other hand, when I returned home to New Mexico I never wanted to leave. I recognized the blessing of having such wonderful choices in my life, but I felt in limbo. I wanted to share Alaska with people from my New Mexico life, so I invited two friends, Marina and Deb, to come up with me.

Susannah,

Imagine that your spring vacation is nearing an end. Hope it was a good one. I am at the cafe in downtown Seward for breakfast. 6:15 a.m. and the Yukon is still going strong next door.

Ride down yesterday was out of sight. Sunny blue sky with mountains like vanilla ice cream. Had a salad at the Apollo and put the skiff in the water. Talked to a fellow at the ramp who was patching a boat he had found at the dump. Plans on heading out to Day Harbor to stake land. The land rush to Day Harbor and Blying Sound has Seward in a frenzie. Hope he doesn't end up like Larry Cope.

Stopped by the Breeze Inn. They had a band and the place was sleezier than ever. Slept on the boat which I plan to work on all day today and hopefully get in the water next weekend.

Sold the davit boom that I had found in the trash in Seward $75.00 (not bad). Guess Alaskans will buy almost anything. I know I do my part in this regard.

Hope to spend tonight on Fox I. if the water stays calm. Will be nice for Tutka. When I said, "Tutka get in the boat," he ran from the top of the ramp out to the end of the dock and jumped into the new skiff (the right one) yesterday.

The Iditarod is over. Susan Butcher came in second again—pretty exciting race though quite warm with only one day of race below zero.

Well, the paper just came and I have run out of stuff to say except "hurry up and come back." I still miss you and love you.

Love, Fletch

P.S. Anxious to meet your friends. Sure a lot for you guys to do out on the island. I'll leave a skiff so you can go to Sunny Cove, the spit, etc. Maybe catch a big halibut for everyone in your spare time.

Dear Fletch,

You will never believe what happened to the car. I decided not to take it back to the Texaco because this could be costing Roy too much money. I am going to call him tonight if I can find his number, and ask him what he would like me to do. It may be best to take it to a Cadillac dealer. But Roy will have to send me money. I seriously am beginning to doubt if I will drive it up. It has broken so many times now it has given me a complex. It died last week along the interstate near the new Indian bingo place. I had to cross the freeway (both directions) and crawl under a barbed wire fence across a pasture and go into the Bingo place to use the phone. It was very interesting in there, crowded with all sorts of different kinds of people. Yesterday a.m. I was on a busy one-way street when steam came curling out and it gave me this weird adrenaline rush.

Love, Susannah

Beyond the Door

Marina and Deb and I drove to Seattle from Albuquerque in a Cadillac. The pink car belonged to the mom of Fletcher's friend Roy, who had moved to Seattle from Texas, so she could be closer to Roy without actually having to live in Alaska. Now she needed this car brought to Seattle. I was glad to help and figured I could save some money. We had Roy's Texaco card for gas.

After Colorado, there were no more Texacos, so Marina and Deb and I began using the money we each had with us for gas. In Wyoming we got struck by lightening. The car just died on the highway and I managed to coast it off to the side—a hard job without the power steering—and it wouldn't go again until after the storm passed.

On the Saturday of our plane reservations, we arrived in Seattle, parked the Cadillac downtown, did some sightseeing while someone towed the Cadillac away. We had $22.00 left between us and 45 minutes before our flight left. We rode the bus to the impound lot, signed a promissory note, raced the Cadillac to the airport, and left it for Roy's mom. I was glad to leave it.

Fletcher met us at the airport in Anchorage and took us out to dinner.

"How was your trip?"

Marina said, "Great! An adventure!"

Deb said, "Yeah! There was still two feet of snow in Yellowstone. We saw a wild coyote right by the road—thank God we were in the car. But a tornado struck us in Wyoming and the car died, and the tent blew down while we were in it in Montana."

"I couldn't sleep that night," Marina said dryly.

"The tent shook all night—it was *loud*. We were at a campground with a hot springs pool," Deb said. "I was so cold I almost got in the pool for the night!"

"There wasn't anyone else there, Deb," Marina said. "You could've done it."

"Ooh. The wind was awful," said Deb.

The plan was for Fletch to take us to Fox Island, stay the night, and then leave on Sunday. He had one more week of school in

Anchorage. Marina, Deb and I would spend that week on Fox Island and then Fletch would return the following weekend.

I had begun to be concerned about the five days on Fox Island part of the plan. Debbie hadn't held up especially well so far. Camping in a tent buffeted by frigid winds in Montana and getting struck by lightening in the pink Cadillac in Wyoming had done nothing to enhance her sense of adventure. I discovered what "not an outdoor type" meant. Marina on the other hand had grown up on a farm in Questa. She had been a leader for Outward Bound. She seemed energized by our adventure so far. The other problem was that Deb and Marina weren't turning out to have much in common, and I had listened with alarm when they spoke testily to one another. Feeling discouraged, I questioned my judgement in bringing friends when I could have spent time alone with Fletch before the season began on Fox Island.

When we stood on the beach the next afternoon and watched him leave, it seemed to get extra quiet as the sound of the boat's engine finally faded. I knew it was unlikely we'd see anyone else during our stay.

The sun would shine far into the night in a week or two, but this was earlier than I'd arrived before, and the twilight was still fairly dark. I could even see a star. A cold, lonely wind sent us indoors, where I stoked the fire and put on some music, and in a while, as we sipped red wine and enjoyed a round of gin rummy, my slight sense of unease lifted a little.

Suddenly Tutka began barking outside. I didn't want to alarm anyone, but I'd never heard him bark with such fierce intensity.

I tried to think what it could be. A porcupine? I didn't think a pudgy little porcupine would cause such alarm. I could hear that Tutka was down near the old A-frame cabin, so I grabbed the binoculars, because you can see better in the dark with binoculars, but I still couldn't see Tutka or whatever it was that he barked at with such ferocity. So I walked closer, almost to the Middle cabin, and brought the binoculars to my eyes again. To my dismay, Tutka confronted a huge black bear—she, or he, shifted from foot to foot and looked to be at least 800 pounds. I yelled, "Tutka, come!" He broke away and ran to me. We ran back into the cabin. I slammed the latch bar into place and put the lock-peg in its hole.

"Well, it's a bear," I said, my back up against the door.

Debbie said, "Oh God!"

Marina said, "He can't get in here, calm down."

"No, he'll go away, you're right," I said.

"We just surprised him and he'll avoid us now," said Marina.

I wondered if it had been dumb of me to call Tutka. It had been an instantaneous, protective reaction. What if the bear had naturally just chased after him? And don't let anyone tell you a black bear is nothing to be concerned with. Bears have personalities like anyone else, and some of them are mischievous, some are mean, some are big fat buffoons, some are sweet and trusting. Some are more paranoid and suspicious than others, just like people, and some are more fearful than others. Also, bears can learn to expect things of people— that's why people should never, ever feed wild animals that are big and powerful or have sharp claws and teeth and can learn to expect and demand things from people. Moose and sea lions are also in this category. Plenty of people have been killed by black bears in Alaska, and black bears tend to eat you all up, unlike grizzlies, who often just gnaw your leg or head and bury you in leaves, not that it matters after you're dead.

It seemed so dark. It seemed like we were alone on an island with a big black bear, which was true. This was not a little spooky, it was a *lot* spooky. But it was also, for some reason, the funniest thing that had happened on the whole trip so far. Even Debbie thought so. After barricading the door, I picked up the radio, called for the marine operator and asked her to dial a phone patch to Fletch's number in Anchorage. He said, "Are you sure it wasn't a porcupine?" We didn't want to leave the cabin, and we even put a sheet of plywood over the hole where the stairs came up to the second floor. We put the biggest, heaviest overstuffed chair on the plywood along with a case of vegetable oil, and went to bed. Around 3:30 a.m., as dawn was just barely hinting its arrival in the sky across the bay, we woke to the sound of something walking toward the cabin. We gathered at the window expecting to see the bear. But the terrible, frightening sound was only a big sea otter lumbering along the path with a fish in its mouth. The bear was never seen again.

Fletcher and Neal and his other buddies did not believe there *was* a bear. They had all kinds of fun teasing us when they showed up on Fox Island that Friday night. Fletcher said all the people on their boats in the harbor who listened in on the radio "got a kick" out of my telling him about the bear. But it wasn't a day later that a wise old boat captain, whose boat was named *Big Red*, told me that bears do sometimes swim from the mainland to an island, if the distance is not far. Around the side of Fox Island there is a long spit of land that reaches nearly to the peninsula that divides Resurrection Bay from Day Harbor. I told Fletcher what the captain of *Big Red* said right away but still he teased me and said it was a big porcupine and the binoculars had made it look bigger. Then a few days later I was digging up alder trees to transplant by the outhouse when I came across a pile of bear manure. Fletcher was in the process of hauling a 50-pound propane tank up the beach when I interrupted him to prove I was right. I think he believed me then, but was never sure because he would still tease me and get that twinkle in his eyes.

The bear incident on the first night had somehow dissolved the tension between Marina and Deb. Over the week, ever on the alert for the bear, we had fished from the beach, watched wildlife, decorated the cabins inside and out, taken a tour in the skiff. When Fletch returned he took us beachcombing, and Deb found a whale skeleton which we loaded bone-by-bone into the skiff and reassembled on the beach in front of the Middle cabin.

What happened with Marina and Deb after they left was interesting to me. Marina wrote that on the way they'd had to stay over in Seattle. She and Deb never found anything in common and this had produced an uncomfortable, disorienting feeling in the hotel room that night. She said she couldn't sleep and lay there staring up at the ceiling, listening to the night sounds of the city. Then in the darkness, she got an idea of what she wanted to do with her life: go to law school. Her insight was even more specific: she would work with water issues in rural New Mexico. She was now in the process of applying to law school and was already enrolled in summer courses. I found it fascinating and enviable that direction could come so mysteriously to Marina, starting her on a whole new, self-directed life. A week or so later I received a letter from Deb on creamy-white stationery decorated with kittens. She thanked me, saying she would never forget her Alaska adventure, and, she said, on the airplane back to Albuquerque from Seattle, she had decided to become a missionary. She was on her way to Guatemala the following week.

Studio on the Lake

We didn't build any more cabins that year, but by mid-summer we completed a smaller project, a studio for me attached to the back wall of the Main cabin, my own room where I could paint and sell my work. It was built on pilings from three telephone poles that over the past two summers had conveniently floated onto nearby beaches. My studio hung out over the lake with three walls of windows looking out on the water and Mamanowatum in the background. In the corner on the fourth wall, the back wall, John cut a hole for the doorway leading into the Main cabin.

Over the summer I worked on the finishing touches of my studio when I could, and painted at my table overlooking the lake. My canvases were smooth, flat rocks that I gathered on walks along the beach. As I worked, I gazed out at a long view of the lake with Mamamowatum beyond, framed in the valley between two of Fox Island's spruce-covered peaks, and mirrored in the lake. I kept binoculars on my table to watch for otters, and to study the mother Old Squaw and her ducklings. Sometimes she and her babies would sit in a row on a dead tree that lay in the shallow end of the lake near my window, and I wanted to paint that. For a long painting, like a duck with seven ducklings, I looked for long rocks. For puffins, I looked for puffin-shaped rocks. For halibut I looked for rocks of a golden hue. Looking for the right rocks was just part of the pleasure. I painted the wildlife that lived all around, sea lions roaring and tossing their heads, killer whales on end with their heads out of the water (a behavior called "spy-hopping"), eagles flying between steep-sided islands, sea otters, cormorants. I painted boats and kayaks, and colorful floats on a gray beach, a white seagull perched on one of the floats. While I painted I listened to music. The stereo was hooked up to a bank of batteries. These were kept charged by a solar panel on the cabin roof. The batteries and solar panel also ran the marine radio.

Guests enjoyed visiting me in my studio. At the end of their stay, they came to buy my paintings. Sometimes it was hard to give up a favorite work that had been especially challenging. On these I put "Not for Sale" stickers. But the rest I sold as souvenirs wrapped in tissue and tucked into boxes for the trip home.

With late summer sunlight slanting in through my windows, my eyes about a foot from a rock on my table, my paint-tipped brush poised for a minute detail, I heard the cabin door open. Footsteps followed by the clacking of Tutka's claws across the plank floor added up to Fletch.

"Susannah!"

"Yes! I'm back here, in my studio!"

Clomp, clomp, clomp, I heard him walk back while I worked. He came to my doorway and stood a moment.

"You're happy, aren't you," he declared, smiling. "I can always tell when you're happy because you sing. I could hear you a while ago outside." My eyes, moments ago concentrating on the colors and form of a tiny scene, took him in. He'd just come from the shower, his hair was fluffy and wet, and he leaned there in my doorway, surrounded by the golden hue of my unfinished studio walls, looking handsome and healthy. He wore a green wool sweater, blue jeans and old boat shoes, and carried a coil of rope—a man in his element. "What are you working on?" he said, beside me. "Is this for Joan?"

"Yeah. She wants a floatplane taking off from a lake. She gave me this picture but the plane's not taking off. I have to make that part up."

"Be sure you charge her enough for it," he said.

"I'll try," I said.

He said, "Susannah, do you like being with me?"

I set down my brush, stood up and hugged him. "Yes, I do. I love you. Do you love me?"

He pulled up a stool and sat down beside me. We faced each other and he held my hand. "Mmm-hmm. I think we're a good couple, don't you?" he said, in his understated way. "I'm a lot older than you, though. What do you think of that in terms of a long-term relationship?"

"Oh, I don't think it's a problem," I said, sounding more sure than I was. I sometimes felt inquisitive and emotional compared to him, seeking meaning everywhere, and wanting to talk about it. He seemed content to just *be*. And often I felt grateful that he tolerated me. I wasn't sure if that was a good thing or not: to be grateful for being tolerated.

"Do you think we'll get married someday?" he said. Was he sort of proposing?

"I could see us doing that," I said.

"Maybe it's better not to. Look at Sam and Carlene. They've been together sixteen years and they're not married. And they've got a bigger age difference than us. They seem like a happy couple, don't you think?"

"They sure seem like it," I agreed. They did seem happy and they were an inspiration to me. Like us, they'd built a wilderness lodge.

They ran it in the winter instead of the summer, and instead of using boats, they used sleds and dogs. Everything they did together was an adventure. My father wasn't happy that Fletch and I weren't married, I knew. As for me, I didn't have any strong feelings about it. I didn't want to appear to be pressuring Fletch even the slightest bit. If he wanted to ask me to get married, I wanted it to be because he chose the idea. Under those conditions, I reasoned, his asking me would be an irrefutable declaration of love. For sure I would be able to stop wondering. But, thinking of my studio, the time and effort that went into building it, and the very fact that I had it, I was reminded that this was evidence of Fletch's love for me.

He said, "Maybe they're still together because they're *not* married."

"What was your marriage like, Fletch?"

"I thought okay. But I found out Yvonne wasn't happy with me. Or she just wasn't happy, period. I really never knew. She didn't treat me very good."

Was she that much of a mystery to him? I wondered. Then I am too. "Are she and I at all alike?" I asked.

"She's very creative like you are," he said, "so in that way, you're alike. A way that you're different is she wore an awful lot of make-up."

Okay, good. So maybe she *was* hard to know, hard to get close to, aloof and cold. I'm not like that, I said to myself. I can be as close to someone as it is possible to be. I can give to someone more than they've ever been given. I am warm. Maybe in time…

"Do you think you'd enjoy spending part of the winter with me in Anchorage?" he said.

"You know what? I was hoping you'd bring that up again," I said, bouncing. "You mentioned that last year, remember? I want to! I'll think about taking a semester off after this one. I don't know if it's a good idea, though."

"Why?"

"Well, by the time I graduate I will have been in college almost seven years."

"It might do you good to take some time off. I'd enjoy showing you some of the places I like to go in the winter. We work so hard all summer, sometimes I wish we had more time together to take some trips on our own. We could visit Fox Island in the winter."

I had started out the summer feeling displaced and unsure, trying with Marina and Deb to merge my two lives. I'd felt envy when the trip somehow brought a sure direction to both their lives. Where did *I* belong? Alaska? With Fletch? New Mexico? I needed a sign. But then I'd become absorbed in wilderness life as the summer had progressed, and it had once again been easy to set aside my concerns. I'd worked hard helping to run the lodge, painting rocks and fixing up my studio whenever I could. Now, as our third summer together was almost over, I had serious things to think about again. I liked the idea of not being away from Fletch a whole winter this time. It wasn't an insight, like Marina had in the Seattle motel room, but nevertheless I decided I would go home for only one semester. I would take a break from school then, and return to Alaska in December, staying the remainder of the winter with Fletch and on through the following summer. Then I would have only one more year of school, the last half of which would be full-time student teaching.

Dear Fletch,

It's wonderful to be back home in New Mexico but I do miss you. My dogs were happy to see me. Sunday we all (Mama, Daddy, me and the dogs) hiked over to a canyon a couple miles from here and built a fire and cooked steaks, baked potatoes, and garlic bread. We also each had a couple cold beers. They asked about my summer. I said I was going back in December! I think by now they know I'll finish school so they weren't against the idea. Thanks for sending the photos. Your idea of traveling to Eagle for Christmas sounds great!

It's now Tuesday night. I'm tired and I guess a little down. Mama and I got to talking about her childhood in Montana tonight. She told me how she had made pets of two different hens when she was little. She said on the farm a person doesn't usually make friends with the animals, since you know what happens to them.

Well, she had hens as pets two different times. The first time her mom put too much lice powder on Mama's hen and it died. The second hen she had as a pet would come to her if she called and would follow her around. She called it Henny Penny. One time a man came to buy a chicken and they had their chickens out running around loose to forage. Her mom and dad couldn't catch a chicken for him. Finally, they asked her to call her hen. The man said he would give her a nickel. Well, they were adults and she was a child, so she called her hen, and of course the hen came.

You asked about how come I chose to go into teaching. It started in my youth. In Casper I taught every little kid in the neighborhood how to fish and rope and cook on a fire and stuff. I was the one setting up the jumping courses and planning the trail rides and talking about constellations. I like kids, and I have this love of knowledge and learning, because there's so many wonders!! I also had to claim a major at some point. I don't know what teaching in public schools is going to be like. I continue to have doubts about being a teacher. But I do like kids and the idea of having summers off!

Love, Susannah

Dear Susannah,

Sure was good to talk to you last night. After talking with you I settled in to watch a show on PBS on what they called sea otters. It was filmed in the Shetland Islands. The otters that they were following were much more like our land otters on Fox Island. This photographer had gone to extreme lengths to get his pictures, according to the narration. It was good but he could have saved a lot of time and energy by sitting on a log in front of our cabin with his camera and watching our otters come and go. Sometimes, I think I almost take some of what we have experienced for granted. Anyway, it made me get out some pictures of Resurrection Bay and Fox I. The green of summer is so inviting compared with the barrenness that has enveloped the area now.

Went for a little run tonight after school. Tutka reminds me of Jack, the dog we had until I was about 5. He would go totally crazy when my Dad would pick up his shotgun which meant they were about to go duck hunting. Tutka does the same when I begin to put on my running gear or pick up my skis. I am sure he doesn't miss the snow as it is a lot easier for him without it. Plus he will be outlawed from the trail once the skiers get on it.

I have been reading one of your Christmas presents during silent reading at school. Hope you don't mind. The whole school is supposed to take 25 minutes after lunch and read. Speaking of Christmas presents. Don't worry about anything for me. I know that you are short or should I say void of finances right now. I am also pretty low so don't expect much from this end. Just being with you will satisfy me. If the same is true for you, we'll be all set.

Love, Fletch

Dear Fletch,

This morning I left the house with the dogs and we headed up toward the ranch. It's not really a ranch, but an old adobe place that was added on to over the years making a long structure of connecting rooms. I used to spend a lot of time there when I knew the people who lived there. I was almost to the ranch when a puppy came frisking out of the trees as happy as could be to see Sara and Gustoff. It ran under them trying to find milk. Of course, Sara jumped and spun around and Gustoff got confused, too. I picked the puppy up and saw that it was skinny with a dull coat. I decided to continue to the ranch and ask if they knew whose it was.

There was no one home but there were two other puppies that were plump and shiny. Other than that, the markings were the same. I decided they must have given this puppy away, and it had run away and was almost back to the ranch when I found it, or when it found me. I went around back and found the dog shed where there was food and water. The puppy was glad.

Well, I'm tired and better get some good rest tonight. Just two more weeks!

Love, Susannah

Christmas Above the Arctic Circle

I arrived in Anchorage in the dead of winter, just in time for the shortest day of the year—December 21, the winter solstice. How different it was from summer! Fletch had hung Christmas lights on the caribou antlers above the wood stove in his house. The colors reflected onto the window that framed the long night's blackness. Now, the daylight lasted only a few hours and even then, it was more akin to twilight. Night was as fathomless as only night in the far north in winter can be: black, frigid, and glittery, like outer space. Fletch's house was in a forest of tall spruce and birch trees. It was made of honey-colored logs and it was dark inside. I opened my eyes bigger but everything stayed dim, all the time. Still, this small log house that Fletch had built himself, six years previous, after his divorce, was beautiful and well constructed. As I looked around, it was evident he was a bachelor, from the rust-colored shag carpet to the shop light which served to illuminate the pantry, but it had a wonderful coziness. The living room had high, open-beam ceilings and a loft with a railing extended across the back half, above the kitchen. The boughs of the spruce trees around his house sagged under enormous burdens of snow. Sometimes the snow would slip off a bough with a big WHOOSH! and the branch, unencumbered, would whip upward, causing a smoke of fine ice crystals to fly out and cascade down. Fletch had a woodpile just outside his door and an ax and wedge on a big stump for splitting wood. We fed the stove constantly. Tutka had a coat of thick fur and looked even more bear-like.

This time of year in Alaska the main thing is, it's dark most of the time. Or maybe the main thing is, it's cold. Fletcher had made arrangements for us and Anne and Neal to fly to Eagle, Alaska to visit teacher friends there. In the summer you can drive to Eagle, but not in winter. We had to drive to Fairbanks and then hire a bush pilot. When we got in the small plane, the pilot said we couldn't fly if the cloud ceiling wasn't at least 500 feet. In order to find out just where the cloud ceiling was, the pilot flew us up to it, and declared, "Right at 500 feet! We're *go* for Eagle!" Deep, gray clouds hung just above the airplane, wisping over the top of the plane above our heads, and below, the dreary winter landscape of interior Alaska extended without end: snow, *taiga*, and muskeg, looking raw and melancholy in the sepia dusk that passes for day. Taiga is the name for boggy, sub-arctic forests, and muskeg is wetland caused by permafrost. A layer of permanent ice—permafrost—is just a foot or so under the topsoil, so in the summer the topsoil can't drain, and it is just lumpy and wet. The spruce trees that grow up out of it I named "everdeads." These black-looking trees are about as big around as pipe cleaners, angled every which-way, sometimes straight, sometimes curved, sometimes curved in an arch all the way over to the ground. I could not understand why they tried to grow in muskeg; they were obviously struggling. I thought that by now spruce trees would have found a way to adapt and be happy in muskeg—maybe by just staying little—or that some other plant would have come in to make the muskeg home, and just taken over. Maybe it will happen yet in a million years or so, but meanwhile these everdead forests in Alaska go on and on.

We rode bundled up in down coats, hats, and mittens. Finally some shape came to the land below, and we prepared to set down in the village. Eagle is situated between a bluff and the beach on the Yukon River. Our hosts, Frank and Linda, met us at the airstrip with a three-wheeler pulling a big sled.

They had built themselves a squat log cabin with a root cellar right under the floor of their kitchen. You could open a heavy lid in the floor and climb down a ladder and be in a room with canned goods, jars, roots, and fruit all around. They had a real white baby. I never saw such white skin—like milk. But he was happy and cooed on his blankets in the warm cabin. Outside by the door of their mudroom they had half a frozen moose hanging from the eave of the cabin. It was as hard as a boulder hanging there. You had to be careful not to bump your head on it when you went outside. Frank used a saw to cut it up for meals. Ducks and geese, which for some reason didn't freeze, waddled around the cabin yard getting in the way. A short ways away they had 18 sled dogs, each chained to its own straw-filled house. A few other people in Eagle had sled dogs, but most used snow machines or three-wheelers to get around.

The morning after our arrival, Anne, Neal, Frank, Fletcher and I went for a ski, and ended up getting lost. We had started by crossing the Yukon and then skied off into the woods on a nice, wide snow-machine trail under new snow, perfect for skiing. But trails went everywhere and at last Frank said, "Fletch, do you have any idea which trail is the one we came in on?" But none of us knew. Frank took the one he thought was right, but finally none of them looked right. It was bitter cold, and dark by one-thirty in the afternoon.

Over the next four hours we skied over every kind of terrain—

across muskeg, up and down steep little hills and valleys. Sometimes we skied in a fairyland of deep powder, past the tops of trees. Occasionally the clouds parted as they sailed across the night sky, giving us the quarter moon for light. But most of the time our headlamps flashed through the spindly spruce trees creating black shadows that lurched like drunkards. We stopped to rest. Neal said, "Do any of these trails look familiar yet, Frank?"

Anne said, "Do you *sort of* know where we are?"

Frank said, "The reason there's so many trails is that villagers come on snow machines to this part of the forest for firewood. The whole area isn't far from the village. It's just a matter of finding the right trails." I felt sorry for him as he skied in front of us all, looking for something familiar. Fletch skied behind Frank, I was behind Fletch, and Anne and Neal were behind me.

I called out, "Are you hungry, Anne?" I worried about her, being the smallest of us.

She said, "No, I'm fine. Not hungry at all. I brought some granola bars if you are." I *was* hungry, but I'd had a bite or two for fuel and opted to save the rest in case our situation made a turn for the worse. We were all in fine shape and none of us perceived ourselves to be in a life-threatening situation.

However, we each knew that could change, with a small accident, a drop in temperature, tiredness, or hunger.

After two more hours of trying various trails, Anne spotted a light twinkling in the distance through the forest. The light meant the village was near, which meant the Yukon was near. We had only to cross the Yukon.

Skiing on leaden legs, we arrived at last to a spot where the forest hung out over the banks of the river. The river, wide and luminous in the moonlight, disappeared into darkness in both directions. As far as we could see, the river's ice—stripped of snow-cover by wind—formed crate-sized blocks and jagged ridges, icy pits and slides, pinnacles, sharp edges and crevasses. This conglomeration filled the river from bank to bank.

We each made a choice: We could keep our skis on for the crossing, or we could carry them. It hardly mattered, because either way—walking with skis across jumbled ice blocks, or carrying skis and poles and walking in ski boots—was unbelievably cumbersome.

I kept mine on and thought that they helped by acting as bridges at times. I could position myself between two ice blocks and lurch my weight forward and try not to fall. Of course we all fell many times. With only headlamps for light, we could not correctly perceive the facets of the ice, or any depths or distance. I don't know how long it took. We just put one foot more or less in front of the other and struggled on. When at last we reached the far bank, we skied another mile along a road to the village school, which was the source of the light by the river. At last we reached the school and left our skies outside the door. Inside the warm building, two or three Native families sat on the floor and in folding chairs watching "The Golden Girls" on TV. They were friendly but uncurious—we were just white people—no notice was given or taken that we had been lost. Frank called Linda who called someone with a vehicle, who came and got us.

I had felt a strange elation while crossing the Yukon. In my struggle I had realized that life right then did not seem in any way ordinary, and that, in fact, life was *extraordinary*.

Dogsledding

When it got light enough the next day to see without headlamps, Linda made us ski to a spring and bring back enough spring ice to make ice cream. "We got ice right in the yard!" Frank groused, shoving his hands into his gloves. "It has to be *spring* ice," Linda said. "You *know* it's best with *spring* ice, Frank." The baby sat on her hip looking bemused, one of Linda's braids in his fist. While we were gone, she prepared the other ingredients: duck eggs and real vanilla and what-not. She made each of us take turns turning the crank on the ice cream maker when we got back. Some school teachers are like that—they treat almost everyone like school kids. They're explicit in their instructions. It's quite a good skill. The homemade vanilla ice cream was the most delicious I've ever tasted.

We never ate a normal meal at Frank and Linda's, but the food was splendid, nonetheless. Linda gave each of us a hollow peppermint stick and a softball-sized, juicy orange that she had left outside long enough to get ice crystals inside. The idea was to suck the juice out of the partly frozen orange with the peppermint stick straw. We did this while sitting in their cozy log living room, warmed by the wood stove. After I couldn't get any more juice out, I peeled and ate my orange, and then my peppermint stick. It was good!

Linda served moose burgers for breakfast, sourdough pancakes with blueberry preserves for dinner. At other times we ate syrup snow cones, caribou sausage with cranberry catsup, and pilot crackers with peanut butter and honey.

One strange thing about the Arctic and any place that gets so cold are the outhouses, because the hole is really deep, and if you happen to see down into the hole, there is a frozen stalagmite about 10 or 11 feet tall. You wonder what happens when it gets too close. Someone has to be the one who breaks it.

Frank sent Fletcher and me out the next day to do errands with the dog team. The dogs leapt like ecstatic idiots, howling while Frank manhandled them into their harnesses. "God damn dogs! They're like this every god damn day, god damn it," Frank said.

The dogs knew the routine, and knew exactly where to go, which was good because neither Fletcher nor I knew how to drive them. They took off like we were in a race. I rode in the sled with big black bags of garbage and empty five-gallon water jugs bouncing around me. And away we went to the post office for mail; across the village to the dump to get rid of the garbage; to the water tower to fill and reload six five-gallon jugs; and then to the library to drop off books and to chat with the librarian, for by now the dogs had less energy and lay down in the road like good dogs. We returned, successful in every way, and deposited the water in the kitchen, taking care not to trip over any ducks in the yard or hit our heads on the frozen moose.

Linda, Anne, and Neal waited for us, wearing skis amid the ducks and geese. The dogs, now rested, realized the fun wasn't over, and we blasted down the road again, over a bank and out onto a wide smooth stretch of the Yukon, going like sixty.

This time I stood on the sled runners holding onto the wooden handle and flying on the wide, smooth river toward a pale spot in the sky where the sun would rise at "high noon." We came after a while to a gravel bar where we stopped and tied the dogs to some willows. Anne built a fire and Linda tucked aluminum foil packages filled with moose meat, potatoes, carrots, and onions into it. It made such a pretty sight—the flickering orange flames and silver packages, snow all around; and the dogs curled into furry balls beneath the curving red wands of arctic willow. We warmed ourselves by the fire and waited for the food to heat. It smelled good. We ate as the sun rose and then set behind a distant ribbon of purple mountains to the south.

No One Brings Up Marriage

Back in Anchorage I looked for a job I could keep until it was time to return to Fox Island. I found one as a desk clerk at a nice hotel downtown, working 3:00 to 11:00 p.m. This meant I had to handle the tired people who had reservations but for whom we had no rooms. My boss always overbooked and many nights I sent people across the alley to the Inlet Inn—which was at that time a dingy place owned by the same fellow who owned Sheffield House. He was also the governor of Alaska at the time. I hated watching the exhausted tourists trudge away with their luggage.

Airline crews from Air France stayed at the hotel every time they came through Anchorage, which is the best route to get from major European cities to major Asian cities. One good-looking French pilot was in love with the other desk clerk I worked with. So I guess they got together every few nights when he came through and had a wonderful romance. She was distracted on the nights he was coming in and I had to do most of the work.

The crews would send their laundry out and one time one of the pilot's long johns came back just the right size to fit a petite child. He asked, "What happened?"

I said, "I'm sorry, sir, your long johns shrunk."

" 'Lung zohns'? 'SHRUNK'?" he asked. "What a funny word— 'lung zohns'—'SHRUNK!' Ha, ha! 'SHRUNK!' " He looked around at his group of pilots and attendants saying, "shrunk!" They all laughed, so I did, too. But when I laughed, the pilot got serious again and wanted to talk to my boss, so I let my boss handle it.

One night while I drove home a boy by the name of Stan Oxenhandler ran a red light and totaled Fletch's green Toyota. My head was hurt, but not bleeding, so I walked to the police station on 2nd Street and called. Fletcher answered the phone, but then he dropped it, and went back to sleep or something. I finally called a taxi at 1:00 a.m. When I got home, I saw that Fletcher was drunk. I slept downstairs on the couch. That's the only bad thing Fletcher ever did.

I was now living with Fletch in his winter quarters, sharing in his ordinary life. We both had jobs; we commuted, we existed within the infrastructure of manmade contrivances; we shopped for groceries instead of catching what we ate. On Fridays we went to movies or out for drinks with Anne and Neal. On weekends we went skiing with friends and on nights when I didn't have to work Fletch and I skied on the lighted trails near his school.

I wondered if the reason our friends Sam and Carlene were still together after sixteen years, in spite of their larger age difference, was because the life they shared was a series of one adventure after another. I could see that being a way to stay together happily. So in a way I saw this domestic life in Fletch's home as a test, and it was different from life on Fox Island. The Fletch I knew on Fox Island worked at skilled labor most of the time and spent his leisure time shooting the breeze with guests. Here, he drove a short distance each morning to the school where he'd taught for fifteen years. He finished his workday with a two-, five-, or ten-kilometer ski with the school's cross-country ski team, for which he was the coach. He came home, had dinner, poured himself a glass of red wine, and spent many evenings until bedtime watching television. It's not that he didn't continue dreaming about boats and the water. This he did during the day, pouring over marine catalogs and boat magazines while his students worked on assignments or watched films.

Our happiest times together were ski trips with Anne and Neal or just the two of us. The four of us would drive up the Glenn Highway to a place called Sheep Mountain Lodge, and ski on groomed trails of varying lengths and then eat a hearty dinner and retire to our cabin for the night. Fletch and I found another lodge, much different in character, that we also liked to go to, on the Parks Highway toward Fairbanks. This lodge was a dark, old log building, more specifically called a "road house," with trucks, ATVs and snow-machines parked haphazardly out front along with a few piles of frozen dog manure. Most of the people staying were men who drove trucks or snowplows, or people out for the weekend on snow-machines, three-wheelers, or dog sleds. People in Alaska pack a lot into the long summer days, not so much in winter. At the lodge, Fletch and Tutka and I would take a ski during the day, and by four p.m., dark outside, we would find ourselves sitting with the others in the dining/living room, drinking beer by the fire and telling stories.

Fletcher and I as a couple had very few bad times, and never any *real* bad times. He was so easy-going; he just didn't get mad. We had a few small arguments, mostly because I was sensitive and emotional. The worst times were when I was confused by life, my problems with under-confidence, my lack of direction, almost beyond my ability to function. I had little to go on, virtually no guidance in my present or my past, very little wisdom. I didn't know that I needed to seek wisdom, nor did I know what the sources would be. I had done a great deal of reading, but mostly novels and adventure stories, albeit good ones. Although what I learned from General Psychology or Early Childhood Education was a beginning, of sorts, it was ultimately not a very helpful one. The need for wisdom did not seem to be an issue for Fletch. These problems of mine were hard for him. Compounding my misery at these times, I blamed myself for making him feel bad. I didn't expect Fletch to love me in spite of my difficulties and struggles. I reminded myself of Kevin, being needy and fearing rejection no matter how often or how much I reassured him. But I had to go real far before Fletcher would show any irritation. He was patient. I was lucky.

I whiled away some time over that winter returning to the unsolved problem of whether I should permanently give up my life in New Mexico and buy into Fletcher's dreams—or not. I waited for a sign, an insight, some direction. Perhaps we were both being too careful. Fletch *had* asked me to come to Alaska and live with him, but he seemed content with that and hadn't raised the subject of marriage again. I think what he wanted more than anything was simply someone to share his dream of living on the water and messing around with boats, and to avoid personal situations that were too complicated or risky. I believed my life in New Mexico was a threat to him; he feared that my love for it could lure me away. Probably, he wasn't far wrong. He dealt with things that made him uncomfortable by avoiding thinking or talking about them, and I guess hoping they'd go away. In my own best interest, I refused to say anything that would feel like pressure to him. But it was hard not being able to talk.

The Beginning of Wisdom

During my first winter in Alaska, I at last came upon an insight that I knew would help me in life. Letters from Jack Snow, in his big, scrawled handwriting, stopped coming. I figured he must have died. I took a walk with Tutka while Fletch was at work. What I figured, what I *hoped*, was that somehow Jack had gotten back to his

Arizona country, and *then* died. I trudged over the hard-packed snow on the trail, thinking bitterly, *there's always something tragic going on in life*. And it was as if another Susannah voice said, *that's right—life is hard*. I stopped. "Life is hard," I said out loud. I looked up into the tree branches, continuing to speak aloud, "and here you thought that when you 'grew up' life got easy. That was just all wrong. And you've been awfully frustrated while waiting for that."

Tutka and I came out of the woods behind someone's shed. Sunlight at a low angle reflected off its white, south-facing wall. Though it was below freezing, I felt the sun on my face and, standing there, face tilted up, warm sunlight on my eyelids, I realized that *life was about coping* with hard times, and about appreciating good times *with awareness*. I knew right then that, in time, this small step in understanding would help me take additional steps toward wisdom. Tutka and I walked into the forest again, to go home. Sun rays filtered through the trees, making a quilt of blue shadows and light on the snow. I said a goodbye, and a thank you to my dear friend Jack Snow.

Spring found me skiing with Fletcher, Anne, Neal, and Tutka up at Prospect Heights on the foothills. Fletcher told us about a seventh grade girl on his ski team who had skied under a moose. The moose stood on the trail at the bottom of a hill, and like a cow, couldn't make up its mind whether to move or not when it saw the skiers coming. The girl was going too fast and couldn't go around, so she crouched low and skied under the moose.

It was this ski trip that allowed me to come upon another bit of wisdom. It was about ten above zero, clear and bright, over new, powdery snow. All during the previous night, snowflakes floated earthward from the sky onto the graceful, white-stemmed birches. Each of their millions of twigs and branches held fluffy ridges of snow in the still air and all together they looked like the prettiest lace against the blue sky that could ever be thought up by anyone.

I skied down a long gentle hill, going pretty fast. There are times when you are skiing that you realize, "Okay, I'm going to crash now." I knew I couldn't make the turn at the bottom of the hill. I crashed hard into the deep powder along the side of the trail, coming to an abrupt stop with my face in a baby spruce tree. My crashing into it had crushed its needles, and this crushing released the spruce's scent. It smelled so good. I closed my eyes and lay there breathing it in for a long moment before struggling to my feet. And I skied off happily down the trail.

When I thought back on that day, I realized that you cannot expect your life to be like that all the time. Really good times—charmed days or moments when everything is strung together in a happy way, and you are filled with happiness, living just in that moment—are rare and precious. I remembered a silver miner I'd met a few years back who called them "jewel days." This new understanding about jewel days and jewel moments enhanced my ability to appreciate. Appreciating had begun to replace feelings I'd held of unfulfilled expectations.

Sea Otters

Having come to Alaska in December, I now had the opportunity to journey out to Fox Island in March, when all is still locked in winter, although a glimmer of spring-to-come is heralded by the returning light. Compared to the lower latitudes, the daylight in the far north is so much longer in summer and so much shorter in winter, that the shortening of light in the fall and the lengthening of light in the spring happens rapidly. March is when you really notice it. All of a sudden there are six more minutes of daylight each day, and in only ten days, that's already an hour more. This returning daylight was even more welcome to me than seeing spring's first crocus in the southern latitudes.

Still, it was bitter cold, and plenty dangerous to be on the water. The smart way to deal with bitter cold and dangerous conditions and still have fun is to be prepared, so when we rode in the skiff from the boat harbor in Seward to Fox Island, Fletcher and I wore survival suits. Survival suits are watertight, insulated full-body flotation coats. They are bright orange so if you fall in the water you can just bob around and be visible to rescuers. They cover every part of you from your feet to your head, leaving just a small place to look out of. They even have a whistle attached that you can blow to call for help even if your mouth muscles are getting cold. There are special pockets for hand-held VHF radio, food and flares. Commercial fishermen in Alaska carry survival suits for each person on board and the smart ones don't wait to put them on in bad weather. For some of the winter crabbers and commercial fishermen, modified survival suits are what they wear most of the time on board their boats. Many a fisherman has been saved by donning one.

On this day, gray, choppy water filled Resurrection Bay from shore to shore. Now and then a stiff breeze blew down the bay, taking the tops off the waves. Heavy fog hung just above the mountain ranges on either side. Except for sheer cliffs, the mountains and islands were white with snow, right down to the waterline. The surf had pounded the snow away at the waterline, and here the wet granite—almost black—supported long, bumpy icicles which hung down to just above the reaching waves. The fjords in winter are silent except for the sound that comes from the rhythmic surge of water against granite at the waterline.

Tutka stood in the bow of the aluminum skiff, a large, black silhouette in a gray-and-white landscape, his ears blowing back against his head, his eyes squinting like a sentinel. I looked back at Fletcher in his orange suit, his eyes also squinting out at the water, his mittened hand on the tiller, intent on navigating beyond the icy waves of the open bay into the quieter water of our cove. As we neared the island, I spotted a group of about fifteen sea otters floating on their backs. Waves tossed them, sometimes flipping them, but each time they just rolled the rest of the way over to resume their back-floats. As we came nearer, they held up their whiskery heads and looked at us looking at them. I clutched the side of the skiff in my mittened hands, marveling at the otters, comfortable, warm and nonchalant in their thick waterproof fur, bobbing and rolling in the icy waves, looking like a picture of pure contentment.

Soon the skiff hit the stony beach in Northwest Cove. Here the cabins stood in snow, in the thin strip of spruce forest backed up against the steep sides of the island. Tutka leapt out while Fletcher and I dragged the skiff up the beach, treacherous with ice, above high-tide line, and tied it to a tree. I walked into the cold cabin and started a fire. I looked out the window at Mamamowatum peeking through the blowing fog, and thought about the otters so comfortable out there, at home in the icy sea.

Alone

Back in Anchorage I fought briefly with the practicality-versus-romance issue and happily gave in to temptation, deciding to quit my job before school was out for Fletcher to spend a week alone on Fox Island. It was a pleasure to tell my friends and co-workers that I wasn't *really* a desk clerk, that my *real* life was helping to run a lodge in Resurrection Bay. The bartender of the Penthouse on the top floor was a fishing fool. He made a date to come out with the whole Penthouse gang later in the summer.

Fletcher and I headed out to Fox Island Saturday morning, did some work around the place, and then my solo adventure started when he left Sunday night. Tutka and I watched the boat drone away toward the head of the bay. Fletcher had set up the VHF radio and we had agreed that I would call him Tuesday at 8:00 p.m. via the marine operator. If you called for the marine operator and gave her your call numbers and the phone number you wanted, she could patch you through to a phone. You could hear the phone ring on your radio—which seemed very odd. You still had to talk one at a time, like always on the radio.

On Tuesday morning I decided to see if anyone was within range and had their VHF on. I had learned to enjoy the aimless conversations about the weather or some other topic that you could have on the radio, never knowing whom you might find to talk to. You could call for, say, *The Minot*, and if *The Minot* didn't have their radio on, someone else would call back to you to see what was up. "This is *Fox Islander*, Whiskey Delta niner-two-niner, calling *The Minot*, come in, *Minot*, over."

Nothing.

"*Minot*, this is *Fox Islander*, channel 16, over."

Quietness.

After a few more tries I realized the radio didn't work. I now worried that Fletcher would come all the way from Anchorage if I didn't call him that evening as we had arranged.

Realizing I had no communication with the rest of the world, Resurrection Bay felt even lonelier than usual that morning. It was still early enough in the season that I could be nearly certain the closest people to me were those in their homes and businesses along the streets of Seward, 14 miles away at the head of the bay. I took my raincoat off the peg, and Tutka and I walked along the beach out to the point. Cold rain fell as if it always had, and always would. As the sea surged around the boulders, I felt like we were wild things standing there, I in my long blue raincoat and Tutka in his black coat, both of us dripping like woolly wild animals and cut off from the world. And then, out of the rain, a lone little fishing boat called the *Hoppin' Dog* came fast past the point, bow high, spray flying. The captain saw us and cut the motor. The bow dropped as he plowed to a stop. I tried yelling to him through the sound of the surf, but he motioned me down the beach where it was calmer and motored alongside while I walked, until we came to where he could get in close. I hollered that someone was expecting a call from me, that our radio wasn't working, and would he please call him when they got to Seward. "Glad to!" he shouted. He got Fletch's number and off he went, giving the thumbs-up sign and cheering me. He then disappeared into the rain, leaving Tutka and me standing alone again.

It turned out that the radio had quit because, lacking a charge from the solar panel, we'd used the generator to power it. The surge of power had disabled the transmitter. Now we knew not to use the generator to power the radio.

I did not see another person for the rest of week. I forgot to wind my watch and I didn't know what time it was. I didn't know if I went to bed at 10:00 p.m. or 1:00 a.m., or what time I woke. I knew only whether the tide was low or high, and whether it was coming in or going out. Because the tide range in Resurrection Bay is around 17 feet, when the tide was high it was not far at all from the cabins, whereas when the tide was low, the beach expanded downward, creating a huge kelpy band fifty feet wide. I knew whether or not I was hungry, but perhaps because of the change in daylight, I never knew for sure if I was tired. I wrote in my journal far into the night, built shelving between the wall studs in the Middle cabin, and painted designs onto them. I took long walks, fished from shore, read my book, and since Easter was coming, I dyed Easter eggs.

4

Jewel Days

Killer Whales

The next day was foggy and still, with no rain. Tutka and I walked along the beach toward the quiet end. I looked for suitable painting rocks. Tutka chased ravens, who were having an important conversation on the beach, and who up and left just as he tried to crash their get-together. They settled a short distance away but when Tutka ran amidst them again they flew off and made themselves comfortable on the branches of a dead tree. Suddenly we heard loud outbreathing echoing in the cove. Three killer whales cruised in at high speed, their tall dorsal fins sticking up like black sails. The killers cruised in closer until they swam along the beach just fifteen feet from where we stood. I was so excited I jumped up and down clapping my hands and shouting to Tutka, who was the only person to talk to, "Whales! Whales! Look, Tutka!"

He thought, "I *know* that, I can *see* that," but he was too kind to say anything. I could see the whales entirely and clearly, even their eyes. And I saw that they were rubbing their bellies in the gravel. It must feel good. Yes, I suppose it does. A bit of sense returned to me

and I backed away, calling Tutka. Killer whales dine on seals and I'm certain a dog would taste okay, too.

We watched the whales as they swam along the curve of the beach, and then out into the cove, and then away. The sun came out, and as quiet settled on the cove, I had a peculiar expansive feeling. I felt as if I was connected to everything: the whales who had just seen me, whose black fins I could still see in the sparkly waves of the bay, the ravens chortling in the dead tree, the jays who had followed me and were now waiting in a tree for me to resume my walk, even Mamanowatum, even something else, which I couldn't name.

I walked on. The subtle lappity-lap of the waves and our feet clacking quietly on the rocks were the only sounds. Further along,

I saw something dead floating in the cove. There wasn't much left, just bones really, held together with a bit of fur. Some of the longer bones hung vertically down into the water. I looked around me. Mamanowatum stood mute, indifferent. I was curious. I walked all the way back to the cabin to get the canoe but Tutka was anxious when I wouldn't let him jump in. He ran along the beach, panting as I paddled toward the bones. When I got up to it I thought it was a sea lion's skeleton, but I couldn't keep the canoe straight and lift the skull with the oar. So I pulled the canoe up onto the beach and just waded in, determined. I got the skull and even though it was almost pure white it didn't smell too good. I carried it to the edge of the forest where I leaned it up against a bleached log, and left it there, where it would eventually get cleaner.

In the late evening of Fletcher's last day of school, he arrived from Anchorage with a boat full of provisions and gear, and Anne and Neal. The next day John showed up from Astoria. We picked him up in Seward, and headed out in the boat for a day of pre-season adventuring. During the winter, winds blast the mountain peaks, forming massive snowdrifts that hang out over nothing along the edges of ridges. These drifts are called cornices, and when a cornice breaks off and falls down the mountain side, it's an avalanche. The weather was beginning to warm enough to cause avalanches to break off and thunder down the mountainsides all around us. In the middle of Resurrection Bay Fletcher killed the engine and we bobbed in the water to watch and hear the show.

Rescue

Farther out, as we motored along, we saw movement on a tiny beach. We drew closer, and saw it was an eagle struggling to lift off the beach, its wings beating the air in powerful, impossible slow motion. It appeared to be entrapped in some fish netting that had washed up on the beach. Fletcher brought the boat in closer. What we saw then was the eagle, its talons embedded in gray fur, trying to haul off a live seal pup. The mother seal swam back and forth in the water in front of the beach. As we drifted in just a few yards from shore, the eagle released its intended meal and flew to the top of a dead tree near another eagle, folded its huge, powerful black wings neatly, and watched us, first with one yellow eye, then the other. We exchanged looks, we commented, and we moved on.

The next day, we returned to the same beach. There on the beach lay a baby seal. Was it dead? No, it turned its head slightly as a wave washed over it. Was it the same seal that the eagle had attacked the day before?

We fished nearby, but we all watched the seal. It didn't move. No other seals came. No one spoke.

Then Neal said, "We ought to rescue it."

"No, we shouldn't," argued John. "Let Mother Nature take her course."

"But we could *save* it," I said. "What do you think, Anne?"

"It probably won't survive," she said.

"That eagle has babies to feed," said John. "You wouldn't want to starve those cute little baby eagles, would you?"

"But look," said Neal. "It's still alive. The mother is gone, and so is the eagle. It's just going to die a slow death. I think we should rescue it!"

"How?" said John, "It's not going to jump in the boat with you."

"I'll go ashore in the dinghy and put it in my duffel bag."

I looked at Fletch. He wasn't going to say anything.

"Fletch, let's rescue it," I said. Fletch helped Neal lift our small plastic dinghy overboard and held it steady as Neal got in, and I handed him the oars and the empty duffel bag.

The rest of us watched as he rowed the dinghy toward shore. Near the beach, he paused for the right wave, and when it came, he rowed onto the beach. The seal looked up at Neal as he walked over to it. He knelt beside it for a moment and then gently lifted it into the duffel bag, zipping it shut. He made it back through the surf and soon we helped him into the boat. Neal set the bag down and pulled the zipper open. A gray spotted seal pup with long whiskers and big, watery eyes peered out. It had flippers with claws like dog feet. I was surprised at how big it was, about two and a half feet long, weighing maybe 40 pounds. This gave me a clear idea of the size of the eagle, whose wingspan would have been close to six feet.

An afternoon wind blew. Wet clouds filled in the sky and the sea turned dark and roughened. We had three hours to go to reach Seward. All the while, the seal periodically bleated its fear in a baby voice that I could hardly bear. It was so much in need of help, and I could do nothing for it.

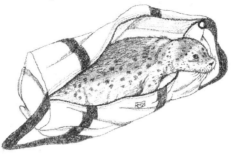

A cold rain began to fall. The boat crashed and jarred through the water. None of us knew if we were doing the right thing. We had stayed off shore and fished for at least an hour before rescuing the seal. I thought, *If they didn't want to rescue the seal, we shouldn't have stayed near it!* But we were all curious. We all wanted to see if the baby would slip into the sea and swim away when Neal approached. We all wanted to see if its mother would come back. Finally Neal had made the decision that had hovered there all the while.

At last we neared Seward, pulled between the outer harbor's rock levees and into the harbor itself, always a relief in rough seas. Neal and I put the seal in a big red plastic fish tub with a wet towel over it and carried the tub between us along the dock and up the ramp. We wanted to take it to a veterinarian. Leaving it in the tub in the back of Fletcher's truck, we went into the Breeze Inn, where local fishermen hung out drinking coffee in the steamy, smoky warmth. "The vet only comes through here once a month," someone said. From the payphone I called the Park Ranger at his home and he met us at Fletcher's truck. He said it was illegal to have the seal. He said we should have left it there, and he said the best thing to do was to let it loose in the sea. He got in his truck and drove away.

Several men had followed out to the truck to see the seal. "Tell you what I'd do," said a sympathetic old fisherman, "feed it evaporated milk with a bit of sugar in it. Warmed up. Take the pup to the Anchorage zoo." "They probably got them nipples at Brown and Hawkins," said another old fisherman. "You just stick 'em on a coke bottle."

So I called the Anchorage zoo from the pay phone on the wall of the Breeze Inn. "The best thing to do is let the seal go," said the zookeeper. "It's best not to interfere," she said gently. She didn't say, "You shouldn't have done it," but I knew by then we had done the wrong thing. Neal knew too. Everyone else, even John, stood around keeping quiet. Neal and I drove to the beach by 6th Street and carried the tub with the seal in it between us, down to the water's edge. We tipped the tub, and as a wave hit, the baby seal swam out. It swam away. Fifty feet away, it poked its head up, as seals do, and it looked back at us. And that was all.

Rockwell Kent, American Illustrator

Soon it was back to work for the three of us. Our first charter of the season—a family from Montana—was scheduled for Wednesday. And then, for weeks afterward, families, groups, friends, people by themselves, couples, all came and kept coming, enjoying life with us for a while at our lodge. I spent my days getting out and putting away fishing poles, organizing gear, welcoming new guests and giving them the tour, helping folks unload and load their gear, taking kids on nature walks, making lunches, coffee, and cider, cleaning the boat, cleaning the cabins, cleaning the outhouses, splitting wood, crewing on the boat, fishing, building fires, cleaning fish, cooking, helping with repairs and maintenance, and painting pictures on rocks whenever I could.

Fletcher and I just had to hang in there long enough to return our guests to Seward and we would have our first days off in a month. It had been four exhausting weeks of rising early and working all day. Especially for Fletcher, who stayed up later telling stories with our visitors. Then, rising earlier than either John or me, he made things ready for the day's fishing, or whatever the guests wanted. The three of us were frazzled and grumpy. For a change, and to get away from John, I decided to ride into Seward with Fletcher that day. On the way a call came over the boat's radio. From what I could hear, it seemed to be someone who wanted to come back out with us to Fox Island. I tried to catch Fletcher's attention by narrowing my eyes at him, with a look that said, *Don't* say yes." He said yes. "Guess who that was!" he said extra cheerfully as he hung up the transmitter. "Chris Kent, Rockwell Kent's grandson! And his sister Kathleen!"

Oh, well, that changed everything. I was curious. After my second summer on Fox Island, Fletch had told me about Rockwell Kent in a letter. I then searched for and found an old hardbound copy of Kent's book *Wilderness—A Journal of Quiet Adventure in Alaska* in a deserted wing of Zimmerman Library on campus. It had seemed like magic to pull from the stacks a book that told with an artist's passion of my island in winter and to read it in my room far away in New Mexico.

It was 1918 when Rockwell Kent, famous illustrator, age 36 and seeking a place to live far from what he felt was a money-hungry, status-seeking, war-loving society, journeyed to Alaska aboard the steamer *Admiral Farragut*. He brought along his young son, age nine. His dream was simple: to live in Alaska, near the sea. In a Seward café he learned of an old man who lived alone on Fox Island. He borrowed a dory, and rowing out into the bay, happened to meet up with the man, an old Swedish farmer who had set up a fox farm on Fox Island. The old man was setting off for Seward for provisions. When he learned of Mr. Kent's search, though, he took Mr. Kent's bowline in hand and towed him and his son to Fox Island. Rockwell wrote about his first sight of Fox Island, "It was truly sheer-sided and immense, and for all we could discover harborless; till in a moment rounding the great headland of its northern end the crescent arms of the harbor were about us,—and we were there!" Happy for company, Mr. Olson invited the travelers to live in one of the goat sheds. It couldn't have been more to Rockwell's liking.

Ashore, Mr. Olson gave his new neighbors a tour of the goat shed, fox corrals, cabin and beach, with goats tagging along through the trees. Rockwell wrote,

> We went down an avenue through the tall spruce trees. The sun flecked our path and fired here and there a flame-colored mushroom that blazed in the forest gloom. Right and left we saw deep vistas, and straight ahead a broad and sunlit space, a valley between hills; there lay the lake. It was a real lake, broad and clean, of many acres in extent, and the whole mountainside lay mirrored in it with the purple zenith sky at our feet. Not a breath disturbed the surface, not a ripple broke along the pebbly beach; it was dead silent here but for maybe the far off sound of surf, and without motion but that high aloft two eagles soared with steady wing searching the mountain tips. Ah, supreme moment! These are the times in life—when nothing happens— but in quietness the soul expands.

With his son's help he fixed up the goat shed until it was a cozy home, and he said he didn't see how people could think they needed a better home than that. There he spent the winter painting and carving wood-blocks for prints, cutting trees for wood, hiking and playing with his son, and writing. Each morning all winter he and Rockwell, Jr. bathed in the ocean or a snow bank. Rockwell's illustrations throughout the book show his passion for extreme conditions and his love of beauty. He said in a letter home,

> The Northern wilderness is terrible. There is discomfort, even misery, in being cold. The gloom of the long and lonely winter nights is appalling and yet do you know I love this misery and court it. Always I have fought and worked and played with a fierce energy, and always as a man of flesh and blood and surging spirit. …We find here life, true life—life rich, resplendent, and full of love.

> To-day was fair at sunrise, cloudy at nine o'clock, and showery all the rest. We worked again with the beloved cross-cut saw, setting ourselves an almost unattainable task—and then surpassing it. And I cleared the thicket for a better view of the mountain to the south; and in the afternoon felled another large tree. Stretched canvas for a while; and painted and drew, and felt the goddess Inspiration returning to me.

> Rockwell went for a walk in the woods; he has a delightful time on his rambles, discovering goat's wool on the bushes, following the paths of the porcupines to their holes, and to-day finding the porcupine himself. He always returns with some marvelous discovery or new enthusiasm over his explorations. He has been practicing writing to-day. He says that if he could only write he would put down the wonderful stories of his dreams.

The fall became winter, and with winter came rain, storms, gales, snow, mist… rain, rain…and the sun went away. When it was up it was only low on the southern horizon, unseen from the north-facing cove. "I look to the sun's going with a kind of dread." But he painted anyway in the semi-light and wrote succinctly and with humor something every artist can understand: "Over to-day's painting I'm filled with pride; it will be equalled by to-morrow's despair over the very same pictures."

I knew of this artist's dilemma through my mother. I would arrive home from school not knowing if I would be welcomed into the house if she were painting. If she was, and she'd had a good day of it, I might be swept into her studio, which smelled of turpentine and oil paints, with barely time to set down my books. She'd have me step back and look at her work, even ask my child's opinion. She would be filled with enthusiasm and good humor and leave her studio, take me to the kitchen for a bowl of ice cream, and ask how school was that day. When my sisters came home, and Daddy, they would each be welcomed into her studio to see her work. But then the next day I might come home to find she'd changed the painting all together. She wouldn't be at peace. She would be stepping back to appraise, striding forward, making jabs at the image with her brushes here and there, trying to fix it. She would be single-minded about some aspect of composition or color that wasn't right. She stayed sequestered with her studio door shut, and my sisters and I knew to leave her be.

Although I loved to paint on rocks and write in my journal, I was far from seeing myself as an artist. Yet even I understood. So much hope and effort goes into presenting to others the joy in one's mind. The blind drive an artist has to create began to seem almost mystical to me. *Why* is there art, and artists? I wondered at the first artists who created images on the cave wall. I thought about my own desire to tell about things in my journal, to chronicle that which I experienced and saw. And the elder Kent wrote in his journal:

> Rockwell has today devoted himself to the goats. He came in this morning in great glee to tell me that they thought *he* was a goat. I agreed with them when he went on to tell me how he had climbed the mountainside with them on all fours pretending to browse and conversing with them in the goats' tongue.

> It is a lovely moonlit night. How late it is again I do not know. I've worked hard the last three nights on an elaborate pen and ink chart of the island. ...I do recollect mighty often that I'm not doing my full part here unless I become a nine year old child for my son's

amusement just as he becomes a four legged creature at times for the astonished goats.

This very night Rockwell and I skated for the third time. Ah, but it was glorious on the lake, the moon high above us in a cloudless sky, the snow and ice on the mountain sides glistening and the spruces black. We skated together hand in hand like sweethearts; going far to one end of the lake in the teeth of the wind and returning before it like full-rigged ships.

All records for winds are broken by what rages tonight. From the north-west it piles into our cove. The windows are coated with salt, and tons of flying water sail in clouds out of the bay hiding the mountains from the base to half their height. Our rafters bend beneath the blast; ice—from we know not where—falls upon us with a thundering noise. The canvases suspended aloft sway and flap, and from end to end of the cabin the breeze roves at will. It's so ridiculously bad and noisy and cold that Rockwell and I just laugh. But the wood is plentiful for we cut some more to-day.

The gale still rages, fortunately not with its utmost fury. This morning Rockwell and I hurried through our chores and then climbed to the low ridge of the island. The snow in the woods is crusted and bore us up well so that we traveled with ease and soon reached the crest. Ah, there it was glorious; such blue and gold and rose! We looked down upon the spit and saw the sea piling upon it; we looked seaward and saw the snow blown from the land, the spray and the mist rising in clouds toward the sun, and the sun, the beautiful sun shone on us.

If I'm out-of-doors busy with the saw or axe I jump at once to my paints when an idea comes. It's a fine life and more and more I realize that for me at least such isolation—not from my friends but from the unfriendly world—is the only right life for me.

I made of my "North Wind" the most beautiful picture that ever was. I stood it facing outwards in the doorway and from far off it still showed as vivid, more vivid, and brilliant than nature itself.

Of Christmas, 1918, on Fox Island, Rockwell Kent wrote:

"Run, Rockwell, out-of-doors and play awhile." Quickly I stow the presents about the tree, hang sticks of candy from it, and light the candles. Rockwell runs for Mr. Olson, and just as they approach the cabin the door opens and fairyland is revealed to them. It is wonderful. The interior is illuminated as never before, as perhaps no cabin interior ever was among these wild mountains. Then all amazed and wondering those two children come in. Who knows which is the more entranced?

When I returned to Fox Island the spring after I read Mr. Kent's book, I searched behind the beach in the woods for Olson's cabins and sheds. Pushing through thickets and brambles, over and under fallen moss-covered trees, around in circles I stumbled with a photocopy of Rockwell's map from his book. At last I stood and said out loud, "It *has* to be *right here*." And so it was. By peering about methodically, the sagging remains of a wire corral were revealed, and there, the water tank for the foxes. A few moldering logs — the foundation of a cabin. I found there, nearly buried in moss, the rusted remains of the wood stove that had warmed the cabin interior so long ago. All had subsided into profound decay, and new life had pushed up and grown tall where the various remains stood. I felt nothing stir my imagination, however, until I looked toward the sea, dazzling through the trees, and I knew this view was Olson's view, this surf sound the sound Olson heard day and night. His footsteps made the same chiming, clacking sound as mine on the pebbly paths as he walked about doing his chores. I could sense Mr. Olson's little homestead of cabins and corrals, the voices of the goats, and the movement of the boy running about on his adventures of discovery.

The son of the junior Rockwell had come to live in Homer, on the other side of the Kenai Peninsula from Seward. His younger sister was visiting him from Massachusetts. The two young Kents drove to Seward hoping to contact a man they had heard about who had a lodge on Fox Island. They waited for us on the dock, Chris, a tall, thin, sandy-haired young man and Kathleen, also tall, with intense, intelligent green eyes and short brown hair.

After introductions Fletch said, "We'll have to meet you back here in two hours. Susannah and I have a few errands to run. Go ahead and load your gear, make yourselves comfortable on the boat if you want to. If you're hungry the Breeze Inn's across the road there, or there's a couple more cafés a mile or so that way."

By evening after we completed our errands in Seward, we were on our way with Chris and Kathleen, bringing the heirs of Rockwell out to Fox Island. Sixty-five years before he had written:

> The gentle breeze came up. With prow high in the air we spanked the wavelets, and the glistening spray flew over us. On we went straight at the dazzling sun and we laughed to think that we were being carried we knew not where. And all the while the strange old man spoke never a word nor turned his head, driving us on as if he feared we might demand to be unloosed.

Unlike silent Mr. Olson, we did talk as we rode out to Fox Island. I couldn't have anticipated the pleasure it would be to meet Chris and Kathleen. Kathleen was my age, interested in writing and opinionated, which I found exciting. She had a short answer for just about anything and it was usually witty and made me laugh. Having her and Chris around was like a vacation after all. They were there as non-paying guests, and either they already knew the Alaska ethic of work for lodging, or they learned while with us because Fletch kept them busy, but also well fed, well-storied, and well-adventured. We didn't take them fishing which lightened our work load. We motored around to the back of the island to the spit that their grandfather had painted from the vantage point of the ridge high above. They stayed only two and half days but we exchanged addresses and made plans for future get-togethers. I suggested to Kathleen that she visit me in New Mexico. "Maybe I'll just do that," she said.

The Wife's Surprise

New groups came every three days or so without a break in between. We loaded our departing guests, their heavy coolers filled with thick slabs of halibut and pretty glacier ice, and their great piles of bags, boxes, backpacks, and gear, first into the skiff from the beach, then into *Fox Islander* from the skiff. Fletcher took them to Seward where they loaded up their vans, trucks, or cars to travel home. While Fletcher waited for new arrivals in the harbor, he hosed out the boat and cleaned it top to bottom, bought groceries, bought boxes of frozen bait herring at the cannery, checked the post office, made phone calls, fueled the boat, ran errands.

While he was away, John and I worked. I helped cut up logs, carried the rounds to the flat area in front of the Main cabin, and split the sections for firewood, until great piles grew around me and I felt capable and strong. I cleaned the cabins, poured lime down the outhouse holes, finished or started a building or maintenance project, worked on trails, and when I could, I found time to paint in my studio. The island was usually quiet with Fletch away, unless

John was using the chain saw. A log would sometimes wash up on our beach and this was always a bonanza; other times we went in search of logs on other beaches. On our beach we would tie the log to a big tree with a long, strong rope. As the tide rose and floated it, we'd pull it up. We used a "come-along" for this. A "come-along" can pull anything. It's like a pulley with a ratchet mechanism that you rig onto a rope, and you just work a long handle back and forth. The ratchet locks down on the rope with each pull of the handle, and whatever you're pulling can't go back, it has to come toward you. We'd pull the log up periodically as the tide rose, until it rested as high up the beach as it could get. Then, when the tide went out, it lay on dry beach. We now had twelve hours until the tide was high again to get the log cut up and hauled away to the woodsheds.

A cedar log as big around as an elephant and longer than a school bus washed up on the beach one night. I figured it had come to us on currents over a thousand miles from southeastern Alaska where the trees grow that big, or maybe even from the giant redwood forests in Washington. Out of a small portion of it, John split enough roof shingles for his cabin, both the woodsheds, and the three outhouses.

Fletcher always called on the radio as he neared the island. When I'd look out the window, I could nearly always see the boat just coming into view at the time he called. Fletcher tied *Fox Islander* to its mooring buoy in the cove and the new arrivals—two couples from Ohio—came ashore. They looked about wonderingly, bubbling with good spirits. I gave them the tour, showing them how to use the wood stove and where the kindling and larger wood pieces were, the right way to operate the propane lights and propane water heater, and where the outhouses and shower were.

The shower was on the back deck of the sauna, outside, out of the wind—sort of. John had built it. It had wood-slat sides but was open on the back, where the island rose up almost vertical. The shower was private, unless it was blueberry season. Then, blueberry picking guests and John tended to go wherever they had to, to get berries, and the steep hillside behind the shower was a good spot for berries. I knew that for some guests, Fox Island Lodge was just too rustic. Once a dignified older woman who had never used an outhouse came out, and was stuck on Fox Island for three days with no choice.

Around the crackling beach fire that evening, we sat on logs sipping dark red wine, and the Ohio couples' stories came out. Both the men were steel-mill laborers and best friends, and the wives were also best friends. The night before, Sam, who had curly red hair, and his wife Sue, and the other couple, had gone to dinner to

celebrate Sam's birthday. The fanciest restaurant in their town was at the airport. What Sam didn't know was that his wife and friends had purchased four airplane tickets. Their luggage was already on the Alaska Airlines jet. As they finished their dinner, Sam's name was paged and when he picked up the white paging telephone he was told his plane to Alaska was boarding. He had left the steel mill that day, an ordinary weekend ahead of him, except for it being his birthday. He thought they had a fishing trip planned. He had had dinner and then found himself on a plane flying north, to Alaska. In Anchorage, they had boarded a bus for Seward, and once in Seward they located the harbor and the *Fox Islander* where Fletch had told Sue it would be, and rode through a glowing summer afternoon to arrive on the beach at Fox Island Saturday evening. Sam kept shaking his head and laughing out loud. He said, "All my life I've dreamed of coming to Alaska."

Sunday dawned to clear skies. We took the boat to Johnstone

Bay and fished for hours, enjoying the scenery and conversation, the lazy day occasionally punctuated by the excitement of catching a good-sized halibut. Sam caught a hundred-pounder, two big lingcod, and several smaller halibut. A pod of killer whales cruised by, astonishing our guests, and on the way home to Fox Island that evening, a group of black and white Dall's porpoise sprinted out from nowhere to our bow to play in its wave. My mind had wandered far afield—up, down, and sideways—out there in stark Johnstone Bay, open to the Northern Pacific. After everyone had gone to bed, I was inspired to add to my repertoire of poems, which now grew to two. I sat at the desk near the wood stove, writing in the glow of the kerosene lantern.

Halibut I Think About While Fishing

The Halibut is a flat fish,
The color of a skipping stone.
Both bulging eyes are on top.
Thinking, *What if I am one of the others—not human—
that swims in the ocean?*
Swimming among the sunbeams.

Looking downward, the halibut is hard to see:

Its top side is as gray as the glacial silt that covers the sea floor.

I swim to the ocean floor.
Puff up a cloud of silt.

Looking up, the halibut is hard to see:
Its bottom side, eyeless, is white like the light above.

I am sitting on the edge.
Gazing into.
We use a heavy line: 80-pound test,
With an eight-ounce ball weight,
And a steel "circle hook,"
Upon which is pierced a four-inch half herring.
As we talk, our lines spin slowly off our reels, the lead weights
carrying the hooks down
into the cold
cloudy
depths.

There the halibut swim in slow undulating forms,
cruising the ocean floor for food.
I think, *When a halibut spies its prey, it flips quickly on*
its edge to snap it up.
I was envisioning this as my line hit the sea floor and went slack.
I could see the flash of its white belly in the darkness.

Here's the other poem I wrote long ago, which my mother approved
of, because it rhymed:

collections of fishes
dried and crusty
collections of dishes
cracked and dusty
collections of keys
old and rusty
collections of peas
moldy and musty
and all of these
collections are trusty
I use them to play with
I know it's childish

Kathleen Kent Visits New Mexico

*When you sit in the sun and let your heels hang out of a
doorway that drops a thousand feet, ideas come to you.*

–Willa Cather, *The Song of the Lark*

I had to return to Albuquerque for my final year of school. Now
it was time to get serious and finish things up. All the arrangements
were made: I'd complete my course work, do my student teaching,
and graduate the following May. Then I'd be free to choose what to
do next. Fletcher had four more years of teaching before he could
retire. We agreed it made sense for me to work the four years as a
teacher, with the same vacations as he—at Christmas, spring break,
and the summer. Then the two of us would expand our open season
on Fox Island to five months and spend the rest of the year doing
something else. Fletcher talked again about buying land in New
Mexico and operating a cross-country ski lodge during the winters.
But I knew he loved the water and boats. New Mexico is a desert.
He said, "What would you think about running charters in the
Caribbean?" It sounded intriguing but far-fetched.

Autumn and my impending return to "reality" found me thinking
about the future again, as hard to set my mind to as ever. I just
couldn't *imagine* it. It was fun to talk about what we might do, but
deep down, planning the future seemed as much like child's play as
ever: "I'll save up $50 and get a palomino and when I'm 18 I'll
move to Montana, and get a job on a ranch, with a trout stream,
and when I'm 26 (*"Wait until you're at least 26 to get married,"* my
mother always said) I'll marry a rancher…" There were too many
damn *variables* lurking out there: Would I be able to get a teaching
job in Anchorage? Would Fletcher keep putting up with me? What
if he started talking about expanding the business again? Would I
want to make a new, "improved" Fox Island Lodge my life? Could I
learn how to put a stop to those bewildering episodes of social
skittishness? Did I want to live on a sailboat for six months of each
year? How could Fletcher afford a sailboat? Would I ever ride a horse
again? Could Fletch really buy land in New Mexico?

Could Fletch ever like New Mexico?

My parents and I had taken the truck to Bernalillo to get hay and when we returned, our door stood open and Janis Joplin's voice came bellowing out. An unfamiliar blue car stood cock-eyed in our drive. Kathleen Kent had arrived from Massachusetts and made herself at home. She came striding out. She had shown up unannounced and unexpected and seemed to have taken over our home, but my mother loved Janis Joplin, discovering her long after the 60s, when she—my mother— was 56, so she was delighted with my young friend right away. We unloaded the hay, filling Trinket's shed to the rafters. Kathleen lit a cigarette and scratched Trinket's cheek through the corral rails, looked out over the corral with its piles of manure here and there on the sun-baked dirt, and beyond to the horizon. I could see Mt. Taylor almost disappearing blue over ninety miles away. "Take me on a drive," she said.

"Okey-dokie!"

"Oh, you girls are going to have fun!" said my mother. "Susie, take my camera with you!"

I had a route I liked to take that went up into the Jemez Mountains, past Jemez Pueblo with the red chile *ristras* hanging from the *portals*, through the village of Jemez Springs and past El Vallo Grande, a *caldero* so vast that the cattle grazing in it look as small as fleas. Then on to the Bandalier cliff dwellings, through the town of Los Alamos, and down the mountain to Santa Fe for a good meal. At Jemez Pueblo we saw a dog chase a burro across the road, then the burro turned on the dog, its ears back and its teeth bared, and chased the dog back across the road and down a hill.

In Jemez Springs where we stopped for cokes at the only store, a bronze plaque over the door read,

AT THIS VERY SPOT 200 YEARS AGO,
NOT A DAMN THING HAPPENED.

We arrived at the cliff dwellings toward dusk, and hiked down into the sandstone canyon from the visitor's center. Beside the small creek that ran along the canyon bottom, a group of deer a few feet from the trail stopped grazing to gaze at us with mild regard. Further on, the last visitors passed us on their way out, and the place was ours. We came to a steep switchback trail that Stone Age feet had worn into the canyon wall. We followed it up, and came to a series of pole ladders, which we climbed, at last stepping out onto the lip of a huge cave. There, secure inside the cave, are the cliff dwellings.

In the dimming light, Kathleen and I explored the small rooms built beside and above one another out of stone and adobe: rooms with small windows and short doorways, rooms with ladders that entered through the roof, and rooms for storage which held tiny ears of corn—the same kind the Anasazi people had grown in the twelfth century. We walked through open areas where women had once gathered, kneeling on the floor to grind corn into cornmeal, their talk bouncing off cave walls, children playing in the peripheries. They ground the corn between oval-shaped stones, which they held in their hands, and dished-out stone slabs on the ground, their mounds of multi-colored cobs growing smaller as the fresh-ground meal filled clay pots.

It was black dark by the time we stepped out to an open area toward the front of the cave where the *kiva* was. The kiva is a sacred place. It's a circular room, dug into the ground, walled with stonework, covered over, and entered by descending a ladder through a hole in the roof. It is where religious ceremonies are conducted and the most profound decisions are made. We didn't climb the ladder down into it, but sat on the edge, our legs dangling into its blackness through the opening. Kathleen lit a cigarette and handed it to me, then lit one for herself. She held her cigarette down in the hole where it lit the room faintly red. "This place blows me away," she said. I felt a little light-headed from the tobacco.

We gazed across the canyon to the opposite canyon wall, rimmed along the top with ponderosa pine. We listened to the night, the faint water sound in the canyon bottom, the rustlings of tiny nocturnals, whispers in the juniper boughs. The deer would be folding their slender legs to curl themselves into nests of grass, their heads resting on each other, their ears twitching off gnats, their sharp black hooves digging into moss, sending up earth smells as they shifted to get comfortable. Stars like pinholes into another world pierced the black sky down to the canyon rims. I focused on the great old branches of a silhouetted ponderosa on the opposite canyon rim. An odd event occurred. The Earth's turning produced the effect of the stars moving through its branches. Then the stars were still again. It must have taken ten minutes but it had felt like a moment. I blinked with a breath of surprise. I took another deep breath and then let it out with a glance toward Kathleen.

She said, "Remember what you told me on Fox Island when I asked you what it was like where you grew up?"

I laughed, still tingling. "You mean about the night sky?"

"That's it."

"I said, imagine you are inside a round room at night and it's so dark you can't see. Stand in the middle with a 50 pound feed sack of those little round bird seeds."

"That's what you said."

"And I said, take a handful and sprinkle them out on the floor like you're feeding chickens."

She said, "Have you ever fed chickens?"

"No, have you?"

"Yes."

"Okay. When you throw the first handful of seeds, they begin to glow. It looks good so you throw more. The room might be turning. The seeds get brighter. Take a step. Throw another handful. The walls and ceiling have disappeared. You smell dirt. Throw some near, throw some far. Each seed stays suspended, each one glows. Skip around! Watch out for cactus! Return to the bag! Throw more handfuls! They shine like white fires. Now the ground is gone. You're skipping in the sky, flinging seeds from the bag. You take the bag, hold its bottom corners, and spin. They all go out there across the sky. There's no round room, only breezes and scents and space."

We were silent for a minute. "A fifty pound bag of bird seeds," she said. "You sure weren't kidding."

I thought about the earth turning again. I thought about how I used to drag my sleeping bag and pillow out the door every night in summer and sleep on the backyard lawn. I thought about my legs dangling in the entrance hole of the kiva. I imagined a whiff of sage smoke drifting up along the walls and out of the entrance hole past my nose. What was time like for the ancient people here?

Time is an odd thing. When you're a child, two or three years old, there is no time. You hear "Wait," and it means nothing. As a school child, my thoughts were often on the desert just beyond the schoolyard fence. When I "returned" after daydreaming myself on a horse across this beckoning expanse, the long black hands of the clock would finally have moved. Summertime lasted forever as my sisters and I hiked over the countryside, in the open space of arroyos, foothills, and mesas across the street from our house, building cook fires at our favorite spots when we got hungry. In summer a child's days are filled with a hundred pastimes begun and enjoyed, without thought to whether there will be time to finish.

I remember a song my mother sang—"Backward, turn backward, oh time in your flight/ Make me a child again just for tonight." Or another favorite, "Time waits for no one/ It passes you by/ It goes on forever/ Like the clouds in the sky." I know now that when one is a mother time goes faster. And I'm told that when one is a grandmother it goes like the wind.

I thought of how waves hitting the beach always gave me a sense of time *before*—long before, to infinity—and of time to come— to infinity. The beginning is where I am right now, and infinity is in both directions from here.

I'd read once that perhaps indigenous peoples thought of time not as something that passes, but as something *they passed through*, along with all other life. They lived through the endlessly repeating cycle of moons. The moon of fawns being born, the moon of new ruffled corn leaves coming up green through the red dirt, the moon of frost turning the tall stalks brown and brittle, the moon the creek freezes, the moon the sun rises directly across the canyon, the moon of fawns being born.

I felt as though *I* passed through time, and maybe that was why the whole concept of planning my life felt foreign to me. I wanted to be content in the cycles, living my little life, but I was made discontent by the onus of *planning for life's stages* like everyone talked about. I liked school because I liked it. I liked Fox Island. I liked riding my horse. I liked Fletch. I liked eating things I caught and grew. I liked learning about rocks from my dad. The little plants that came up in the spring were my friends. I just wanted my own beautiful life. I wondered if, being like this, I had anything to offer others.

I tried to imagine the thoughts and concepts of cliff dwellers whose population in times long past must have reached as high as one thousand souls. Right here they had laughed and loved, and worshiped the sun-father and the moon where their mother dwelled. Daily offerings of gratitude and prayers were made to those above, and great ceremonial dances took place on this very spot. We were on sacred ground.

Susannah,

Received your letter and pictures yesterday. Good to hear from you. Sounds like you and Kathleen had a blast. Neal and Anne seem to be getting along fine. Neal said 'no problems' when I asked so I guess the rough spot is over. Had me worried for a while there. Hate to think of what he'd do without Anne. Had them over for a ski and sauna last weekend and we all had a pretty good time.

Last weekend was unbelievable. I had a charter with a family who are friends of the Hinckleys. There were 5 including a very small baby. They were from Australia. They just wanted to sight see and hang out on the island which was good for me. I could tell that a storm was brewing from the 12-18 foot seas out near the bird rocks which we couldn't get anywhere near. Showed them Bear Glacier but couldn't even get out to the sea lions on Rugged I. So I headed back to our cove where a typical Caribbean "line squall" hit us. We idled in the cove for about an hour while 50K winds whipped through. The annual Seward to Seal Rocks (past Aialik) sailing race was in process and they were having quite a time. We finally made it to the beach where John and a couple from Astoria (John's friends) helped us land. Then the wind picked up and our mooring anchor began to drag. John remembered the big anchor in the shop. As it turned out, I am sure that anchor saved the Fox Islander from blowing up on the beach and total ruin. By evening we had steady 50K winds with gusts to 70K and 6 foot seas in the cove. The boat had 3 anchors out and had dragged them to a point one boat length outside the surf line.

One gust picked up the dory off the beach and flung it 10 ft. in the air until the bow line snapped it back to the beach and kept it from flying over the new cabin. Couldn't believe that the boat and engine were OK. It was impossible to get off the beach to check the Fox Islander. Fired up the sauna for the guests and used it myself to thaw out. Blew 50-70K all night. At 1:00 a.m. there was a mayday from "Maniac" which had broken its mast—"dismasted" off Caines Head. The Jellison came out for the rescue. "Magic" made it to Thumbs Cove where another boat had gone down and there were 10 people on the beach. Musser was holed up in Humpy Cove with his Dad. Sunday with the wind at 40K+, Musser made a run for Seward. His anchor was snagged down so he had to leave it behind. Talked to him and recommended that he rig a sea anchor at least. I figured he didn't carry a spare anchor. About 3 hours after talking to Musser as he passed Thumbs Cove in "green water and 8 foot seas" I heard him calling the Coast Guard. His engine had quit and he was adrift. They told him to throw out a sea anchor which he didn't have. They made it to him in time and towed him in.

He called and asked to use the truck to pull his boat.

I didn't dare bring in 8 people through these conditions so I called Ann and had her get me a sub for my first day of school. We got out to the boat and checked everything out and left Fox I. Monday around 10 a.m.

What an adventure for the grandparents from Australia. I gave them a Kent book which was greatly appreciated. After all this, I cancelled Simpson's Labor Day charter— too physically and emotionally drained—also need to pack canned goods and tools back into Seward.

Think of you a lot. Don't envy your student teaching but do envy your weather. Well, I had better finish this. Plan to head down the highway to Seward in about 2 hours. I am showing a film on geology right now.

Miss you tons,

Fletch

Dear Fletch,

I miss you. Teaching went well, much better than it has been. At the end of the day I got a bunch of hugs from the kids which put me on cloud nine. We have had about three days of cool weather, and the trees on the mountaintop are lovely colors.

I felt philosophical all day on my birthday. I spent a while talking to two boys and their father who were traveling by mule and wagon from Loving, New Mexico to Idaho. Loving is down south. The dad looked dusty and tougher than leather. What an adventure. It was fascinating talking to them and looking over their outfit and mules.

Friday evening Katy and Steve took me to dinner, up the Tram to the crest of the Sandias. ("Longest tram in the world.") We pigged out.

Just had breakfast, cleaned up my room and am sitting at my desk writing to you. I can't help but gaze once in a while out of my window. It is breezy outside, sort of windy, but sunny. A fall day in New Mexico has a special quality I love. I hope someday you'll see how it feels, too. Yesterday I went riding and everything was so perfect I felt like quitting school and living in a shed.

You asked what I think about getting a bigger boat. I really am still becoming acquainted with boat and sea life. I am fond of it although I am also fond with land life, where I can move about under my own power. What I'm saying is that I don't know enough about how things would be with a bigger boat and running daily tours into Aialik to say much on what I think about it. To be honest, I might be apt to feel a sense of guilt about it. Aialik is such a secluded and mystical place. To me it's like a holy place. That is the poetic aspect of the idea to me.

On the realistic side I guess it would be pleasant to travel there every day or every few days, and to see and experience others enjoying it. Some people would be awestruck and you know I would like seeing that.

I am not one to think in a business way. I keep thinking how much I'd rather just have the boat we have, take our friends and other people on tours or fishing occasionally, and travel about exploring the rest of the time. But that probably makes no business sense. Perhaps you will need to keep reminding me that we need to make money in order to live on Fox Island,

and have a boat.

It's not that I'm not capable of thinking in a business sense. Would you consider the possibilities of renting the cabins long term as a way of making money? What about people's two-week vacations? Or someone's month-long adventure? Or an artist's or writer's dream to live at a place like Fox Island? Another idea is to do longer outings with people, like to Montague Island. They could have themes like "The Sea Life of Prince William Sound" or "The History of the Kenai."

How about the way it is? I think we really got all the systems down this summer. As we get more organized and familiar with our jobs, things go more smooth and enjoyably. I like our Fox Island life. I could see doing the same again (with a few changes).

You asked what I thought about selling the Fox Islander and getting a bigger boat. I guess I thought of a lot to say. Tell me more about this tours idea. How would it be? And tell me about my ideas, what do you think of them? Sometimes I think I have some uneducated or not-so-good ideas and you don't want to insult me so you don't say anything.

I know you don't like to write down deep thoughts. I don't understand your ways of thinking deep thoughts, but I know you think them because I've been amazed by your insights before. I am going to move to Alaska, probably, on the basis of what I can infer. But I really would like to know how you feel, how you think it is going to be. I feel sure enough to take this step, but I would like to know more. If you see and like my ideas, my hopes for the future, let me know. If not, let me know. If you think our plans are compatible, say so. Tell me more about how it is going to be. Would you like me to try writing professionally if I could? Or do artwork? With your ideas would I have the time and space to do that? Would you mind if I spent my own time and money buying land in New Mexico? Would you like land here?

If I were settled in a small town, teaching, raising horses and writing, and had been doing so for some time, would I expect you to forget your dreams from your own heart and join me in mine? I hope not. Is this what you hope from me? I hope not, because I don't think I can do that. My own ideas (writing, owning land) are dear to me. Is that okay with you because we could somehow probably join our dreams.

Now quite a bit of the day has passed, and I've still got lesson plans to make. One more week in the school and then back to UNM for a while, then back to the school full time. I will consider getting back on campus a vacation!

I hope the days continue to fly by. I am lonely for you.

Love, Susannah

Dear Fletch,

Well, it's finally November! The weather has turned warm again after some days of rain and snow. It's around 60-65 degrees. There is still a smidgen of snow on top of the Sandias. Last weekend I got to get outside helping my parents get wood. It's beautiful outside with winds that play around amongst the piñon trees, winds that come from far away. Here at the house, now and then comes the smell of snow, wood smoke, dinner cooking, someone's dryer going. The sky is as clear as it can get, so that means here in Placitas we have a view that goes 90 miles to the west. I can see Mt. Taylor and if I look north I can see the Sangre de Cristos. When you get to see it you will think it is different than anything you've seen. I just now thought of the view of pure white Denali from Anchorage. Denali looks like a ghost when its shadows are the exact same color as the sky around it.

Last night when I came home from Katy's there were a million stars in the sky, and it was amazing to see how they twinkled. I'd never seen them twinkle like that, and I don't know why they were doing it. I saw three falling stars, too. This is the month to be thankful and I was thankful that I could take the time to stand out there and ponder the heavens, the night wind, and not have the headache that's been with me for a couple weeks.

I helped Katy last night address wedding invitations, make inserts telling about the reception, and make maps. She's getting married in San Rafael. Poor thing's under so much stress having moved out of her apartment and having to board her dogs and cats at the vets where she works. Steve is not much help. He watches TV, drinks beer and his way of comforting her is to tease and tickle her. Still, he's a nice guy and I think Katy found herself a good one. I'm not much help being at least as stressed as she is. But last night I put in quite a few hours and I think it took a load off her shoulders.

We also watched a movie called The 25th Day with Anthony Quinn in it. This guy is living in Romania with his wife and child when WWII happens. A policeman who has been ordered to gather up all Jews gathers Quinn up even though he isn't a Jew, because he wants Quinn's wife. So Quinn is sent to a labor camp and for a year and a half he is a "Jew." Then he escapes to Hungary. He can't say he's Romanian there because they didn't like Romanians in Hungary at that time. So he gets called a Hungarian volunteer and is sent to another labor camp.

He's working in a factory there when he is noticed by a high-ranking SS man who is a scientist and he says that Quinn's features prove Quinn is of pure German stock. Quinn is immediately made a high-ranking SS man with his picture on all the magazines. So then he's a guard at a labor camp, and he meets one of his friends from seven years ago, now, who is now a prisoner. As the Germans begin to lose the war, he escapes with a bunch of prisoners and they all go to an American military place that is now present. There they are all taken back to Oremberg again, which is now taken over by Americans. They live there for three months or so, in the barracks.

Quinn has never heard from his wife, nor she from him because all their letters have been intercepted. She was once forced to sign a paper that divorced them because he was a Jew, but he isn't sure if she meant it or not and she gets awfully befuddled seeing him in SS uniform on the magazine covers.

Quinn is the best natured guy possible, innocent and provincial and makes some dumb comments here and there that could get him in trouble, like saying he's Romanian in Hungary. He's hapless and the whole movie is about how war is a big crazy machine that is apart and unrelated to the lives of people. Quinn is always being told, "you're a Jew, you're Hungarian, you're German," then finally, "You're a nazi."

At the end of the movie he's tried in American court for being a nazi. But at court his defender asked him "do you know why you are here?" and he answers "I don't know why I've been anywhere in the last eight years."

Also, the defender reads to the court a letter from Quinn's wife, that was just recently intercepted by the Red Cross. It's the first time in eight years Quinn has heard from her and the letter is read in public. The letter clarifies much of what's happened to him, and she also tells of their two young boys and of herself being raped by some German officers and having a baby that is now two.

He is acquitted, he takes a train to where she is, and after the train has gone and the people have all dispersed, he sees her and their sons, and the blond baby. They both feel awkward.

The ending is quite unlike any ending I've ever seen. It was happy, but here's this couple who hardly know each other any more. Their love for each other is the only aspect of their relationship that has been constant. They're finally reunited; Quinn smiles to the blond child and shakes the hands of his boys. Then an American reporter with a camera appears, arranging them, lurching around them clicking, telling them Smile! Smile! Takes one picture after another. At the very end, the pictures show a grimace of anguish on Quinn's face—and the movie's over!

I learned about WWII from it and so maybe it would be a good one to show to your classes. It was over at 2:15 a.m. then Katy was asleep and I watched part of Indira Ghandi's funeral and then I drove home to Placitas and that's when I saw the twinkling stars.

Not much else has been happening. Now that it's afternoon I better get out of my pajamas and start figuring out what I need to get done. It's a beautiful day, and I'm thinking of you.

Love, Susannah

Student Teaching at Alvarado Elementary

Back at school, a student again. When it came time to choose what grade to teach, I chose innocent, adorable first graders. And everything went great for a while. I lived with my parents again, Ned and I resumed our weekend horseback rides at first; the school was a pleasant drive each morning through cottonwood groves on Old 85 with occasional glimpses of the river. At first I only taught certain things for limited times—like the "word of the day," or an arithmetic lesson—or I taught small groups of five or six children in "committees." This was fun, and I was good at it. I taught them about popcorn in a lesson about the Indians who lived in what is now the northeast United States. "Can you imagine what the Indians thought when they first found out that this kind of corn popped? It would be like if your mom put a pot of beans on the stove and they all started banging around and shooting out of the pan." A little girl delighted me with a burst of giggles.

But then things went haywire. I began to be given responsibility for the whole class, 27 children, and I couldn't control the whole class. There were children in it who were discipline problems. There were two boys who made fart sounds and laughed like hyenas. There was an Indian boy named Antler (adopted by white parents) who was interested in everything except his schoolwork. He constantly found bugs in the classroom, climbed on the bookshelves, and under the tables. There was a boy who brought his Cabbage Patch doll to school and threw it up on to the ceiling fan, where it spun around a few times and then flew off. There was the girl who got great pleasure out of being just plain ornery. There was the girl who cried and said, "NO!" and ripped up other students' work. There was the girl who refused to do anything but draw.

I was in awe of the actual teacher, Mrs. Schweinbraten, whom I had been assigned to, and who was supposed to be my "mentor." She was a beautiful *señora*, with long, black hair, dark eyes, and red lips. She was self-assured and civilized, unlike me. She could gain perfect control of the class in less than half a minute, using a voice so quiet she was hard to hear. She spoke in velvet tones, guiding, manipulating. Whether she was gliding about the room, or sitting perfectly still, smiling like Buddha, or giving stern—but beautiful—

looks, she functioned as a teacher with supreme confidence, whereas for me, classroom management was turning out to be a complete mystery. I sensed I had a lot to offer—I even thought I would be a far better teacher, thinking of teaching in its purest and highest form, than Mrs. Schweinbraten, if the children would just behave.

In too many ways, I was still a child myself. I wanted Antler to be able to wander out the door of the classroom into the sunshine and look for bugs. I, too, thought the doll on the fan was funny, though in my role as student teacher I was mortified. I wanted the girl to be able to draw pictures, and learn through her artwork. I understood the confusion and fear of the child who cried and struck out in anger—something was terribly wrong at home. I just plain didn't like the boys who made fart sounds or the ornery girl who taunted me. Somehow, I needed to conjure up at least the appearance of maturity, but I just didn't know how. Mrs. Schweinbraten and I were no matched pair. She'd never encountered a young woman or a prospective teacher like me.

I thought about my problems and went to others for advice. Mark, my professor with whom I'd had a sort of romance between the covers of my journal, and who I considered my mentor, had come to expect so much from me that it was excruciating. But when I told him I was in trouble, he gave some good advice. He suggested I go out and buy a puppet. Children that age have a hard time distinguishing between what is real and what isn't, he said, and the puppet could focus their attention—and be my helper and ally. Mark's idea worked. I introduced the puppet, a koala bear. I told them the story of how he had accidentally gotten on a plane in Australia and ended up here, and he missed his home and needed new friends. The puppet hugged my shoulder and nuzzled my neck, turning to look shyly at the children. I said they needed to speak quietly to him, so they wouldn't scare him, and to take turns. I guess I was pretty good at creating a voice and persona for the puppet. The children were as quiet as mice, and anyway, I was desperate, which probably gave my performance a certain potency. I allowed the children to raise their hands and ask the puppet questions, and we all listened to his answers. The children loved the puppet. He indeed was my friend, and theirs. He came out at special times, in the morning, before the last bell, and if I needed him real bad.

I had noticed also that the children became attentive and quiet whenever I drew on the chalkboard, which I naturally did as part of many lessons. So I continued doing this, and also gave a short daily art lesson. All the children looked forward to this each day. These two techniques were uniquely "me," and they worked well.

From there I had to find my style. I had to fly. I had to give my own rhythm and character to each minute of each school day. I had to bring those kids along to life with me as their teacher. My strengths were my only hope while I struggled to find management techniques and to grow in confidence.

Mrs. Schweinbraten, however, had her own challenges with regard to me. She struggled with our differences, and with having to give up her control of her class, and soon she began to interfere in earnest. With her as their teacher, I didn't think the children's natural thirst for learning was being fulfilled. I did not think she was creative in her teaching. The children seemed mesmerized by her and I could not deny that she was a master at management. I stayed in awe of her in this regard, as she began to discourage my efforts and to replace my newly minted techniques—my big hopes— with her own suggestions, which I was unable to carry out. Each interference set me back down a hill which had to be climbed again with dwindling energy. I had no wherewithal at the time to assert myself. I went into a critical loss of confidence. At last she didn't even allow me to choose the "word of the day;" my words like "burro" and "starlight" had to be replaced with words from a standardized curriculum, from a book which sat at all times on her desk. As my responsibility for the whole class continued to increase each day, as is the practice in student teaching, things rapidly became worse. In addition, I spent every evening and most of the weekends preparing for school. I became exhausted and discouraged. Finally, in late April, after four months, after the children had gone home for the day, in abject defeat I said, "The class is yours, Roberta. I won't be coming back tomorrow." She was very sweet and understanding. I may have been wise enough to know that Roberta had sabotaged me, and that she acted sweet because she had succeeded in driving me away. But if I had some sense of this, my damaged self-esteem was more than enough to override such self-protective thoughts. I believed she felt sorry for me because I had had to admit defeat. Eleanor

Roosevelt said, "No one can make you feel inferior without your consent." I guess I gave Roberta consent. Mrs. Roosevelt also said, "You gain strength, courage and confidence by every experience in which you really stop to look fear in the face. You are able to say to yourself, 'I lived through this horror. I can take the next thing that comes along.' You must do the thing you think you cannot do." I was only ready to get as far away from my failure as possible, physically, emotionally, and spiritually. I hoped to avoid anything like it for the rest of my life.

I drove home feeling as if my soul had collapsed like an empty paper bag. I said nothing to my parents, or Ned, or Fletcher at first. I didn't even want to think what Mark thought of me or what the whole Department of Education was saying. I got on Trinket and rode, slowly on gentle terrain, for Trinket was old now. Her front legs had an odd stiffness and she would sometimes stop, not to graze, not to think about doing something ornery, like she might have in the old days. She'd just stop. I dismounted and led her. I rode and walked Trinket every day for three weeks while my college classmates completed their student teaching. In May, they graduated.

I stayed away from the phone, but finally Mark had called enough times for me to feel pressured into calling him back at his office in the College of Education. He was angry, but not at me. He said things had been handled wrong, ranted about my student/teacher liaison not dealing effectively with the situation, about how I should have been matched with a different teacher whose style might have been more like my own. *How can anyone tell what my 'style' is or what I'm like?* I thought. *I don't fit anywhere that any of them is used to.*

I figured Mark was just being nice, but he did cheer me up.

After saying goodbye to Mark, I got out a letter Fletch had written a few weeks before and reread it.

Susannah,

Saturday afternoon Tutka and I took the skiff out to the island. It was pretty rough so we followed the east shoreline and ducked into Thumbs Cove for a breather before crossing over to Fox I. We landed about half way down the beach to stay away from the surf in front of the cabin. I used the block and tackle and pulled the boat up above high tide which was no easy job as dark fell. But what a beautiful night with a full moon and clear sky. The lake is pretty well frozen but I wouldn't risk walking on it. Tutka had a great time exploring his old haunts. I made up a good dinner for Tutka which I figured he deserved after the cold ride out.

Had a nice quiet evening and didn't have to worry about the boat at anchor as usual, but the marine forecast was for increasing winds to 25-30 knots with no let up before Tues. So I became a bit concerned and decided to head back by first light. What a ride in! Took one wave over the bow and bounced around for two hours fighting 6 foot seas. My fingertips were starting to get frostbite inside my rubber gloves. Poor Tutka was about frozen but we made it and I learned a lesson about winter boating— don't do it in heavy seas and under time restraints.

Plan to stay in town next few weekends to work on the house. I am a bit sore today from the hauling, dragging and bouncing around.

That's about all for now—Take care and don't give up. I know you won't.

Love, Fletch

When I finally called Fletch and told him how I'd quit school three weeks shy of graduating, he was good to me. He said things like, "Don't worry about it. That teacher failed you. Your guidance person didn't know what she was doing. Come on back up here; we have work to do. Tutka misses you." He also said, "Susannah, I'd like you to think about moving up here, for good. Will you think about it?"

I hated to think how disappointed he must be that I wouldn't be getting a teaching job in the fall. But as far as I could tell, that made no difference. He wanted me. My spirits began to lift in anticipation of Fox Island, my little world where I was becoming ever more competent. It was a relief to leave New Mexico that spring. I left the budding cottonwoods along the Rio Grande, my friends, my parents, my horse, and the roads and trails along which I rode, and, with Fletch's proposal in mind, I left without a backward glance.

—⟡5⟡—

Always Tie Your Own Horse

The Drunkards

The first charter of the season was a doozy, and my troubles in distant New Mexico evaporated from my memory. This group had heard about us from the bartender at the Penthouse Bar, which was in Sheffield House Hotel where I'd worked the previous winter. They had rented a motor home in Anchorage and all but the driver arrived at the harbor drunk as skunks. Fletcher didn't know what to think when the group of six men stumbled down the ramp and along the dock and practically fell into the boat. Somehow they managed to get their gear loaded, and after their one-hour ride, they managed to transfer from *Fox Islander* into the skiff and from the skiff onto the beach.

John and I were ready to help with the gear. Guests always brought so much gear and luggage that even *they* seemed baffled by the huge volume piled on the beach. Besides this, there might be propane tanks, groceries, lumber, and any number of other items to carry up and stow away. John did not think highly of anyone who didn't pitch right in on this job of hauling *all* the gear, not just his own.

He expected all guests, including children, to help carry the gear up the beach with the rest of us, and if they didn't, he'd be likely to say something. Most guests just naturally did haul their own gear and help with the rest. But on this day John stood by in amazement as a well-tanned, inebriated Australian man lurched out of the skiff onto the beach, picked up a large, frisbee-sized flat rock, and began to spin in circles like a discus thrower. With mighty effort and a terrific grunt he released the rock. It flopped to the ground and he flew through the air horizontally and landed quite a ways out in the water. He stood up shouting and dripping saltwater as Fletcher ran into the water to help him get his footing and wade ashore. His friends were incapacitated with laughter, practically falling down. I wondered, how did he reverse the action like that? Scientifically speaking, could such a feat ever be repeated? We three stole glances at each other, dumbfounded, and wondered if it was going to be a long and dangerous few days.

The group, as it turned out, was a lot of fun, not that I wanted any more of our guests to be like them. They brought a whole case of fine, expensive red wine, the best I'd ever tasted. They brought an entire lamb and a spit they'd had someone weld especially for this outing, for roasting over a fire. We got into the spirit of their fun and celebrated with them each evening.

John had built a sauna the previous year. Inside was a 50-gallon barrel for a stove into which he had rigged a three-inch air intake pipe from the floor, which, like the cabin floors, was a few feet above the ground on pilings. This intake pipe caused the fire to roar with life. We would usually get nearly as hot in there as the rocks on the stove we threw water on to make steam. When we couldn't stand it any more we'd run out—naked and hot as hell—and jump into the canoe, which we had positioned just outside the sauna door at the top of the beach. Fletcher would give the canoe a shove, leap in like a bob sledder, and we'd shoot down the beach—a long ride if the tide was out—and jet out into the water, where we'd all dive in one direction—the plan, anyway—tipping ourselves into the ocean. Thus fortified, we'd swim back to shore. Fletcher and another semi-responsible party would haul the half-sunk canoe to shore and empty it. We'd all drag it back up the beach, reposition it, and crowd once again into the sauna, grabbing another cold beer off the porch on the way in.

That was the time Fletcher bragged so much about the new Bruce anchor he had ordered, which lay on its coil of rope on the floor of the boat. It had finally come to Seward from Fisheries Supply Company in Seattle. It so happened that this was the same group who, upon returning to the cove after a day's fishing, stood and watched while Fletcher dropped the new Bruce anchor overboard forgetting to first tie the rope to it. The Australian said, "Gee, Mate, what'd you do *that* for?"

John's presence in my world continued to make life difficult. There was nothing John thought he could not do, and there was nothing he tried that he did not think he was good at. John wanted a bathtub; he dug a large tub-sized hole in the forest floor a ways past the big cabin, and lined the hole with a dense, thick padding of soft moss. He topped this with a lining of heavy, black rubber sheeting. He suspended a 50-gallon barrel that he had gotten out of the Seward dump—he got a lot of the stuff he needed from the dump—between two trees with chains. He put a "T" in the water line and ran two hoses from the "T": one went straight to the bathtub, and one made a detour to the barrel. From the barrel he ran another hose to the bathtub and then he attached spigots to the ends of both of these hoses. He then filled the barrel with water

and built a fire under it. Soon he had hot and cold running water. The temperature of the outdoor bath could be made just right by operating the hot and cold spigots. And it was like heaven to recline in cushiony comfort there, after a hard day's work, looking up at the tree tops and breathing the fresh, clean air, watching the bright flames whip about under the barrel, and listening to the waves crashing on the beach. John's presence, as confounding as it was, benefited me. I never knew what he would accomplish next, and watched his endeavors with curiosity and sometimes alarm.

John had his place fixed up like he wanted. He replaced his picture window downstairs with an even bigger picture window, so that practically the whole front of the cabin was glass. He had five kinds of radios: a VHF marine radio, a hand-held VHF, a ham radio, a regular radio, and one he'd made out of a coil of copper wire that you listened to with head phones. Unfortunately, you could only get the Seward station on that one, which at that time had a deejay who tried to be very encouraging about the rain every day. She played only a few songs. "Muskrat Susie"—how I hated it. "Raindrops Keep Falling on My Head"—whose idea was that in all this rain? "By the Time I Get to Phoenix"—so damn long! Get there already! "Leaving on a Jet Plane"—I couldn't take it anymore! Paul Harvey was next, "good day," and after that, the forecast—rain. Rain at night, rain in the day. Rain for the next three weeks. The deejay's cheery, chirrupy, syrupy voice (like cough syrup) would then come on to promise personally, "Don't you worry, we'll have a sun-shiny day before the summer's out."

Antennas sprouted from the tops of John's spruce trees. All around his stove, he used refrigerator shelves to make drying racks for kindling and clothing, and he loosened a floorboard so he could lift it to sweep dirt and dust under his cabin. Long gone were the days of hauling water to the old cabin. John didn't have a propane on-demand hot water heater like Fletcher and I had in our cabin and in the guests' cabin. But he still had hot and cold running water. He made his hot water by attaching a hose from the main line that filled an upstairs storage tank, which, when he turned on the hot water spigot, drained into a copper tube which coiled around his stove pipe. The water came out piping hot. He got the things he needed—the refrigerator racks, the water tank, and the copper tubing—from the Seward dump.

John sometimes cooked in his cabin. Most notable were his cinnamon rolls. He made the cinnamon rolls up in his cabin and brought them over to bake in our cabin, which had a propane stove with an oven. He was proud of the cinnamon rolls. They were his own recipe. When they were ready, he'd walk down the trail wearing an apron and oven mitts, carrying the cinnamon rolls fresh and hot in their baking pan to share with the guests. The rolls weighed about two and a half pounds each even though they were regular-size. If they weren't eaten within five minutes of being oven-fresh, they couldn't be eaten at all, for they hardened like *adobes*. They were good, though.

Winter in Anchorage

By the end of my fifth Alaska season, my New Mexico identity lay unrecognized under my competencies and my love for the far North. I had mastered an inventory of useful skills. I identified with the Alaskan outdoor life, and this is how folks knew me now. Fox Island had become my life. I still knew in sober, realistic moments that it would be sensible to get a "real" job, but I mostly thought of a job in terms of a way to earn money during the winter until it was time to return to Fox Island. Fletcher didn't want me to go back to New Mexico, and I didn't consider it. He and I drove through Turnagain Pass and along Turnagain Arm back to Anchorage, back to our log home in the foothills of the Chugach. Fletcher had an unattractive chrome and black-vinyl couch that I had left alone when living with him before. Now I bought an inexpensive sofa that looked pretty good for a while, to replace it. He had a plywood floor in the kitchen, stained with grease and other crud. I scoured it clean and laid flooring. He had big silver shop lights rigged up with extension cords to illuminate the pantry and one for a porch light on the front. I got a book on wiring and wired the place and put up nice lights. I bought a desk for myself and had my mother send up some of my books. All of this, while Fletch was at school teaching.

Termination dust, the first light dusting of snow on the mountains, showed up one morning in late August, while the birch on the lower foothills were still yellow, and the sky a pretty autumn blue. A week later, the day I had my first job interview downtown, ice covered the entire city of Anchorage. I wore big, felt-lined boots with my nice clothes and had to hold on to parked cars to keep from falling as I made my way along the sidewalk from the bus stop to my interview. Fletcher had not replaced the green Toyota that had been totaled by Stan Oxenhandler, but that was okay because I liked riding the bus. To catch the bus I walked a mile down our dirt road—which was called "Our Road," to a paved road, and while I waited, I watched the ravens on the telephone poles. I shared their interest in traffic mishaps on days like this, when cars slipped off the road into the ditches. I envied the ravens, as I waited to go to work, for being able to fly off to the wilderness at will, leaving the city behind in a matter of minutes.

My interview was at Patrick's Alaska Grocery. I would be a clerk taking orders and doing the paperwork, inside all day, and the job paid $6.00 an hour. It's just a job, I told myself. I accepted. Patrick's shipped groceries all over, to far-flung villages of Alaska, and most of the customers were Alaska Natives. I don't think they went to the post office to get their groceries. I think they went directly to the airstrip with their four-wheelers and snow-machines.

Certain villages had certain things they liked to order. King Salmon people ordered cases of baby corncobs in cans. Shungnak people liked black olives. In Selawik they ordered canned bacon and pilot crackers. In Holy Cross they liked mandarin oranges. We shipped boxed milk, baby formula, fruit and vegetables, and cases and cases of canned bacon, canned butter, and pilot crackers. Everyone liked "Shasta pop," though its high sugar content made it heavy and more expensive to ship. I took orders from McGrath, Aniak, Galena, Sleetmute, Bethel, Emmonak, Kotlik, Koyuk, Anaktuvuk Pass, Shaktulik, Scammon Bay, Goodnews Bay, and everyone else who wasn't getting groceries shipped from Seattle or Fairbanks. Some of them ordered to stock small stores. I hated to think what things cost in those stores. I loved talking to the Native people, hearing how they pronounced their villages' names, especially Kwethluk, which is raven language. I made the best of my job at Patrick's, typing up our order forms and decorating them with drawings of vegetables and mandarin oranges and baby formula at first, and later moose, caribou, snow-machines, and things that weren't directly related to groceries.

Shortly I applied for and got a job at the Arctic Environmental Information and Data Center, part of the University of Alaska. There I worked with scientists who studied all aspects of Arctic and sub-Arctic life, volcanoes, avalanches, permafrost, earthquakes, sea ice, growing seasons, treeless zones, and even one who studied time's effect on concrete by periodically visiting and analyzing bunkers along the coast that were built during World War II. Even though I was only a clerk, this was a great job with terrific potential, and good pay. I was there when Mt. Saint Augustine blew across Cook Inlet, and stood at the windows watching its ash plume with the scientists, listening to their talk, watching their activity. I also filled orders for publications and learned some about editing and writing books.

Natasha

In early November I had a day off and flew in a Cessna to visit my friend Natasha, whom I had worked with at the Sheffield House, and who now lived in Tyonek. Natasha had black curly hair and bright black eyes. Her father was a Russian Orthodox priest in Chicago, where she had just moved from when I met her. She had married the hotel maintenance man, Greg Hamsun, a big Norwegian from Pennsylvania. I thought Greg and Natasha had come remarkably far since arriving only a year ago from their homes in the Lower 48. She was now married and employed as a schoolteacher in the Alaskan bush, and Greg now had a pilot's license and owned a Cessna, a four-wheeler, a pickup truck, and all kinds of hunting equipment. Plus he'd bought Fletcher's red one-ton truck.

Tyonek, a Native village, is across Knik Arm from Anchorage, about forty miles away if you're a crow. In the winter, if you have all day, it's possible to drive around the head of the inlet to Tyonek. The State maintains an "ice road" across the frozen land and on various frozen waterways. Most of the time it's more practical to take a small plane, if you have one. Greg met me at Merrill Field and an hour later we were over Tyonek. He buzzed their house to let Natasha know we had arrived. She soon met us at the airstrip in Tyonek with their four-wheeler.

Natasha made stuffed cabbage and fish pie, Ukrainian recipes, for dinner. And over dinner, I told my student teaching story. I knew Natasha and Greg had been curious. And it didn't feel too bad to tell about what had happened. It was even a relief to have my failure out where I could face it.

Natasha and I walked out of her house the next morning to go to school. The old one-ton flatbed that had hauled loads of lumber and other items to the Seward harbor for us now lived in Tyonek, and looked like all the other vehicles in the village—sorry indeed, but still useful. Some kids had written on it with black markers: "We love Mrs. Hamsun." Natasha and one other teacher comprised the teaching staff at the village school. Hers was a small classroom of first, second, and third graders; the other teacher taught fourth, fifth, and sixth. We walked in our heavy boots and warm coats across a pond, up a steep hill, and past a yard lumpy with broken-down snow machines buried in the snow. As we walked and talked, Natasha asked me to come and teach an art lesson to her class later that day.

It didn't matter to the kids, when I came back for the art lesson at 2:30, that I drove to the classroom door on a three-wheeler and wore my heavy boots into the classroom, stacking my coat and hat and mittens on Natasha's desk. That was normal to them. Greg had taken me on a tour of the village and the country around it, and I'd hurried to get to school in time. Natasha said, "This is the person I told you about! She's here to teach the art lesson. Do you all have your tablets and markers out?" She sat down in the back of the room with an encouraging smile, and there I was, in front of a classroom of little, expectant faces again. I wrote, "Scribble Art" on the blackboard.

"Who would like to come up and draw a scribble to get our art class started today?" I showed them what I meant and erased it. The children only giggled shyly. I said,

"It isn't hard...see?" and I did it again. I smiled at a boy who looked like he might have the nerve to come forward. I brought the chalk to him.

"You get to be first!" The skinny boy in short Levi's—just a little bit less shy than the others—came forward, drew a big scribble, and hurried back to his seat to a quiet chorus of giggles.

"Hmm," I said, tilting my head, "I *think* I might see a picture here…hmm…yes, *here* it is!" and in a few seconds with a few lines and dots I turned the scribble into a mother duck with a duckling following behind. When I turned around, hands shot up, waving eagerly. I thought, *Thank goodness for Mama and her ways of keeping us entertained on long trips.* Another scribble became a moose, and another a boat, and the children began to say, "Me! Me!" So I said, "I'll tell you what, each of you may draw a scribble and hand it to your neighbor. Then you can make your own pictures!"

Over the next half-hour they drew and then colored their pictures. "This is my father's fish camp," said one girl. "It's my favorite place and then I like our duck-hunting shack."

"This is a whale! It's eating a fish!"

"This is a sad bunny, teacher, see?"

"Hey, teacher! Do trains have chimneys?"

"Hey, *Teacher!*"

Flying over the inlet in Greg's Cessna the next morning, looking down at the round "ice pans" bumping each other in the silty gray water, I decided that I would redo my student teaching, not at UNM, in Albuquerque, but at UAA, in Anchorage. However, I still wanted to graduate from UNM. I had a feeling the Education Department at UNM would help me work something out. I called Mark when I returned home. He contacted the head of the Education Department at UNM, and by Christmas arrangements had been made between the departments for me to student teach in Anchorage, and to graduate—from UNM—in May.

Student Teaching in Anchorage

My second attempt at student teaching took place at a school less than a mile from Fletcher's house. On my first day, I walked to my new school in the dark of night—the sun wouldn't rise until mid-morning, sometime around the science lesson, long after spelling and English. I walked on a trail through snowy woods, across a footbridge over Little Campbell Creek, frozen like black glass between high, round snow banks. Next I walked through an opening in the school's chain-link fence and into the play yard, where the snow was thoroughly trampled, and up to the doors of the school. I paused at the double doors. I may have even had my hand on the handle, but I stood there for a moment in the dark. I took a deep breath and went inside.

I had chosen this time to teach 5th grade. The real teacher—or, as they called them at UNM, the "cooperating teacher" with whom I would work and whose class I would teach—was Miss Patty Barrett. At the University of Alaska they say, "master teacher." And Miss Patty Barrett, a slender woman who wore her shoulder-length auburn hair parted on the side and flipped up on the ends, was truly a master. She was creative, efficient, dedicated, and could wither an ornery kid with a glare that would surely stop a grizzly.

I discovered right away that I related better to ten-year-olds than I had to six-year-olds. At ten, children wonder about all manner of things, much in the way that I did. I was thankful that they had progressed in their schooling to deeper subjects such as writing, social studies, and science. It was easier for me to get excited about teaching those subjects than the alphabet or addition and subtraction. I was grateful too, that in Miss Patty Barrett I had a constant inspiration. Not only that, Patty supported my teaching style. Her written evaluations of me—which were all being forwarded to UNM—positively glowed. To add even more to my chances of success, I had Fletch at home. With Fletch I could discuss any management problems I may have had during the day, and he would listen carefully and then set me on my way to handling them effectively, coaching me on how to handle students' behavior problems. I was delighted with this help. *He's so good!* I thought. *I wonder if I'll ever be able to know what to do on my own.*

I liked to sit and ponder the subject matter, get ideas, and create my own lessons. This is the kind of leeway I needed, and Patty said it was fine as long as they learned what was required. Each evening after dinner I sat at my desk in the loft and worked on the next day's lessons. My desk faced the upstairs window with a view of spruce boughs; it felt like I lived in a tree. Snowflakes drifted through the boughs one night as I sat preparing for a history unit on Indians, specifically covering the time just before and after the first European settlers showed up. I became impatient with the textbook's descriptions—the short, tidy history of what happened, and the lists of vocabulary words—sterile information not really well connected in any meaningful sense. I closed the book and started digging through a cardboard box of my stuff. I found a NASA calendar of photographs taken from space. At that time, in the mid-eighties, such photographs were not common. I brought this to school with me the next day and held a picture up before the class. "It's a photograph taken from the space shuttle; can you guess what it's of?" After looking at it for a while, they could see that it was a photo of the United States at night, sprinkled and splotched with light from all the towns and cities pretty much all over the place. You could see the shape of the nation from the cities along the coasts and around the Great Lakes. In the interior were big and little bright splotches: Denver, Salt Lake City, Missoula, Dallas/Ft. Worth, Kansas City, Indianapolis, Atlanta, Winston-Salem, and the others. "Before the Europeans gathered their hope and courage and crossed the ocean in their wooden ships," I said, still holding the photograph before them, "this same view from space would have been completely black. You would see no lights at all—nothing."

The kids were silent for a while, then an incredulous boy with a sort of a nervousness in his voice challenged me, "Well, what about campfires?"

"A campfire is just a tiny pinprick of light swallowed up by the dark," I said.

Someone else said, "Cool."

"Yeah!" And I knew it was time to begin the fifth-grade unit on Indians.

In the end I graduated, without pomp, but with a gratifying sense of accomplishment. I received my diploma from UNM in the mail, and ended that chapter of my life. It looked like our plans for our future—teaching in the winter, adventuring in the summer—would come to pass. For now, spring had come. The promise of warm breezes called us outdoors. I was released for the time being from serious thoughts. Our season on Fox Island was ahead and much had to be done. Fletch had contacted a man who, like him, had claimed land in the cove years ago. He'd offered to buy the man's claim, and the offer was accepted. The land was about halfway toward the quiet end of the beach in our cove, just past the ruins of old Olsen's fox farm, and separated from our cabins by two more claims, which Fletch hoped to eventually buy. He planned for the three of us, and whomever else we could get to help, to build another cabin on the new property this summer.

"Red in Tooth and Claw"

Fletcher, Tutka, and I left Anchorage late, in pouring rain, rolling into the parking lot at the Seward Harbor already tired, and hurrying in our rain gear to load the boat and get out to Fox Island before dark. In the dusk near the island, we spied a large orange float almost entirely submerged. It looked suspicious, low in the water, as if whatever was on the other end wasn't resting on the bottom, as a crab pot or an anchor would be. So we decided to pull it up with the pot puller. The pot puller, a steel davit with a block and winch, was located on the back deck and could be swung out over the side of the boat when it was needed.

After a few turns of the puller, as the slimy old rope began to pile up on the deck, we discovered that the float was attached to a long-line (a commercial halibut rig with many hooks, that has an anchor on one end, and a float on the other). Whirr, whirr, the pot puller pulled. At the puller's controls, I stopped it and started it, as Fletcher removed various creatures from the hooks and coiled the line into a pile. First came three halibut, next an eel, a skate, more halibut of various sizes, many big lingcod, more skates and eels, and on, and on. More than half were long dead. Many were near dead. The live things had fed on the dead ones, and got caught, and so on, and so on. Fletcher said the long-line had probably been blown into deep water during a gale, and its anchor had drifted off the bottom, so that it had spent who knows how long fishing wherever it went. This one had way more than the usual number of hooks—at least a couple hundred—and thousands of feet of line. As we worked I thought angrily that whoever set it was greedy and foolish. But Fletcher said the open season for long-lining is so short—just 24 hours—that fishermen have to try to do the best they can. Even if the opening happens to be during a storm, they go out.

An hour of pulling the long-line became two, then three, then four, until cold seeped into my bones and weariness overcame my mind. Still we released the living and dead creatures into the sea, until sometime in the very early morning. And still the hooks kept coming. We finally tied the float back on and towed the line until its anchor set in the bottom of our cove. We would finish it the next day. We anchored the boat and rowed ashore, hauling the heavy skiff up the beach. Then we entered our cold cabin, dragged up the stairs, and fell into bed.

The dawn came fresh and pretty, though cold. We finished pulling up the rest of the long-line as Neal and Anne motored into the cove in their new boat, a 21-foot Bayliner. Ashore, they helped us unclip the hooks and clean and stow the line, and at last we put the long-line to rest in the shop.

During dinner that evening a school of dolly varden came in to our cove and began to rise—an irresistible invitation to get out the spinning rod. We hurried to finish our meal, grabbed our fishing poles, and headed down to the water. Anne caught one, then Neal, and then the laughter and shouting started:

"Don't HORSE it!"

"Give it some LINE!"

"Tighten your DRAG!"

"You got it!" and anything else people yell to each other when the fishing is good and spirits are high. Tutka raced back and forth between us, barking. Since dollies survive in fresh water, we put a few small ones in the lake, and kept a couple for breakfast, and several more to pickle in gallon jars.

While winter gales had raged on the Pacific, objects had fallen from hands, homes, boats, and businesses, into the ocean from all around the whole Pacific Rim. These are some of the places around the Pacific Rim: Russia, China, Japan, Taiwan, the Philippines, the Mariana Islands, Hawaii, the United States, and Canada. Giant waves had sloshed the flotsam from these places up, down, and sideways and for hundreds, even thousands, of miles, finally blowing some of it over the tops of Alaska's remote beaches. And when our waters were calm enough, and safe, we could round a headland that reaches far into the Gulf of Alaska, and head into neighboring fjords, expanding the number of beaches to explore. Anne and Neal, and another couple, Nan and Robert and their dog, Bucky, were along with Fletcher, Tutka, and me that day.

Fletcher liked to use our dory, a wide boat with flared-out sides and a rounded bottom, for beachcombing because it handled surf well and held a lot of loot. No matter what we went ashore in, it took skill, strength, and timing to get through the surf and land safely on a beach. I watched Fletcher, our trusted captain. What wasn't obvious in the aplomb with which he captained a boat and interacted with the ocean was the pleasure he derived from sharing these experiences with others. Being both in his element and providing the means for others to have adventures here made Fletch a happy man. But unlike me, he didn't emote. He only made occasional comments, saying at the end of an especially wonderful day, something like, "Did you notice how happy Anne and Neal were today?" He'd chuckle. "They started joking around with each other. I haven't seen them like that in a long time. I think they had a good time, don't you?" And being an emotive person, these insights of his, these comments few and far between, tended to surprise me. Sometimes it would make tears come to my eyes. I had to remind myself over and over how deeply he felt things—that he *did* feel things deeply; he just didn't express it much.

With the wind blowing the curls in his beard out from his neck he looked just like a painting by Winslow Homer. I sat on the boat seat in my life jacket, admiring him. He rode relaxed and intent, hand on the throttle, eyes on the waves. When a big one came along and began to lift the dory, he gunned the motor, bearing all six of us and the two dogs ashore in a rush. Then, just before grounding, he killed the engine, tilting up the shaft in one motion to keep the propeller out of the gravel. The wave finished the job by carrying the dory high enough onto the beach for us to leap out, hold it steady, and get ready to haul it further with the next big wave, now that it was much lighter without us in it. We stood in water halfway up our boots and waited, holding the sides of the dory, ready. The dogs had leapt out and were already running around on the beach. Here comes the right wave! Go! We hauled the dory all the way onto dry beach with that one. Because the tide was coming in, Fletcher had brought a few pole-sized logs to place in front of the dory so we could roll it yet further up the beach. Since the incoming tide has just six hours to travel 17 feet, it comes in fast. If the tide took our dory, it would be awfully cold getting back out to the boat, which would be considerably farther away from us at high tide.

Fletcher tied the dory to a big tree and we started off to explore a beach that few had walked upon. Beyond the beach sat lower land with trees, and farther back, a lake. Even though these beaches had been trod upon by few, even though a tiny number of people had seen the clear lakes that lay behind many of them, some of these lakes held thousands of plastic bottles of all colors mixed up in great rafts of driftwood. This is because, out in the great oceans of this hemisphere, a damn lot of those who travel upon them or work on the docks and in the harbors, use detergent such as "Joy" and "Dawn" to break up their oil and gas spills. Then they fling the emptied plastic bottles onto the sea.

Among the driftwood in the lake or on the beach, we also found big orange inflated fishing floats (the kind that are good for making swings), small oval net floats, hard plastic floats, and even metal floats. We found lighted buoys, buckets, nets, boxes and crates, and rope of all sizes up to three inches in diameter—those would be off barges and cargo ships. We even found a bomb once. We found glass floats from Japan, nestled in low-growing beach peas or gray gnarled driftwood. Life rings, oars, life jackets, spools of copper tubing, sheets of Plexiglas, hatch covers, and tools. Fly fishing poles, nine-foot surf-fishing poles, halibut fishing poles, and cane poles. Gloves, boots, children's shoes, elegant plastic dishes from Japan, hats. Once I found a corked green wine bottle with an envelope inside, but the envelope was empty. That still puzzles me. But best of all, lumber: from 2 x 4's to 2 x 12's, and sheets of the finest three-quarter-inch marine plywood. It might be worn, with barnacles hanging on it, but it was all good, and we'd use it.

It was fun and hard work, walking on the rocky shoreline of a long beach, carrying stuff. Neal yelled, "Hey, Susannah! I found a glass float! It's *red*!" How rare would *that* be? I thought, and hurried toward him. Glass floats were always either green or blue, once in a great while amber, but *never* red. Neal walked to meet me holding the little red float out.

"*Gosh!*" I reached for it—and was handed a light bulb by Neal who grinned a big grin and even did a dance. I laughed and punched

him on the arm. "Why, you—!" Still, though, the red light bulb was miraculous, for it had remained unbroken.

All along we kept a watchful eye on the water, for we knew that if a breeze roughed up the sea we must hurry back to the dory and out through the surf while we still could. I trusted Fletcher's judgment and felt secure. I was full of happiness and anticipation at being on an adventure. Yet at moments I felt a tinge of slight anxiety. Like any day, sunny days could be deceptive. It would be unlikely, but still it was not unusual, and I knew it, for outings in Alaska to turn to survival situations. I'd heard the stories. If we were far from the dory when the wind came up, by the time we hurried back the surf could already be too big for us to make it out to the boat. And then, what if the *Fox Islander* drug anchor in the wind and drifted away? What if it bashed up against the rocky beach?

I heard yelling far up the beach and could see Fletcher motioning to us on the edge of the woods. Neal and I ran, and came upon the others gazing at a scene, in the moss-hung forest behind the beach, that raised the hair on the back of our necks: a crude skiff made of worn planks, overturned and propped up with forked branches, and under it, three down sleeping bags, decaying. Boots, clothing, and blankets lay scattered about. There was a fire circle and a pile of wood under a rotting piece of canvas, a rusty bow saw, two axes, and a fishing pole leaning up against a log, and lying over the log, a belt with a sheath attached, and a knife in the sheath. Near the fire circle was a two-foot pile of dark blue mussel shells. I lifted the heavy, brittle material of a wet sleeping bag and in the folds, I found a leather wallet, with a few bills and identification inside. The pale, smiling man in the picture was Ray Martin Castings, from Ohio. Also in the wallet were two licenses for commercial halibut fishing for two different years. I spied a small first aid kit and opened it to find a pair of glasses and a set of keys.

We dreaded what else we might find: the bodies. Or a few bones left by bears and other scavengers. We began to search around, but after an hour we had found nothing more. Finally, down at the farthest end of the beach from the camp, we found the tangled, mangled remains of a boat: a mess of ropes, cables, engine, anchors, and hydraulic gear, with a few shattered pieces of blue-painted plywood—all that remained of the hull—and all this mostly buried into the beach. The wrecking of it had been so violent, even the anchors were bent. The blue plywood, the huge rope reel with rope on it, and hundreds of steel hooks told us it was a homemade commercial halibut boat. We found a brass propeller and shaft and one Plexiglas window. As we salvaged the rope, we speculated and watched for grizzlies. When they wrecked, they must have gathered what they could for survival from the boat and went to the most protected part of the cove to set up camp. Did they have survival suits? Did a passing boat eventually see them and rescue them? If a boat did come by and rescue them, why didn't they take the wallet, keys and glasses with them? Or anything else? Did they die?

In town the next day Fletcher turned in the wallet, glasses, and keys to the Coast Guard, and the Coast Guard cutter *Jellison* made the two-hour trip from Seward to investigate. An article appeared in the next week's *Seward Phoenix Log*. There had been three men aboard the boat *Sally Ann*. Witnesses had seen them in the Seward harbor working on their boat before leaving; it had collected a foot of water in its bilge. No one knew if they got it fixed. There was a warrant out for the arrest of Ray Martin Castings, but police would not say what the crime had been. The three had left the harbor in November. They were never seen again. Some people believed that Ray Castings had set it up to look as if he and his boat mates had perished. Perhaps another boat took them there; they went ashore and set up the camp, then went back out to the other boat and let the *Sally Ann* loose in the driving wind where she would wreck on the beach. But the coast guard had found handfuls of blond hair that had been pulled out by the roots. No one ever found any trace of bodies. It was thought that in the spring bears had gotten them.

I wondered if the long-line we had pulled up earlier in the week could have been theirs, and concluded it must have been.

Tides

Tidal range is affected by the moon, the sun, the shape and depth of the ocean's bottom, the size of the ocean, and the shape of the ocean's contours.

Along the girth of the earth the sun and moon are often situated in such a way that as the moon pulls one way, the sun pulls another, and the tides don't amount to much. Also, in small bodies of water—ponds, lakes, even small seas—the ebb and flow is barely observable.

Alaska, being near the North Pole, periodically receives the pull of both the sun and the moon in unison. They pull on the immense body of water that is the Pacific and the water is funneled into Resurrection Bay and other fjords that are wide at their mouths and narrow in their bodies, that extend far inland, and that become more and more shallow toward their ends. This contour creates extreme tide ranges up to thirty feet.

The bore tide in Turnagain Arm of Cook Inlet rushes in so fast it actually forms a ridge or wall of water. As the story goes, once a duck hunter got his legs stuck in the fine, interlocking glacial silt as he walked far out onto the mudflats at low tide. As the tide came in he was becoming buried in water. He used the barrel of his rifle to breathe through, hoping the tide would not cover the very tip of the barrel as he struggled to keep it above the water. Someone far away on shore saw him out there, ran to their car and drove to call for help. Eventually a helicopter came to rescue him and began to pull him out but by then he was locked in glacial silt and was pulled in half. Or so the legend goes.

Fletcher told me about a time he was anchored in Kachemak Bay, fishing. The tidal range is even greater in Kachemak than Resurrection Bay. When the tide runs, it carries your bait, hook, and weight far out (or in) so that instead of seeing your line go straight down to the bottom you see it going out from your pole at an angle and there's nothing you can do but put heavier weights on. You can put on 10-ounce weights, then 12-ounce weights, until it's no fun any more. It takes too long and tires the shoulder muscles to bring up or let down in over 200 feet of water with the tide running. On this occasion, Fletcher had the anchor down and the tide was rising fast. The running tide had carried the boat and dragged the anchor. Suddenly the anchor snagged on something below in the deep. He tried to haul it up but the winch couldn't budge it.

If a boat is stuck to the bottom with the anchor, the sea can come over the side in minutes. The only thing to do is to untie or cut the anchor rope—quick! Fletcher untied the rope from the cleat.

The rope began whizzing off the big coil, which lay on the deck, and over the side of the boat. He picked up most of the big coil and threw it in. He tied a huge orange float on the end and threw that in. WHOOSH! The float sucked under.

Fletch said he always wondered what the anchor was snagged on—maybe a wreck. And now, so did I.

Food

The day our first guests of the season came out, I spent the day alone, bushwacking through the forest. My mission was to locate and fix a break in the water hose, so my staying behind had a measure of legitimacy, but the real reason was that my old gremlin had come back to haunt me. I felt shy and skittish, wanting earnestly to be alone, yet lonely. I carried a screwdriver and knife in a sheath, and as long as I was going to journey into Fox Island's dark interior, I brought lunch and a canteen and a baggy of dog food for Tutka, plus a bow saw and hatchet. I had it in mind to make a hiking trail.

Life on a small island can feel restricted, especially a densely forested island without trails. My new trail would lead to the low spot in the ridge behind the lake, and follow the steep ridge up to the summit. There the hiker would top out on a treeless knoll and a dizzying, 360° view of Resurrection Bay, several of the neighboring fjords to the east and west, and nothing but the great Northern Pacific to the south. A few small songbirds might twitter about in the alders there on Fox Island's summit; eagles and ravens might fly at eye level or above, but most of the hundreds of thousands of sea birds and shore birds—auklets, petrels, ducks, oystercatchers, murres, puffins, gulls, grebes and cormorants—live and fly in the regions far below.

After locating the break in the water line, which I accomplished by lifting the PVC hose periodically to see if it was heavy with water or not, I fixed it. Fixing the water line usually meant re-connecting two sections of pipe and putting hose clamps on a joint that had been joined with a connector but no clamps. Afterward I began marking and cutting my trail. My goal was to mark and cut as far as the ridge, which drops off shear on the other side to the narrows between Fox Island and the peninsula. Once I reached it, I continued cutting away brush another twenty yards up the spine of the ridge, then rested with Tutka beside me, watching waves break bright white and soundless at the base of the cliff far below. The summit, as far away as the distance which I had marked and cut, would have to wait. Toward afternoon I returned to the cabins, leaving the canopied forest for the sunny beach, and stepped indoors long enough to call Fletcher on the radio, to see how much time I had before I needed to get ready for company. He said they were having a great time fishing and wouldn't be back for several hours. I walked up the beach looking for rocks to paint on. I found a dead eagle down by the cave and kept some feathers.

My solo adventure and long hours alone that day had given me an enthusiasm for wine, food, and camaraderie. I looked forward to the feast we had planned that evening. I took a shower on the back deck of the sauna, built a fire on the beach, and checked to see that the wine was nestled in ice. Fletcher and our guests returned at 8:00.

Among the many pleasant things in life is eating with a good appetite stoked by work and play outdoors. Most of our evening meals on Fox Island were glorious feasts. This doesn't mean complicated food, just simple, fresh food, and plenty of it. Fresh-caught halibut deep fried in beer batter or grilled or baked; salmon grilled outdoors over a fire of our own alder wood; snow-white tanner crab (called "snow crab" on the market) dipped in melted butter. Big, fresh shrimp in the shell, crunchy stir-fried vegetables over steamy rice, and good, wholesome homemade bread with butter, red wine, and cold spring water.

Fletcher often stopped to pull up crab pots on his way back to the island after a day of fishing. He put the guests to work on this job and many others. It added to their experience and helped with the workload. Harvesting crab started with the crab pots being set somewhere around 300 feet down, with a big orange float marking the spot. After a night and a day, the pot was ready to pull. Fletcher gave someone the job of hooking the float with the boat-hook as he maneuvered the boat up to it. This wasn't easy if the sea was rough, and he had to watch that the rope didn't get in the propeller.

Sometimes it took a few passes before the float was hooked and brought on board. Then Fletcher coiled the slack in the line. He fed the line over the block and between the two steel disks of the pot puller and the puller began its work. He carefully coiled the wet rope as it came in, wearing rubber gloves, pulling off bits of seaweed and long strands of jellyfish slime. While this was going on, everyone waited to see the pot coming up. Fletcher also had to watch for the ascending crab pot, for he had to stop the puller before the heavy pot hit the boat. It was a welded "rebar" cage, about three feet wide and deep by five feet long, covered with heavy netting, with one-way funnel openings on either end that the crabs crawled into to get the bait. Finally he hauled it up through the water the last two or three feet by hand and with someone's help, lifted it aboard. If there were any crabs, he removed them from the pot and tossed them into a fish tub or a bucket. The pot was then re-baited with a halibut carcass, and dropped over the side again.

If John or I hadn't gone along that day, we prepared for Fletcher and the guests' return by dragging the fish cleaning tables out from under the Main cabin, building a fire on the beach, and setting a large galvanized wash-tub, the sort that cowboys used to bathe in, full of water over the fire for boiling the crab. Also from under the cabin we hauled out the big buckets for fish guts and large plastic tubs for the big carcasses. We put on our Helly Hansen rain gear—

bib overalls and sometimes the matching coats. My outfit was dark green (the better to walk through the forest unseen). John's was traditional bright yellow. We uncoiled the hose that would be used to spray off each other and the tables and the beach after fish cleaning was finished. By now the boat was attached to the mooring and everyone was climbing over the side into the skiff. We waited at the waterline to greet the guests—with laughter and congratulations to whoever caught the big one—and to help haul up the fish and gear. Halibut bigger than fifty pounds were too big to fillet on the tables so these we hung between two trees. If a fish were really large, we would hang it from a scale so guests could have their picture taken with it. Fletch always positioned them with their fish just so, to get the best look for their photos. To clean the fish, John and I used sharp fillet knives. Guests usually wanted to help and if they didn't know how to fillet already, one of us taught them. Really big halibut made fillets four or five inches thick. Some would be saved out for the evening meal, and the rest packed in ice for the guests to take back with them. We saved the carcasses to bait crab pots.

We got ice any time we were near a tidewater glacier. Fletch would sidle the boat up beside some sparkly little bergs and then use a big salmon-fishing net to "capture" them. We had to be careful not to try to get one that was too big, because glacier ice is extremely dense, and, therefore, extremely heavy. Guests were constantly going after the biggest berg that would fit in the net and then discovering that it was far too heavy to lift—and it wasn't easy to get the net back out from under the big ones. Even a berg about half the size of the net was too heavy. Those the size of cement blocks were manageable. The ice was astonishingly pretty—sculpted into fascinating shapes by the saltwater, clear and diamond-bright. It had tiny specks of matter in it. I told our guests those specks had been frozen into place 2,000 years ago, during the time of Jesus—just the type of marvelous fact I enjoyed sharing. In a cooler this ice remained unmelted for weeks.

Around the point on Fox Island was an avalanche chute that emptied onto a V-shaped boulder-strewn beach, and if the previous winter's snowfall had been heavy, snow lay in this place well into July. Although it was nearby, it was hard work getting this snow because the water off the point surged in and out among the rocks, and the beach was nothing more than a steep pile of jagged boulders. We had to land the skiff without getting it pounded against the rocks, tie it to a rock, and walk up to the snow carrying shovels and coolers. The snow itself was wet and heavy, but a cooler-full kept our food cold a good long while.

For dinners we often combined our fresh-caught food with food our guests brought, potluck style. Grown-ups and kids, families and friends sat around the big dining table Fletch and I had made. Outside the endless summer sunset filled the picture windows. Stories were told, and crab leg after crab leg was broken into, the succulent, white meat dipped into glass dishes of melted butter. We ate like gluttons after a day working and playing in the fresh air. Ten-gallon buckets sat on the floor around the table, for crab shells. These were full at the end of the meal.

But each summer there were also a few food disasters on Fox Island, such as John's cinnamon rolls when they had been out of the oven long enough to set up. It was late summer at the time of ripe blueberries, when a particularly unfortunate meal took place. That evening we sat down to plates piled with red chili stew and fresh baked cornbread, both made by our guest, a teacher friend of Fletcher's, Mona Cronk. I'd made beer-batter halibut and rice, and John had spent the afternoon picking blueberries for dessert.

Mona's stew was an abomination. I took a bite and carefully glanced sideways at Fletcher, who stirred his around with his fork like a child who hopes to give the appearance of actually eating. The stew burgeoned with four-inch strings of tough meat and teeny bones, all conglomerated into a pulpy mass of squished beans and other matter in a red sauce. I recalled Mona Cronk speaking proudly of her backyard farm, where she raised rabbits. The table was not completely quiet, but while I waited to see how everything would play out, I noticed that it was definitely much quieter than normal. When the voices dwindled and only the sound of clinking silverware remained, Mona Cronk cleared her throat and commented that she guessed the rabbit she'd killed for the stew was too old. That gave everyone permission to laugh and chuckle and not eat the stew, and Fletcher took a big bite of hot oven-fresh cornbread, which he set down again right away with a look of surprise. Mona Cronk croaked, "My *cornbread*! It's *horrible*!" There on the counter sat a big yellow plastic bottle of Joy dishwashing detergent she'd mistaken for cooking oil.

Finally, a small portion of the blueberries John brought to the table proved to have worms in them. He didn't concern himself with tiny worms, or at least felt like he oughtn't to, so he was extra

assertive about how they didn't bother him a bit. Such a thing would be nonsense. Further, it was nonsense, in John's way of thinking, for anyone else to raise a fuss. He'd pop the wormy blueberries in his mouth—even as the worm looked out to see what all the commotion was about. This was especially entertaining for children, and he'd say, "Their naturally sweet taste reminds me of wild hickory nuts."

I was more careful when preparing berries. The berries with worms floated to the top in a bowl of water (along with the worm they had some air in them), and I'd cull them out. But John would go no further than to proudly walk up the path offering the freshly picked bowl-full of berries just as they were.

That evening, beer-batter halibut and steamy white rice saved the meal. Nothing could be better than fresh, firm, delicious chunks of halibut fried quick and crispy in a golden beer-batter crust and dipped in tartar sauce or melted butter, or sprinkled with juice squeezed right out of a lemon slice.

Rarely, but sometimes, a halibut would have worms: several dozen little white curly-cues, about the size of the spring in a ballpoint pen, coiled in the belly meat. This whole section could easily be cut out and used for crab bait, but it was possible to miss some if you were a less careful person.

One gloomy day a few weeks after our disastrous meal, I had a bad experience with wormy halibut and a bewildered guest. Occasionally a guest or a group seemed somehow lost, unsure. They'd traveled from Seward for a long hour through rain and tossing waves, past gray shoreline, and soaked, black forests, conveyed in a boat captained by a bearded, tired-looking man. Then they'd found themselves marooned in an endless downpour for three days on a dismal island in a wilderness with three ragged people and a huge black dog.

One of the guests—a young woman—was not much of an outdoor type and I guessed that she'd come along to please her husband. It was wretched summer weather: rain, wind, 50° all night and all day, gray. With no other choice but to carry on, Fletcher and the guests, including the young woman, had gone out that day in search of good fishing, and they'd done well. But, in spite of the good luck, her anxiety had not been soothed by a day spent tossing about in the Gulf of Alaska. John noticed her misery, and felt compassion. There were countless times when people were outraged and affronted by John, but I believe he was a compassionate man through and through. He built up the fire in the guests' cabin, fried up a batch of beer-batter halibut and took it right over, golden hot on a paper-towel-covered plate. The cabin was crowded and warm, full of steam and piles of wet gear. While the men reveled in the day's fishing, and John told tall tales, the woman sat bundled in a sweater beside the stove, with the plate of halibut on her lap, daintily pulling it apart and eating it. Then I noticed her looking hard at the piece she held in her fingers. It was full of little worms cooked into protein-white curly-cues.

I always regretted that I had been standing next to her, for the woman looked up at me with an expression I had never seen and will never forget: a mixture utterly forlorn and sick, with a glint of accusation. There was nothing that could be said, or done. Fletcher, John, and I wrote the whole experience off as a complete failure of the sort we hoped would never occur again.

Over the radio, John told Fletcher to tell our guests to come down to his cabin for some fish chowder when they got back. Gathered in John's cabin as his guests, we learned too late that the chowder he used was some that someone else had cooked up the week before, that I had finally left on the deck for Tutka or the birds or whatever came along. It had sat on the deck a day and a half, and Tutka and the birds had eaten only a little of it. I'm sure John's sense of frugality was insulted at the sight of it there, all crudded up and neglected, and he felt it must be reclaimed. Looking into the pot there on his wood stove, I saw that the volume had increased, and I wondered what else he had added to it. John's refrigerator was a Styrofoam-lined plywood box with open ends covered with burlap. It sat in his woodshed. Water dripped out of punctured hoses onto the burlap, creating cooling by evaporation. He usually kept glacier ice or avalanche snow in it too, and it did stay cold. But he saved everything in there. Bait herring, octopus tentacles, butter, bursting black bananas, small fish slipping out of their baggies, knotted bread bags containing old dinner buns or salad or pancakes, all jumbled in together. Fletcher wanted to be tactful in front of the guests and prevent them from having to eat the chowder, without hurting John's feelings. And as Fletcher was a master of diplomacy and tactfulness, I watched carefully to see how he would handle the situation. He looked at the gummy-sided pot and gave a hearty laugh. "*Ho* Ho Ho! Why don't you all get your gear put away, and grab a beer, and Susannah and I will fix up a plate of beer batter halibut. That chowder's from last week, and I meant to leave it out on the deck for Tutka. John, where's that big fresh fillet you saved out?" It was fascinating the way he would change the order of things, keep anyone from feeling bad, put himself in the position of having performed the oversight, and make up small falsehoods to attain his diplomacy and set people in motion. When the mistake was clearly mine alone, or John's, such as forgetting to bring the outboard motor in out of a gale, Fletch would say, "I meant to bring that outboard in last night."

At which time John or I, whoever had made the mistake, would say, "Oh, I can do that right now." I learned this aspect of diplomacy from Fletcher, and it sure has helped.

Marooned

Fletcher had scheduled a week off for us in late June, during my father's visit from New Mexico, to work around the place and take a short trip. Anne and Neal had come out to help build our fourth cabin on Fletch's new property down toward the quiet end of the beach, a ways past the spot where Mr. Olsen, the fox farmer, had lived. The new cabin was my favorite. Situated back in the woods, it was hidden from sight, yet from inside you could see the cove through the trees. It was a short walk both to the beach in front of the cabin, and to the lake in back. It was similar in design to the Main cabin, but smaller, so that it had a sturdy, cozy feeling, more like a cottage. It became known as "the Woods cabin." Secluded and distant from the other three cabins, it became a favorite for romantic couples and for those who planned a longer stay of a week or two. On the lakeshore where the path ended stood a great old spruce stump about five feet tall. John had taken the chain saw and cut a right-angled chunk out of it, slightly reclined, so that it was a chair where you could sit and look out at the lake. As with the Middle cabin and the Main cabin, John oversaw the construction of this new one, working off a plan Fletch and I had drawn up. It was almost complete. I could hear John's hammer as he worked alone, bent on finishing it while we were away.

First, a few things needed to be done, and Fletcher wrote out job lists for each of us on index cards, which we carried around in our back pockets.

Mine read:

1. FLOWERS/PLANTER
2. FINISH NAILING DECK BOARDS
3. STACK WOOD

The day was overcast and cool, perfect for work outdoors. Fletch was on the boat in the cove. On the deck of the Main cabin, Daddy used the circular saw and hammer, building a box seat that would hold life jackets and the batteries we used for the radio. Anne worked on the beach near the Middle cabin, getting ready to paint oars. Neal had the task of hanging several hundred floats, which we had found on beaches, between two trees on a rope (Fletch had said, "There's a few floats lying in the woods behind John's cabin.") I began stacking wood on the deck of the Main cabin.

Daddy laid a board over the edge of the deck. "Come over here and stand on this for me, Susie." He made the cut and I stepped off. "Let's measure this space," he said, handing me the tip of the measuring tape.

He said, "Have you and Fletch given any thought to getting married?"

"We've given some thought to it," I said. He got another board in position and I stood on it.

"Well, you should."

"Why do you think so?" I was curious. A few years ago my parents had been furious with Anne for living with Neal before she married him. I'd never seen them so upset with her. I'd never seen them upset with her at all. Her cohabiting caused a furor in their lives and in mine, since I was living at home witnessing their feelings. But neither had said a word to me about my living situation until now. I figured it was because they were just relieved that I was with someone mature and financially stable. I knew Daddy liked Fletch. My parents didn't have the expectations for me they had for Anne or Betsy. Maybe they were just going along with who I was. Maybe they'd tired some of raising children. When I was still little my mother had begun granting herself more and more time to paint, had begun to go riding with her friends, stopped being a Girl Scout leader. By the time I'd come along she was happy to just let me loose on my horse. I was happy, too.

Daddy said, "A woman living with a man is being taken advantage of."

"Oh, Daddy, I don't feel that way!"

"Well you should," he said. "Does he pay you for your work here?"

"A little, not much. Pretty much everything goes back into the business."

"Does he pay John?" he said.

"I think so," I said.

"He's made enough to buy another lot," Daddy said. "It's just not right. You should get married and if he won't marry you, you should leave."

"Well it's not like he won't marry me; it's not like that, Daddy. I'm here because I want to be. I like this life."

"You don't have any legal claim to any of this."

This sounded far-fetched to me. *Legal claim*. What was I supposed to do, hire an attorney? This life was like a gift from the Fates, like a good dream made real. Hardly anyone got to live this way. I lived in the midst of such beauty and mystery that when I thought about it, it could make me laugh with tears in my eyes. I was friends with the mother duck, friends with the porcupines, friends with the otters. I used to take a mirror outside just to look at myself being where I was. It wasn't something quantifiable in figures on paper. I said, "I don't need any legal claim."

"He should marry you!"

"He's a good man, Daddy. You like him, don't you? Are you mad at him?"

"Fletch is hard to get mad at," Daddy said mildly.

Just then Fletcher hollered from the boat, and pointed. A humpback whale was swimming past him with her calf. The baby was larger than the boat and the mother must have been sixty feet long. Black, wet water monsters. Daddy ran for his camera. I could see Tutka beside Fletch with his paws up on the side of the boat, ears forward. We stood on the crest of the beach and watched the mother and calf. Their every exhalation was a misty geyser that said, "PUFFF." A big "PUFFF" for the big whale and a smaller "PFFF" for the smaller whale. They traveled through and even after they were out of sight we could still see and hear their outbreathing.

The next morning we packed and left for our excursion into Aialik Bay. It took four hours to get well into it, a narrow fjord with mountains almost leaning out over the water. Atop the great gathering of mountains on its western end rests one thousand square miles of accumulated ice and snow called the Harding Ice Field. It buries the mountains' tops. Just a few peaks rise from it. But Harding

Ice Field doesn't just sit there. All that ice is heavy, so glaciers form and flow powerfully, inexorably, down every available crease where a flow can get started. Many of these are nameless glaciers scouring remote valleys. A few are tidewater glaciers, meaning that they flow into the ocean. Aialik was a lonely, mysterious place of ocean, rock, ice, snow, mist, and waterfalls. Humans rarely visited. We were the only ones there.

We fished in a small cove, secluded in a soft atmosphere of low foggy clouds and quiet seas. The fishing was slow, our voices quiet. I could hear the lap of the sea against the hull of the boat as we gently rocked. Not far from us, a gray whale cruised past a granite outcrop over and over, like a lion pacing in the zoo. He was small and covered with barnacles. Anne caught a small halibut, about eighteen inches long, the size called a "chicken halibut," because it's a good size for dinner.

We set the anchor for the evening and rowed the skiff ashore to explore at a rocky beach. At some time in the past the State must have made this land available to claim. Someone had ventured out here and had built a hut out of a section of metal Quonset with a plywood front and back, on a knoll above the beach. "Look at all the bear shit!" said Neal. Black piles lay plopped here and there in the grass and wildflowers.

"This place must make an awful roar in a heavy rain," I said. "If you were by yourself, you'd go nuts. If it rained, it would be too loud; when it stopped, it would seem much too quiet."

"And then you'd listen for the sound of twigs snapping," said Anne, sidestepping a pile of manure.

Neal said, "The walls would be cold, unless you had a good fire going for a while, and then they might get too hot."

"It's cute, though," said Anne, noting the tidy curtains and flower boxes.

Fletch said, "Let's see what's down this trail." We followed him down the trail that led behind the hut. I figured it probably led to the outhouse. To my utter delight, we stepped out of the woods onto a whole new beach in a whole new bay.

"Fletch! Did you know this was here?"

"Yes, I've seen it on the charts. Thought I'd surprise you. I didn't know it was a *sandy* beach, though. It's pretty nice, isn't it?" Fletcher knew from reading the charts that the peninsula at this spot is low and narrow—no more than one hundred feet wide. The beach wasn't only made of sand—it was *black* sand. The atmosphere was muted, silver-toned, enchanting. Our surroundings looked like a work of art. Brilliant wet greenery in the form of devil's club and hemlock fringed the black beach. A large orange float had come to rest on the sand, so bright it looked like it had a light bulb on inside. I stood mesmerized as Fletcher, in blue jeans, black rubber boots and a red wool sweater walked silently toward the float. (This beach made no sound, unlike all the rest). The strange beauty affected us all. We stood near each other and found ourselves speaking quietly. (Maybe also because of all the bear sign around.) After a while, we left the tiny beach in Harris Bay and hiked back to the small rocky beach in Aialik and built a fire to warm ourselves and cook supper. It was a lovely dinner spot with logs to sit on, and we watched the gray whale cruising back and forth, back and forth.

We slept on the boat in that cove, and after setting two shrimp pots the following morning, we headed deeper into the fjord. For the next two beaches, the weather was still nice. The second beach had a carcass of a sea lion on it, the size of a small horse but a lot rounder. It looked very peaceful lying there, but it had a gaping hole in its side where you could see its ribs. Two golden eagles that had been perched on it pushed off and flew away as we approached.

Back on the *Fox Islander*, we made way deeper yet into Aialik, close along the shore. We saw a mother black bear with two tiny cubs walking across a rockslide high on the mountainside above us. One half of the barren gray slide was covered with snow—an old avalanche—and alongside it a waterfall rushed. These elements made vertical stripes of still white—the old avalanche, rushing white—the waterfall, and unstable gray—the rock slide, bordered by the bright green of the alder forest on either side. The mother bear and her small cubs were black specks moving across it. They had crossed the avalanche and waded the tumbling water, traversed the rocky slide, and were reentering the forest.

All the while, clouds gathered and the wind increased. The change in weather could mean that we might have to hole up for a day or two. We anchored near Pedersen Glacier, and using the skiff, found passage into a stark, misty lake through its narrow outlet in the beach. Little icebergs knocked about in it, fallen from the glacier which humped alongside it on its north end. Getting back out of the lake was difficult as the tide had begun rushing in through the outlet. At full power, the outboard roaring above the sound of rapids, we made only about half a knot against the current. We gradually made way. I trusted that Fletcher could navigate the rapids and avoid any sandbars, and he did.

Later we ate dinner ashore at a place sheltered from the wind by an outcropping. As I reached to get a pot out of the fire, I laid my hand upon a hot rock and burnt it. I spent the rest of the evening with my hand in a blue plastic bowl of ice water. Enough had gone wrong—the worsening weather, the difficulty getting out of the lake, the burnt hand—to introduce an uncomfortable uneasiness. Although we didn't have to worry about darkness coming on, the heavy clouds made gloom out of the twilight. Fletcher said we'd check the shrimp pots and then anchor across the bay for the night, on the more sheltered side. Our pots had sixty-two big shrimp and an octopus inside. As soon as we stowed the pots and our fresh-caught food, we motored across the fjord, buffeted by wind, to find shelter. Fletch was wakeful all night, watching that we didn't drag anchor in the increasing wind.

The following day the misty blowing rain had become hard, driven rain. We headed for escape around Cape Aialik, but were turned back by the seas. We could not go ashore, either, because we needed to be on the boat if it dragged anchor. We took shelter in a cove and after a while another boat came in from the open waters of the Gulf. Fletcher spoke with the captain on the radio, "*Fox Islander* calling *Kodiak Star*, over."

"This is *Kodiak Star*, *Fox Islander*."

"How's the weather out there?"

"It's a mess, and no end in sight," said the captain. "They just had a hell of a storm off the coast of Australia. I'll be keeping you company for the night."

"We're moving up to the next cove over," said Fletch. "The bottom's too soft here."

"Thanks for the info."

They chatted about the weather and their boats for a while—the captain was a commercial fisherman heading for Kodiak—and we motored away, finding anchorage in Three Hole Bay. It offered more protection, but there was no beach so we still couldn't go ashore. We didn't have a stove, so we couldn't eat the shrimp. Without much food left, we each ate a bowl of warm oatmeal with canned peaches and canned milk, using some hot water we'd saved in the thermos the night before. The boat rocked, swinging around at anchor, making wide arcs as the wind came first from one direction, then another.

Once out of Three Hole Bay the following morning, we again encountered intimidating waves and a banshee wind. Massive green swells drove in from one direction, piling up against exposed cliffs in explosions of white; the wind howled from another direction. "It's a 'contrary sea,'" yelled Fletch. "These swells come from that storm near Australia." The whipped-up waves created by our local wind tossed along on top of them in a fury of confusion. Once again, we retreated and spent another night in Three Hole Bay. We ate hash cold from the can, and just before bed Anne concocted a meal of maple syrup, condensed milk, and powdered milk in the thermos—nearly the last of our food. She shook it up, poured us each a small cup, and it was very good. We had not been off the boat for more than 24 hours.

Morning came with slightly calmer weather. "What's for breakfast?" asked Neal. "Let's see. We have a box of freeze-dried potatoes, sixty-two shrimp and one octopus." Once again we headed out of Three Hole Bay to check on the seas at the Cape. The swells from Australia remained, but the wind had diminished. We kept an anxious eye on the 16 foot skiff we towed, as it surfed this way and that over the foam-streaked swells. The skiff could turn sideways on a big wave, plow into it, and fill with water, pulling us down. I saw Fletch hitch up his sweater to have quick access to his knife, to cut the tow rope if necessary. After an hour we made our way around Cape Aialik and headed into Resurrection Bay. By mid-morning we made Fox Island. My legs felt wobbly as I stepped ashore. John met us at the water's edge, capable, helpful, and fascinated with our tale. We were soon indoors with a fine fire going in the wood stove, safe from the elements inside the strong walls we'd built, the weather a dramatic scene beyond the windows. We put the shrimp on to boil and began retelling our stories over coffee and John's fresh cinnamon rolls.

— 6 —

Points of No Return

A "Real" Job

Another summer was over. It was time for me to find a teaching job. I'd been filling out paperwork all summer, sending it with Fletch to mail from Seward. But an event had occurred which turned my fate. Alaska's typically exciting oil economy had dropped into a pit. We returned to find that homes in Anchorage had cost their owners tens of thousands of dollars more than they were now worth. A caravan of motor homes, pick-ups, and cars, loaded with belongings and modern-day settlers, rolled down Alaska's highway, while others left on jet planes for better prospects in the Lower 48. Businesses closed by the dozen, and "For Sale" signs appeared everywhere. Alaska's population had dropped, and there were no teaching jobs.

I refused to go through the gauntlet of substitute teaching, which our teacher friends told me I had to do for any hope of gaining a permanent job. Substituting was my only choice, they said. I remembered too well how my third grade class—myself included—used to torment a certain substitute at Mt. Taylor Elementary. Those were harrowing days for poor Mrs. Minihan. And even we kids were glad when Mrs. DeSmet came back and regained control of us. With the unthinkable prospect of substitute teaching looming before me, I wished once again that I had never gone into education. I tentatively believed I could succeed as a regular teacher; I could rely, if necessary, on Fletcher's support. But I quailed at the thought of substituting. I supposed Fletcher was disappointed in me, but he said nothing.

My sister Betsy worked at Alaska Legal Services, and told me of a job opening. I applied, and was hired as a receptionist. Legal Services, sometimes called Legal Aid Societies, exist in every state and receive their funding from a variety of federal, state, and local sources. They handle civil cases for those whose income comes in below the federal poverty level. We had a local and statewide office in Anchorage, and outpost offices in other towns and villages across

the state. I worked in the statewide office. I had to sit at a desk and answer the phone seven hours a day, in the reception area, a place with no windows. But the types of cases the statewide office handled were interesting. In between phone calls, I typed legal briefs, using a word processor for the first time. My first case had to do with Indians in Southeastern Alaska. A New York art dealer had somehow gotten ahold of some of their house poles. House poles represent the history, the identity, the stories of the Tlingit people. The art dealer would not give them back, saying that certain members of certain clans in the tribe had authorized him to take them. Eventually Legal Services won that case for the majority of the Tlingits and the house poles were returned.

I then typed a brief about sea otters. Sea otters were hunted to near extinction by the late 1800s and it is against the law now to hunt them in Alaska unless you are an Alaska Native and are using the pelts for "traditional purposes." A woman from a village in the Aleutians had made teddy bears from sea otter pelts, and had sold them at a craft fair, and some people felt this wasn't a "traditional use." It didn't matter what I thought; I just typed the briefs, enjoying the stories, and the writing styles of the various lawyers with whom I worked, and watched the development of their cases with keen interest.

After a while I was freed from the reception desk and took a job working with the lawyers, editing their briefs, helping with research, and other legal secretary-type tasks. I liked this work, and made a good wage. My new office had windows facing the Chugach. I still found myself looking out of windows, just as I had as a child in school, but I felt myself taking to this "real" job. Maybe this would be a good job to consider as a career. It was unlikely I'd ever make a living on Fox Island, I thought, and besides, when I remembered my father's concern and tried to think like a sensible person, it did make me uncomfortable knowing that I had no claim there. Daddy seemed to be pretty sure about how *he* saw the situation. Maybe I *was* being stupid. I liked to think I was as free as a bird. But maybe I *was* dependent on Fletch. If I didn't have a real career, like this one, with a nice paycheck, how would I ever buy land in New Mexico, or anywhere? If we did break up, I'd be left with only memories. Then there were Fletch's plans to worry about. Little voices said if I gave up Fox Island then I wouldn't have to worry about Fletch's plans; I could have this great career, with savings piling up in my bank account. I could make my parents proud. Other voices said, *Huh. You can't give up Fox Island, you can't work at a real job in the summer time.*

During my lunch hour one day I walked along 4th Avenue and met up with someone I had worked with at the Arctic Environmental Information and Data Center. I liked her a lot. Her name was Jill and she was one of the State's two avalanche experts. She had written and published a small book about avalanches for which I had filled orders, which was my first contact with someone who had written a book. She had impressed me as being a self-directed person who had come far in her chosen field, and since it was a career that involved the outdoors, she stayed in my mind. We chatted briefly and I learned that she and a friend had spent the summer in small boats—she in a row boat, he in a kayak—rowing and paddling the Inside Passage from Seattle to Skagway. I said, "You must be in great shape!" She bounced on her toes and said, "Yes! I feel like I could just—just—*break* things!"

Fletch Wants a New Boat

Fletcher declared that the original *Fox Islander* was too small. He wanted a bigger boat, one with the lines of a New England lobster boat. He already had it planned. It would be 36 feet, with a diesel engine, plenty of back deck room for fishing and handling crab pots, kayaks, and cargo, more interior space for seating during bad weather, a small galley, and a flying bridge on top for good weather. He told me he had already contacted a boat builder in Massachusetts, and by Thanksgiving we could go have a look at it. He was happy showing me pictures of lobster boats in his *Commercial Fisherman* magazine. They were beautiful. I never saw lines on a boat as pretty as those, and those were working boats, not playthings. The idea of beauty and function combined has always pleased me. "Why don't you write Kathleen and let her know we're coming?" he said. The Thanksgiving trip to see the new boat would be my first time east of the Mississippi.

We left Anchorage at night dressed against the bitter cold. Twelve hours later, we stepped off the plane onto the tarmac of a small airport in Rhode Island, into a balmy sixty-degree morning, under a pale New England sky that smelled of the sea. We found our bags and drove first to Kathleen's house in Massachusetts. How different New England was from Alaska or New Mexico! My first impression was that it was like driving through the world's biggest neighborhood park. Square, white houses sat prettily on curved roads in bare-branched hardwood forests, every detail just so. The architecture fit in nicely with the surroundings. In Anchorage, most of the construction was new, and much of it was big and ugly. Most of it had gone up rapidly beginning with the pipeline oil boom days in the '70s. In New England the sense of change was slow and comfortable, more of the refining and adapting variety, less of the conquering and altering variety.

I realized I was where most of the U.S. history I'd learned in school had taken place. Fletcher pointed out that Europe contained far more antiquity, was far older, but to me this place might as well have been a foreign country when it came to how different it was from what I'd seen.

Kathleen's sister, Clara, invited us to Thanksgiving dinner. She and her husband owned a home that was built not long after the Revolutionary War. As we sat with beers before dinner, their baby boy asked the same question of Fletcher over and over, that sounded like, "Shu shu se suh?" He was so earnest and cute looking up at Fletch, and we began to make funny guesses about what he was asking. Watching Fletch, I was reminded of our very first charter in Kachemak Bay years ago, before we knew each other very well. The family we took out that day had four small children, and I remembered my pleasure at watching Fletch interact with them, and how they were drawn to him. Now here it was almost five and half years later. Thanksgiving in Providence. I felt content.

Early the next morning, we left for Falmouth, on Cape Cod, where the new boat was being built. Along the way we stopped for breakfast at a small diner where our meals cost $2.15 each. Fletcher told the waitress we would have had to pay $6.00 for the same breakfast in Alaska. Every time he mentioned we were from Alaska people began asking questions. Fletcher exaggerated, telling people we have more friends with dog teams than snow machines, that we live in a log cabin, etc. Later, I ribbed him about the dog team remark, saying he shouldn't make a practice of exaggerating or "enhancing" fact, but he pointed out it's true: we did know more people with dog teams than snow machines. We knew two people with dog teams. And our house was made of logs.

In the cavernous interior of Marine Industries, Inc. we spent the day with the builder, going over every portion of the new boat.

Afterward we returned to Falmouth for a few beers and some camaraderie at the local pub. Fletcher looked at the menu and said,

"I'll have three 'kwayhogs.'" This food was spelled "quahog" on the menu. Fletch's pronunciation set several of our new *compadres* at the bar to chuckling. We soon learned that the word is pronounced "kwohog", and I didn't even know what it was.

They said, "Where are *you* from?" and when Fletcher said, "Alaska" they gathered close while he told them about log cabins, dog teams, and seventy-five degrees below zero, how you try to throw hot coffee out of your mug and it makes a frozen arc from your cup on down, an arc that doesn't quite reach the ground. They stared at him. He said, "You don't pee outside when it's that cold."

The quahog turned out to be a huge stuffed clam about as big as a man's fist. I didn't believe any of the things they told us about quahogs.

The next day we left at dawn, back to the small airport at Providence. Airborne again, after just three days, it was as if New England had all been a dream.

The new *Fox Islander* was finished by late March. Fletch sold the old Bayliner and arranged for the new boat to be carried by truck via Interstate from Falmouth to Lake Union in Seattle.

Back in November at the harbor on Cape Cod, he and I had strolled along the docks, looking at boats of all kinds, and I'd found myself noticing and admiring them as before I'd admired horses.

Before that, a boat had more or less been just a boat. Now I saw them in a new light. I felt this continuing shift to new realms of possibility in life, to this whole new life direction, this ever-deepening involvement, while at the same time struggling to quell my anxiety about what the new boat *meant*. Over dinner one night I said, "Are we going to start bringing out bigger groups?"

"No, Susannah, my Coast Guard license is for carrying six passengers, like it has been." He said this wearily, as if I'd badgered him. I felt disappointed in myself, but forged on.

"Will this new boat mean we're going to charge more? I don't think I can take it if things get too fancy on Fox Island."

"We need to get more of the higher-end tourist trade, and we have to take more people out. I plan to build another cabin, and add a bigger dining room onto the side of our cabin. That way we'll have a large common area where people can come hang out when the weather's bad. One whole wall could be bookshelves; you'd like that, wouldn't you? And we need flush toilets. I'll probably buy another boat in a year or two and hire another driver."

"Then you're going to put in a dock?"

"I don't know if that's feasible. Might be."

"But don't we do alright?"

"Wouldn't you like to make a good income from this someday?"

"Yes, but what if our regular clients won't be able to continue coming out?"

"They will."

"Fletch, I can't stand the thought of developing Fox Island more than we have."

"I'm glad you feel that way," he said. "You've always provided our environmental conscience out there. But we need to start making more income. We're going to need to hire some help at some point, a boat driver, maybe a cook. We'll do it in a way you're comfortable with. I think that's part of why people keep coming back, Susannah, because of your influence."

This comforted me some. But my aversion to development ran deep. I knew myself enough to know it wouldn't just go away. Too many times, growing up in the West, I'd seen the death of places I felt connected to. Landscapes were the definition of me, my soul to the soul of the land, places in which I was alive and aware, in love with life, and grateful. Sometimes the land I loved seemed defenseless, there to be bought and traded by unknowing agents, routed, changed, and too often, ruined. My night dreams that winter began to be about condos on Fox Island, even roads and neighborhoods on the slope behind the lake, unheeding people, blaring televisions. I thought, *I should be practical and safe and stay at this good job I have. But I can't not return to Fox Island. Anyway, wouldn't it be wonderful for Fletch if I just stood by him? For him, shouldn't I just shut up about my principles? Shouldn't I gladly and selflessly accept a position in life as his steadfast partner and mate?* It'd be great if I could do that, I knew. Anyone would want that. I wanted to give that to him.

Along with my confusion came troubled thoughts about Fletch and me. Underlying tensions over our differing desires took their toll, making conversation on some topics difficult or non-existent. I spoke to myself about what a good man he was, and about how good he was to me. Was one person supposed to lead and one supposed to follow? Fox Island would need my influence in the years to come, he had said, and what a wonderful life it was. How fortunate I was. I could buck myself up this way, convince myself, forget my worries. We'd have harmony and fun. At these times, I could see Fletch was happy, for he was happy when I was. Then at other times his plans sounded like something I could not abide in good conscience and I would think, *Fletch doesn't see things as I do*, and I doubted he ever would.

My childhood home was on the last street on the edge of town, and then there was nothing but open desert country until you came to a ranch about sixty miles distant. About a quarter mile from our home, and parallel to my street, was a dirt track called Lobo Canyon Road. From the time I was a little scabby-kneed girl, I left my house and crossed my street skipping or running—sometimes galloping— on my way to adventure. For me then, there was some kind of enchantment going on. The culture of other children—what they wanted, the toys, the TV shows they watched—I hardly knew. I just knew that I had the biggest front yard in the world, full of canyons and caves, lizards, horny toads, cattle, bones, mesas and mountains to climb, wind and grass, the occasional cowboy on horseback, sunrises and sunsets, and innumerable discoveries waiting to be made.

Eventually, Valencia County paved Lobo Canyon Road and then they built a school bus yard beside it. The bulldozing for the bus yard happened suddenly. In the morning as I headed out the door on my walk to school it was the same old sunlit desert, with lizards scurrying amid sagebrush, but when I returned home I stared at a great swath—acres—that had been laid bare; the sage, dirt, rocks and grasses pushed into hills around the perimeter, and a shiny chain-link fence laid out ready to enclose it. Country I had recently ridden across on Trinket, jumping sagebrush at a full gallop, and in earlier childhood, skipped across, now graded flat and stark and ready to receive steel buildings.

This was the background that formed my uneasiness with the changes that were coming to Fox Island, an uneasiness that came and went throughout that winter. Then finally, in March and April, optimism prevailed. As the days grew longer, as winter melted away in cold rivulets, as new grass pushed its way into the light and leaves unfurled from buds, as another Fox Island summer approached, Fletch caught me up in his simple enthusiasm to be on the water in his boat. I neither wanted to spoil his fun or miss out on any myself. And if Fletcher didn't see things as I did, I loved him all the same. We planned to fly to Seattle and return in the new *Fox Islander* as soon as school was out.

Voyage by Boat from Seattle to Fox Island

I quit my good job at Alaska Legal Services—common sense and my concerns borne away on springtime breezes. John finished his school year and drove up from Astoria with a truckload of gallon jars for pickling dolly varden, and cases of gold-tone cans for canning salmon (he said the cases "fell" into the back of his truck at an Astoria water-front cannery). Because his camper shell was full of gallon pickle jars and gold cans, he had had to camp in a tent on his way up. May is a wet time of year to travel in the Yukon Territory and Alaska. Heavy, old snow still lies on the ground, ready to decay into melt water, trickling away, but not far, to lie in puddles upon the soggy ground. John said he'd slept on picnic tables when they were available, to avoid sleeping in muck. He had already agreed, grudgingly, to take care of Tutka on Fox Island while we were away. He said, "Sure, I'll take care of the old fart bag." Thus reassured, Fletch and I flew to Seattle to sail the new boat on the second half of its journey to Fox Island.

Four of us convened for the trip: Fletcher, myself, Neal, and Fletch's friend Troy, an accountant from Vermont. We worked in pairs or alone, following Fletch's instructions, buying equipment, charts, tide and current tables, food and supplies, and stowing, rigging, checking fittings and equipment, followed by more stowing and rigging.

The new *Fox Islander*'s lobster boat hull made it nearly one-of-a-kind on the West Coast, at the time. This boat was not luxurious. Her materials were basic. She was beautiful, graceful, powerful. She was a working boat. The colors were white with red bottom paint, trimmed in gray and black, with teak handholds and chrome railings. Examining her 36-foot length in three 12-foot segments, the first, or bow-end segment, was a large forward deck with a V-shaped berth below. The middle segment Main cabin contained the controls and indoor seating, windows and galley—with the flying bridge on top of it. The rear segment was the spacious aft deck.

The forward deck was enclosed in railing and was suitable for riding on in calm weather, even sun bathing, if the opportunity arose. Beneath the forward deck the lower cabin contained a "V" berth: two red vinyl-upholstered beds along the sides coming together in the bow. One could hear the sound of water on the hull in bed, a "clunk-swoosh-gurgle" sound. Storage compartments lined the area above and below the berths and the forward-most area in the bow. A small head, or toilet, completed the interior of the lower cabin.

Three slatted wooden steps on a ship's ladder led up from the lower cabin to the Main cabin, which was surrounded by windows, had red seats, a red dining table, and along the other side behind the captain's seat, a small galley with red counter tops. The captain's seat and ship's wheel were situated in front of an array of high-tech navigational equipment. The front windows looked out over the forward deck, and met up with the long side windows on both sides, providing a wrap-around view.

A narrow-windowed door on the back of the Main cabin opened onto the aft deck. The aft deck had far more room than the original *Fox Islander*, with gunwales all around, wide enough to sit on. Cleats and pole-holders occurred at regular intervals along all three gunwales. Big hatch covers flush with the deck provided access to the boat's engine and bilge.

Attached to the back wall that enclosed the Main cabin, and just beside the doorway, a silver ladder led to the flying bridge. It had its own captain's chair, a low Plexiglas windshield, and its own set of controls so that the boat could be piloted from either the inside cabin or up on the bridge. The captain's seat in the Main cabin, the forward deck, and the flying bridge were my favorite places.

Seattle to Port Townsend
On an early June afternoon, with a low growl, the new boat's big diesel engine eased us backward from the dock. Once clear, Captain Fletch pushed the shift lever to *Forward* and we prepared to leave

Lake Union. The *Fox Islander* had been tested in the Atlantic, made the journey across the landmass of North America by truck, been outfitted in a fresh water lake in Seattle, and was now destined for its future in the Northern Pacific.

Since Lake Union is a ways above sea level, those wishing to enter the Pacific Ocean must leave the lake via "The Locks" at the lake's far west end. Waiting for our turn in the lock, we tied up in a holding area, left the boat and stood at an observation rail. Far below, a big tug and several sailboats ascended as water surged into the lock. Finally the water reached lake-level and a great gate opened. Men untied the boats and motored out. Then it was our turn to edge in and tie up along with two small barges and a cruising sailboat. We secured the boat to cleats forward and aft, and stood on the deck watching workers and spectators recede far above us into the light as the water drained and our surrounding space towered above like a huge, algae-covered elevator shaft. At the other end of the lock gates opened, and we untied and motored out onto the Pacific. As we sailed away, Seattle's waterfront disappeared from view first, then her tall buildings and then finally only mighty Mt. Ranier was visible, snow covered and mutely glowing through Seattle's light smog.

Right away, the depth sounder read four feet. I wasn't used to seeing Fletch as concerned as he was for a moment, but he determined that it was only a malfunction in the depth sounder, and we weren't about to run aground. Otherwise, our passage to Port Townsend, our first night's stopping place, across Puget Sound from Seattle, was uneventful. After docking, Neal, Troy and I took an evening stroll through the charming town with its giant trees and lovely gardens. Fletcher had found the problem with the depth sounder by the time we returned and I could see he was more relaxed than he had been in days. Months of preparation were over, everything was in order, the journey had begun. He said, "Susannah, tomorrow we'll leave early and celebrate with a vacation day in Victoria!"

Port Townsend to Victoria, British Columbia
We neared Victoria by mid-morning, and I had crossed the border

into my second foreign country. I recalled the time when, a few years earlier, I rode north from Albuquerque with five friends and a big gray husky in a blue station wagon. A few miles out of Santa Fe we decided to pull a U-turn and head south for Mexico, instead. We'd arrived in Juarez ten hours later in time for some disco dancing in a few of the city's seedy nightspots. Comparing the danger in Juarez to the dangers I considered now before me—crime and corruption in a teeming Mexican border town versus wind and waves in the Northern Pacific—I knew which sort I preferred, although powerful water always held a particular fear for me. I recognized that fear first, I suppose, at age six when I shuddered to think that my friend Mark Forest had moved to the edge of Hoover Dam. However, I had studied the charts, and I knew that for the most part, the Inside Passage was a network of inside, protected waterways with a few exceptions. I'd think about the exceptions and the crossing the Gulf some other time.

We left the boat tied to a dock, climbed the harbor ramp and beheld a regal, northern metropolis. Carriages, mopeds, bicycles, and people on foot criss-crossed along wide, clean avenues in the fresh, bright light. In this clear light, with its formal gardens, elegant, domed buildings, towering evergreens, and cobbled streets, Victoria showed me the prettiest city I'd ever seen. It seemed a perfect place from which to journey into a labyrinth of dark wilderness. At the end of the day, after a restaurant dinner, we sat on the *Fox Islander's* back deck, under the soft harbor lights, sipping wine and talking. I saw many boats bobbing with the movements of people doing the same as us. Some were cooking on grills that hung out over the rails of their boats. There were retired couples in cabin cruisers, rafted to one or two other boats, old friends who'd taken many trips together. There were families on sailboats. Some were out for a day or two of island hopping. Some lived on their boats full-time. Tomorrow morning they'd go south, or north, or stay for a while in the Victoria harbor. I looked around me and thought, *I'm in this world now. I belong to this society, the Offshore People.* We sat between two other boats, the *Twizzle* and the *Mary J.*, visiting and telling stories far into the night. No, they said, they'd cruised the Inside Passage for thirty years. They had friends who'd gone the whole way more than once. But they wouldn't care to cross the Gulf.

"How long you taking for the trip up?" asked the *Twizzle's* captain, Ben.

"Should take us around fifteen to twenty days at the rate we'll be traveling," said Fletch, "we'll take two or three days to cross the Gulf."

"You going straight across?"

"No. We may stop in Icy Bay."

"Might not be able to get in there. Yakutat's your better choice."

"What about Lituya?"

"In weather, you mean?"

"Or just to see it."

"People do it. I sure wouldn't. You've heard of what happened there? I'd be spooked."

"What happened there?" I asked.

"Okay," said Ben, "Vicki, where's my wine?" He filled his glass, lit a cigarette, and sat back. He tilted up his head and exhaled. Then he focused his gaze on me.

"Okay," he said.

I zipped my jacket shut and pulled the collar up around my neck.

"Now understand there's this sand bar across the entrance to Lituya. They call it *La Chaussee*. You know French?"

"Uh-uh."

"It means 'The Chopper.' Unless the sea is right, you can't even get in there. Now. Lituya Bay is narrow with an island right in the middle, called Cenotaph. Means monolith, or gravestone. Three tidewater glaciers flow in at the upper end. Otherwise it has almost no shoreline." He described Lituya's nearly vertical sides with his hands. "Deep, deep lake," he said. "Full of icebergs over near the glaciers. Treacherous."

"And it has this bar across the entrance," said his wife. "The Chopper."

I looked from her back to her husband.

"Young lady, this whole coast is earthquake country. You know about the Good Friday earthquake in '64. Well, this one happened in '58, in July, during a good commercial fishing season, and Susannah, it knocked the needle off the seismograph in Seattle."

"It registered eight on the Richter scale at the University of California," said Vicki.

Ben continued, "The epicenter was just fifty miles south of Lituya. That same night, anchored in Lituya were three boats, the *Edrie*, with a father and his young son on board, and the *Sunmore*, and *Badger*, each with a husband and wife on board, just like you two."

I felt momentary pleasure out of his assumption that Fletch and I were married.

"It was a pretty evening, just like this one, long summer twilight, no wind, calm there in the bay like this glass of wine. Still and deep. Calm. Howard, now I think that's the name of the captain on the *Edrie*. Howard and his son saw thousands of gulls swirling around Cenotaph Island. Now, don't you think they knew something was gonna' happen? You watch the animals, young lady. The animals know things we don't know."

"That's right, honey," said Vicki.

"Howard and his son had gone to bed. All of a sudden Howard gets flung outa' bed! His boat is pitching like a, like a—"

"Mechanical bull!" said Vicki.

"That's right. 'Well *hell*,' says Howard, 'we drug anchor, we're on the bar!' He runs up on deck and stops there because he sees what no one we know has ever seen. The earthquake is happening and the mountains *jumping* like, like—"

"Popcorn!" says his wife.

"Exactly right, like the biggest, tallest, 15,000 foot-high popcorn only they don't sound like popcorn, Vicki," he said toward his wife.

"They're roaring," she said.

"That's right! No! No! They're *groaning*. 'Cause they're coming apart. And avalanches busting off their sides along with cliffs and forests and it's all spewing clouds of snow and dirt. Howard, he's deafened and just frozen there on the deck of the *Edrie*. And then, he sees a wall of water come from the eastern end of the bay. He watches it sweep over Cenotaph Island, ripping out trees by the roots, bounce off the eastern shore, and head straight toward him! And then he moves. His kid was standing behind him hanging onto the boat. He gets him in a life jacket, starts the engine and tries to pull anchor. But it won't pull! He lets out every last bit of chain as the wave reaches them. It gets under them, they rise. You see the Empress Hotel there?"

I looked away from him toward the Empress, majestic and glowing in the evening light, the flags on her turrets not stirred by the slightest breeze.

"That's how high the wave lifted them. The anchor chain snaps and the short end whips around the pilot house of *Edrie*. Howard gets on the radio 'cause he wants his wife to know what happened. He shouts, 'Mayday! Mayday! This is the *Edrie* in Lituya Bay! All hell has broke loose! I think we've had it. Good-bye.' Then he goes back to fighting the wave."

"They're riding the wave as it heads back toward the western shore, carrying them and icebergs of all sizes and trees. He's horsing the boat around the trees and bergs, trying to run the *Edrie* off the wave before it crashes against the shore. Meanwhile the radio is full of voices—they'd all felt the 'quake too, of course, all along the coast—trying to account for loved ones. Howard and his son made it off the wave, and rode it again and then again. As it finally began to settle down, he got back on the radio, trying to fit his call in with the others. 'Have you seen *the Badger?*' 'This is *Markham* base calling for *Markham*, come in *Markham*!' '*Edrie*, this is *Miss Lilly*, we're on our way if there's anything we can do—.' 'Mayday! Mayday!' '*Sunmore, Sunmore!* This is *Badger* calling, over!' 'Were there any other boats in the bay?' someone asks Howard. He says 'I didn't see any come in, unless they were behind the island. If there were any behind the island, they've had it.' "

"What about the young couples on the *Badger* and the *Sunmore?*" I almost shouted.

"Well now, they weren't both young couples. One was an old couple, like us, on an old boat like the *Twizzle*. The other was a young couple on a brand-new boat just like you two. They survived and their stories are as incredible as that one—"

And so went the evening under the spell of Ben's stories, with Fletch adding a few and then it was Neal's turn, and all of us settling into the perfect night in the Victoria harbor.

We planned to leave early the next morning, and woke before 6:00, but Ben was up and suggested to Fletcher that we leave later. "Extreme tides today," he said. "Which means extra high and extra low, which means extra fast. So leaving on an outgoing tide would just slow you down. All that water falling ten feet over six hours moves very quickly, especially through narrow passages." He said the tidal current in some places can reach 15 knots. Considering that the topmost speed of *Fox Islander* was about 16 knots, I knew I wouldn't want that kind of current pushing against us. Fletch said, "Yep, I see what you mean."

"Good! I think I'll take a walk then," said Neal, grabbing up his pack. "I'll stop by the shower and let Troy know we won't be leaving 'til after noon."

Fletch backed down the ladder and motioned to me. "Let's get a little more 'rest,' " he said with a smile.

Victoria to Nanaimo, British Columbia, Along the East Side of Vancouver Island

We left at slack tide later in the day, waving "so long" to Ben and Vicki. "Good luck! Be careful!" they called as we motored out. Slack tide is the moment when the tide stops going one way and just before it begins to go the other. Moments later, when the tide began to come in, it gave us a few extra knots, which got us to our next anchorage about the time we would have arrived had we left at dawn on an outgoing tide.

We made Nanaimo, B.C., that evening, docking at the fuel dock until we could get moorage. Downtown Nanaimo roared with raucous shouts and laughter and the screeching of brakes. I decided this meant it was either Thursday, Friday, or Saturday. I was afraid I wouldn't sleep, but I slept well, waking in the bunk I shared with Fletch the following morning after we'd gotten underway. Fletcher had decided to leave very early since this day we were to cross a great distance over the Strait of Georgia—a stretch of open water but still behind the protection of Vancouver Island. Riding there on the red boat bed, cozy in covers, I remembered camping trips when Daddy and Mama would wake early and get on the road. We girls would still be asleep in the camper bed above the cab of the pickup truck. We'd be on our way to Montana, and I'd sleep on, rocked in the motion of the truck, snug as a bug.

Fletch lay beside me, resting but not asleep, and in the berth opposite, Neal snored gently. I raised up on my elbows and looked up the passageway, and there sat Troy at the helm. This concerned me because Troy, a big, doe-eyed man with a sweet temperament, had narcolepsy. I had already seen him fall asleep at dinner twice back in Seattle, again sitting on a bench along the street in Victoria, and once while sitting at the table in the boat looking at charts with Fletcher. But, I figured, Fletch had turned the helm over to him, and Fletch could be counted on to never do anything unwise. I could tell the waters of the Strait were calm; I knew Troy had just gotten up, so he would be well rested, and I saw he held a steaming cup of coffee in his hand. So I lay back for a minute and finished my pleasant reverie of traveling to Montana in those days long past.

Nanaimo to Campbell River, Traveling in the Strait of Georgia

I awoke again just as we got sideways to a long fetch in the Strait of Georgia. Fetch is the distance over open water which wind can blow, and if the fetch is long and the wind strong, big waves occur. With waves and a steady wind pushing against the side of the boat, we began to feel a sickening pitch-roll motion. I had to clutch every handhold as I got out of bed and made my way upstairs with difficulty. Every loose object on the boat skidded and banged across the floor in a mess. In spite of all this, I felt good. Fletch had already gotten up again and was at the helm. The autopilot kept us faithfully on course, and the movement of the boat, though relatively violent, wasn't much worse than some I'd experienced on board the old boat going around Cape Aialik.

Fletch had shown me how he programmed the autopilot by entering into it the latitude and longitude for each way point, or segment. Latitude and longitude coordinates are determined by the use of navigational charts and the Loran C. The autopilot was somehow in cahoots with a big special compass that rode deep in the bow of the boat somewhere where it was isolated from any local magnetic forces, and it was also connected with the boat's steering mechanism. The autopilot wouldn't let us point anywhere except toward the coordinates we set. If we twisted on top of a wave, pointing toward 340 degrees north/northwest instead of 330 north/northwest, the autopilot brought us back with a resolute lurch. The Loran C kept track of our course. Using charts, Fletcher programmed each segment necessary for negotiating the day's waters into the Loran C before getting under way. He programmed in zigs and zags in long and short segments to avoid islands, rocks, and shorelines between our beginning spot and ending spot. The Loran C, in turn, received a signal from towers located on land. Its gray screen with black letters and numbers displayed the desired course and the actual course moment-by-moment. We checked it frequently to be sure we weren't off, because you could drift a certain distance sideways on a current, say, and the autopilot would faithfully take you toward the coordinates you'd programmed into it, only now since you had drifted, there could be a small island or jutting shoreline or slightly submerged rocks between you and those coordinates. The radar was good for comparing the shoreline on the chart with the actual shoreline to be sure they matched, and for keeping track of other boats, in the fog or at night. I liked the way the big round screen on the radar glowed our faces green in the night, and the way the signal swept around it like a clock hand that could reveal the unseen. The depth-sounder saw the ocean bottom up to 800 feet, and displayed the sea-floor contour that was directly below the boat at the moment when the sonar signal hit the bottom and bounced back up. It showed a picture of that contour from one instant past to a few moments past, depending on the width of the display you selected. The depth-sounder could also be set to show fish that were below the boat. In rough water, the tipping of the boat this way and that sent the sonar signal out at an angle and made the depth sounder less reliable. In spite of the sophisticated equipment, we had no way other than our eyes to detect logs and other debris in our path. Water-logged telephone-pole-size logs, that float vertically, with only a few inches of one end above water are called "dead-heads" or "widow-makers."

We left behind the cold, playful wind and uncomfortable beam sea and entered quietness through two mountainous, spruce-furred islands, near a place called Comox. I let loose of the handholds, unzipped my jacket and pulled the hood off my head. The sun shone through wisps of mist, and through it I could see the shores of a large island to starboard and Vancouver Island, to port. Behind the few homes and buildings on Vancouver Island the land rolled higher until it tilted up into low mountains that looked like gentle green dinosaurs who had fallen asleep in the snow. I headed up the ladder to the bridge. I found a spot out of the breeze and felt pleasantly warm. I wrote in my journal.

We hoped to travel 75 to 100 miles that day—to Campbell River where a network of narrow channels would bring the scenery within mere yards of us on either side. Somewhere in there we'd find a cove to anchor in for the night, and maybe catch a salmon. I set my journal down and lay back, gazing up at the northern sky, which is peculiarly thin-looking in summer—like aqua-colored cellophane. The boat thrummed beneath me and the air was so fresh—but for the occasional wisp of diesel exhaust—I was sure I was the first person ever to breathe it. The sloppy stretch of water we had endured in the Strait of Georgia would be the worst we'd have to deal with until we left the protection of Vancouver Island, which is a bit over 250 miles long. In the meantime we had another whole day of traveling in well-protected waters.

Campbell River to God's Pocket

Near Comox I realized I had already lost track of the days. Was today the 14th of June? I had tried to keep track of it in my daily journal writings. Most of the time I wrote in my journal while riding on the flying bridge alone or with Fletcher, but sometimes I wrote more than once in a day. Finally I decided it must be the 15th, because we had left Seattle the 11th and spent four nights: Port Townsend, Victoria, Nanaimo, and a cove near Campbell River. After leaving Campbell River we would continue along in the shelter of Vancouver

Island for one more day. We'd stop briefly at Port Hardy near the island's northern tip, and then edge along it, scarcely protected from the vast fetch of Queen Charlotte Sound by scant islands, to spend the night in a place called God's Pocket. God's Pocket is known as one of the good places to wait to cross Queen Charlotte Sound. The Sound is entirely open to the Pacific Ocean. It should be crossed when the tides and weather conditions are good, and everyone usually wants to make the shortest possible crossing of it.

Looking at the charts, I decided that a "strait" is any straight passage where the fetch is long enough for a good wind to blow unobstructed. We'd already crossed Juan de Fuca Strait and the Strait of Georgia. Conditions in them vary depending on many factors that the captain must consider, including the strait's width or narrowness, how many miles of fetch it has, how hard the wind is blowing, which way the wind is blowing, whether it is foggy or not, and what the tide is doing. A "sound," on the other hand, I decided, looking at the gaping blue expanse of Queen Charlotte on the chart, is much larger than a strait and, more importantly, it is completely open to the ocean. Talk about fetch! The warnings in our books about sound crossings were generally more dire than most warnings about the straits we'd encounter. I figured, then, that a "dire strait" was a sound.

In the morning we had made good time on an incoming tide through Seymour Narrows and Race Passage, so named because of the currents. We were up to fifteen knots with five added knots from the current, riding waves like rapids. We had another two-and-a-half hours of incoming tide, then the outgoing would begin to slow us down. Two tugs with great long barges steamed ahead of us; other than those, we saw no one. As we progressed farther north, massive foothills rose steep from the sea. Granite mountaintops rose above the foothills. They still reminded me of dinosaurs asleep in the snow, but closer to stegosaurs than brontosauruses. I no longer saw houses or towns since leaving the Campbell River and only the occasional lonely cabin. I did see numerous logging roads on the foothills, both on Vancouver Island and the mainland. The peculiar kinked logging roads made varicose veins over the gray, eroded mountainsides where lumber companies had done clear-cut timbering. Clear-cut is when they completely remove every last trace of every tree, except the stumps. Some of these clear-cuts are many hundreds of acres. These scenes looked nothing like the living, breathing forest teeming with life that I knew had existed there just months before. I felt certain these forests would never function quite as elegantly, even once they had grown back, or at least not in my lifetime. That didn't seem good at all. In the water we encountered logs and sundry wood which we had to dodge, and sometimes, when there was a great deal of wood debris, we were forced to slow down and push through it. In the afternoon I realized we had spent that entire day approaching and surpassing the two tugs. I looked back and saw that even now the first one we passed was still in sight behind us. They had been moving very close to our speed, which I found amazing, considering that they pushed loads of many thousands of tons.

We pulled into the Port Hardy Harbor to refuel, shower, and get groceries. It was lovely weather and I enjoyed the feel of earth beneath my feet as I walked alone the mile or so to the grocery store. I always looked at towns with the idea that maybe I would move there someday, and I decided that Port Hardy met my criteria. It was a small town with large open spaces and places for kids to play, and very few cars. Here, I decided, I would have plenty of country to explore on foot and on horseback. I walked along. I didn't have the faintest notion if I would have kids, or not. What did Fletch think? I didn't know that either. A gaggle of children crossed the road up ahead on bikes and let their bikes fall as they ran for the swings in a playground. I remembered that family with four children from one of our first charters in Kachemak Bay. Fletch had beached the skiff, and the children, of various heights and in various colored rain coats, scrambled to help Fletcher haul the skiff up and then just seemed to surround him with their enthusiasm and adoration. I remembered his rich laughter. I remembered how good he'd looked among them. The sight had made me feel buoyant, I recalled. This was a memory of a *feeling*, not a *thought*; it hadn't put any ideas in my head to someday be his wife and have children with him. I didn't interpret it or anything. I just remembered it now, as I walked to the grocery store in Port Hardy. If I did have kids, they'd have open space and fresh air and a real community here.

I entered the grocery store and found it well-stocked, then

reached into my pockets and discovered I'd forgotten to bring enough money. I had only eight dollars and a few coins. Knowing Fletch planned to get going again as soon as I returned, and that I didn't have time to walk back and return to the store with more money, I tried to do the best I could. I ended up with four plums, lettuce, milk, a Hershey bar, and a small package of frozen vegetables. Forgetting money was a bad mistake, as groceries would become harder to come by. I walked with less enjoyment back to the boat. But I knew Fletch would be kind about my error, and I was grateful.

From Port Hardy we island-hopped over to God's Pocket, where a log-cabin lodge sat adorned with brilliant flower boxes above a quiet cove, nestled among huge trees. It had a dock (private, thirty cents a foot), and some permanent mooring buoys. About six or seven boats stayed for the night. We fished for a while and caught a small flat fish. We anchored and cooked our fish with vegetables and rice, and later fell asleep to the gentle sounds of water lapping against the hull of the boat, and birdsong in the trees all around.

God's Pocket to Bella Bella
My favorite Inside Passage guidebook, *How To Cruise to Alaska Without Rocking the Boat Too Much*, by Walt Woodward, read:

> You now, indeed, are approaching "fog country." Both
> Queen Charlotte Sound and Queen Charlotte Strait,

or portions of them, can be socked in with impenetrable fog banks. You must have accurate true course lines drawn on the chart, measured and marked for distance as well as heading. These must be drawn before you leave port. And yes, you must draw them even though you have radar. You have a few other things to do before you plunge across the Sound. Listen to Alert Bay's continuous weather broadcast, paying particular attention not only to the forecast, but to actual conditions being reported from Bull Harbour and Egg Island. If the wind from any direction either is predicted or reported at more than 15 knots, don't go; wait for better weather. Augment this by looking at the tops of the trees above you; if they are wildly waving, don't go. If there has been a storm in the nearby Pacific Ocean in the last 24 hours, maybe you shouldn't go; there likely will be a residue of heavy swells. Unless you have absolute faith in your radar and/or your ability at dead reckoning, don't go if there is fog.

Another guidebook read:

The ocean swells in the Sound can be tremendous. If it is sunny when you leave you can still become enclosed in fog in the Sound. The currents coming out of numerous inlets can be treacherous when combined with wind. Mark all your coordinates and routes before heading out.

Fletcher did all of these and determined the tide would be right for leaving at 5:00 the next morning. I got up with him, made coffee while he made last-minute preparations, and stood beside him at the helm as we sailed away, hoping that Troy and Neal would sleep on awhile. It was so seldom we spent any time alone. We quietly motored out of God's Pocket into the Sound. Once out, long, low swells, as long and low as swells can possibly be, and moving as slow as swells can possibly move, ever-so-gently raised us and lowered us. Fletch said, "Susannah, let's take our coffee and go up on the bridge." Around us, the world opened into a vast panorama of morning-blue ocean, crystalline aqua sky, and ghostly blue, far distant mountains. There seemed to be a lack of sound. It dawned on me that our engine noise no longer reverberated off nearby land, but traveled out, unimpeded in the vastness. We were silent for a while, taking it in. Fletch said, "It's nice, isn't it? Times like this almost bring tears to my eyes." I smiled, marveling at this occasion of his expressiveness. He put his arm around me.

When Neal and Troy got up, I made breakfast of granola and plums and juice, and we shared a leisurely meal and sipped coffee on the aft deck, still riding atop gentle ocean swells, being pestered occasionally by seagulls. Later I wrote in my journal and sketched; Neal read his book lying on his back with a pillow under his head on the forward deck; Troy and Fletch rode in the Main cabin talking about old times and looking over charts. Toward late afternoon, after once again entering protected water passages behind a series of islands, we pulled into Bella Bella harbor for fuel and groceries. Bella Bella is an Indian village at the confluence of three passages. Neal and I walked up to a building with the sign "Band Store" written in black on a white background. "Band" means "tribe." I wondered why so many hotels in Canada didn't have actual names, such as "Bayview Inn." They just had a sign in black-and-white that said "HOTEL," like a big generic box, and the same was true for some grocery stores and all liquor stores. The grocery stores that didn't have generic signs were called "Overweighta," which I thought odd, but I decided the name was no more odd than our grocery store in Grants called "Piggly Wiggly."

Villagers walked the roads in Bella Bella, laughing and talking. Children played in the bright, warm sunshine. In spite of all the people being out, when Neal and I approached, it got quiet. Amidst the silence we entered the store, which was small, dim, poorly stocked, and quiet, in spite of several shoppers besides us. No one met our gaze. The magazine racks were jammed with low forms of entertainment—a variety of magazines featuring true crime, monster trucks, pornography, guns, and the rest. It made me sad to think of the transition still being made by these Indians, from vital self-reliance and a spirited heritage in this beautiful, mystical setting, to feeling compelled, now, to feast on garbage.

We anchored that evening in a dark green cove on the same island, north of the village of Bella Bella. When Fletch shut off the engine and the anchor was set in the cove's rocky bottom, I listened carefully. The sea was so still I couldn't even hear the sound of water against the boat. I thought it was silent. Then I began to hear songbirds all around us in the forest, in the twilight. Occasionally a movement flitted from branch to branch, but always, it seemed, on the edge of my vision. A fish rose off the port bow, then another a distance away, and then another close behind me off to starboard, making tiny slap sounds and concentric ripples that went out from the center and disappeared. I went below and found my spinning rod. Neal brought two cold beers and sat and talked on the bridge while I stood on the forward deck, casting off the bow in the direction of ripples. We talked about the Indians' life there—what it must have been like. Then we were silent for a long time listening to bird songs. Neal said, "But don't you think you're over-romanticizing the Indians' life?"

"Oh, no, I think it *was* romantic," I said. "It had to be. Their world in nature was full of portents and meaning, with dreams and visions woven in. Animals were their relatives, and thought of as helpers, or guides." I considered my own summer life in the wilderness compared to my winter life in the city. "Their time was not fractured with interference like traffic and appointments and loud commercials about things they didn't care about. Their lives were all of a piece. They lived simply and directly from the land. Can you imagine how much more meaningful big feasts like

Thanksgiving were, when everything on the table was hunted and harvested? And how much better your appetite would be? And they didn't have to contend with major damage to their natural surroundings."

"Except for earthquakes, landslides, avalanches, floods, and volcanoes," Neal said.

"I mean the kind of damage other people do: One day you come home from work and there's a strip mall going in where you used to pick berries," I said impatiently. "Or the kind where you're not sure the natural systems that support you and every other living thing, are going to be working right when your children have children. It was more consistently peaceful in those days."

"Except for when they warred with their enemies," Neal said. "You sound like you think it was Utopia."

"No, I don't think it was Utopia. The times *we* live in sure aren't Utopia, Neal, any more than it was then. In spite of volcanoes or the problems we have in *our* times, though, there's still no end to goodness."

I decided to change the subject and tell Neal about Qolus the Changeable. Qolus was the wife of Thunderbird. They lived in the heavens, one of the four kingdoms of Reality. The other three were the earth, the underground, and under the sea. Thunderbird was mighty and striking to look at—pure white, I think—with different-colored feathers in his wings. And very, very huge. He made the sun shine when he opened his eyes and made the wind blow when he ruffled his feathers. Thunderbird's wife, Qolus the Changeable, didn't have much to do in the heavens, though, and was bored, so she told Thunderbird she wanted to go to earth. When she went to earth she changed into a man and became the husband of a graceful young girl, Mowita. Mowita was the daughter of Copper Woman and Snot Boy. Snot Boy was an incomplete being whom Copper Woman had picked up off the beach long ago. He was actually mucus, which she had spit out from crying so hard from loneliness. She cried because she had barely lived through a terrible ocean voyage before landing here. She was the only one of four sisters to survive, their vessel had been destroyed in the landing, and now she was completely alone—the only human, the only woman. Even though Snot Boy was incomplete and inept—he built smoky fires and such, and had the physical traits of a whole variety of sea creatures—she understood, somehow, that she should cherish and nurture him. He had come into existence for her, and from her, that day as a sentient being who was the matter of life and suffering…but he *was* of life. And so she nurtured him. She took care of him while he went through his various sea-creature-like growth stages—an anemone, an urchin, a clam, and so forth—transferring him to bigger and bigger sea shells until he looked somewhat like a man and could build fires and walk about on his own. Eventually he fathered her children. Their daughter Mowita was happy with Qolus. Remember, Qolus, who was once Thunderbird's wife in the heavens, is now a man on earth, and his name is Mah Teg Yalah.

Well, up in the heavens Thunderbird eventually got lonely for his wife, Qolus. He began to weep and couldn't stop. He really didn't intend to flood the world with his tears; he didn't want to cause such a catastrophe, but he couldn't stop crying. Copper Woman, being a wise old woman now, knew that the rain would continue for four days for each finger on both hands. Mowita and Mah Teg Yalah built a huge house and jammed the spaces between the logs with pitch, so that when Thunderbird's tears began to flood the earth, the house floated up off the ground. Mowita, Mah Teg Yalah, and the other four daughters of Copper Woman, and the four sons of Mowita and Mah Teg Yalah entered the house, along with some animals. Copper Woman chose to stay behind, though.

After many days, Mah Teg Yalah sent Raven out to see if there was any land anywhere that wasn't flooded. Raven flew back into the house through a window and said there was no land. He sent Raven out again a few days later, and that time Raven brought back a sprig of hemlock and dropped it into the house through the window. Mowita and Mah Teg Yalah knew then that they would see land again when they opened the door of the house, and they did. The animals in the house along with the other four daughters of Copper Woman and Snot Boy, and the four sons of Mowita and Mah Teg Yalah ran outside. These daughters and sons made four couples. These four couples clasped hands and each couple ran off in one of the four directions, to the east, the west, the north, and the south, and became the parents of all the people of the world.

Mowita knew that Mah Teg Yalah wanted to go back to the heavens and be Qolus again, wife of Thunderbird. And she bid him goodbye, giving him one last kiss on the lips. Then, he changed into Qolus and with powerful wings so bright they hurt the eyes, he flew away. Mowita was lonely, but she was self-sufficient, and learned to be content. And the happy thing is that one day her mother, Copper Woman, showed up. But that is a whole other story.

Neal said, "So. The grandfather of everyone is snot?"

"No, the grandfather of everyone is Qolus, wife of Thunderbird. The *great* grandfather is snot which came from Copper Woman."

"Well, I like that story," said Neal.

"Yeah, I do too," I said. "It's strange. But true."

Bella Bella to Bishop's Bay

The Inside Passage, about 1,142 miles long, begins on the south end somewhere near Seattle. Some disagree about the exact place it begins, and its length in miles is disputed because of that. But there's no mistaking where the Inside Passage ends on the north end. You have left Juneau, traveling southwest across Cross Sound. When you reach that north-end spot you should look back into the labyrinth that has been your home because when you face the other three directions you're looking at empty horizons. You just pop out of the protected water you've been in all this time, and that's that. Dead ahead of you, but quite a long ways away, about 5,000 miles, is tiny Midway Island in the Hawaiian Island group. We'd be turning north at the end of the Inside Passage, and would follow the treacherous coastline home to Fox Island. Fletch estimated we'd be at the end of the Inside Passage in about eight days.

For now I sat with Neal on the bridge watching the scenery scoot by close on either side of the boat. Back at our anchorage near Bella Bella, I had made breakfast of bacon, sourdough pancakes covered in strawberries and whipping cream, and icy-cold orange juice, all goodies I had paid a premium for at the Bella Bella Band store. We had left the dark green cove of birdsong and fish ripples, and were now motoring along the side of an island, in a long passage no wider than a typical front lawn, with nothing that needed doing except to enjoy life. Sunlight shone through a break in the fog and made flashing prisms out of the droplets cascading from the tips of billions of spruce needles. Here on the bridge, the boat's engine thrum made a comforting, almost hypnotic, rhythm conducive to daydreaming. Even though a breeze swept down off the mountains and across the Sound, it was offset by the warmth of the sun. I felt the cool, moist air against my face and neck and hands, by now the only parts of me uncovered. I smelled the tree-cleaned air and occasional whiffs of diesel exhaust, and sometimes the rich, dark smell of the ancient forest.

Suddenly I heard high above me the glissading screech of an eagle, and followed the sound to the sky:

Black body, bright tail and head. From high above he sees a
fish, a glint of silver beneath the surface. He folds his wings

against his body and dives, so fast I think he'll crash. At the
last second his wings unfold, his talons drop like landing
gear and break the black surface, a bright salmon struggling,
blood droplets falling, a silver wake vanishing as quickly as
it appeared, and the eagle strains for the sky. I hear "whoosh,
whoosh" as he disappears over a ridge. I look behind and
watch the boat's wake churn out pure white in a big V, and
watch the wake disappear far behind into the green-black
reflections of the spruce forests.

Bishop's Bay to Prince Rupert

We spent that night in a side passage called Bishop's Bay. Here someone had built a pool to collect a natural hot springs and had covered it with a small hut with low, open windows. Four other boats were anchored here—three fishing boats with their rugged, strong-armed crews, taking a break, and a lovely cruising sailboat called the *Grizzly Bear*, with a couple on board who looked like they'd stepped off a movie set. After dinner our various dinghies rested beside each other on the beach as we enjoyed the hot springs: three gray Zodiacs, our brown dory, and the sail-boaters' white lapstrake dinghy with "*Baby Bear*" painted in gold lettering on the stern.

Neal's summer plans were to leave our adventure at Prince Rupert and return to Washington State where he had friends. I dreaded his leaving. With Troy occupying Fletch's time, Neal had been more available for companionship. I'd miss his capricious humor and inquiring mind and the roving topics we'd explored. Neal could handle what I offered in conversation and give back his own ideas in a satisfying way. As for Troy, he was nice, but he seemed shy around me. He would have been speechless with bewilderment had I told *him* the story of Copper Woman. We'd found nothing in common between us and rarely spoke.

At the same time, I was glad to be arriving in Prince Rupert, because it meant I could get a shower, stretch my legs, find a new book, eat a restaurant meal, and maybe even enjoy a cocktail on some outdoor patio. Prince Rupert is the most northern ice-free port in Canada. Lumber barges, commercial fishing boats, and freighters come and go, as well as the British Columbia ferry, the

Alaska ferry, and an occasional cruise ship. In addition, both a paved highway and a railroad connect Prince Rupert to country beyond the Coast Range. In spite of its population (about 20,000) and its access to the world, Prince Rupert is not like any American city. I found it noticeably un-commercial. Window displays in shops along the main street reminded me of school bulletin boards, hand lettered on poster board, decorated with crepe paper and balloons. It seemed much more like a kindly welcome, and not so much like elaborate preparations that had been made to lure us to spend our money. Prior to this I had not realized the extent of commercialism in the United States.

The next morning we helped Neal carry his luggage to the ferry terminal, and off he went on the southbound boat. Fletch, Troy, and I ended up waiting in the safety of Prince Rupert's harbor for a day and a half while a gale blew up out at sea. I stepped into a small book store, a place that like many places, had a VHF radio on to keep in touch with loved-ones who made their living on the water: fishermen, loggers, ferry captains. I looked at knick-knacks and listened to the marine forecast: winds 30 to 40 knots, seas to seven meters. I thought how different land-life was from ocean-life. In town it was just an ordinary windy day.

Ketchikan

Ketchikan, Alaska was our next destination, back in the U.S., where we would pick up Daddy, who was flying in and would be joining us for the second half of the trip.

We thought we were an hour late to meet Daddy at the Ketchikan airport. I was concerned that he would arrive and have to haul his luggage all over the place trying to find the harbor. But just as we approached Ketchikan, a big Alaska Airlines jet came in for a landing right alongside the water. We tied up at a dock in front of the airport and found we were there just in time to meet Daddy as he stepped off the plane. We only thought we were late because we had forgotten to change our watches after leaving Canada. We got his luggage at baggage claim, carried it out the door, and right to the boat. Daddy said that's the first time he'd ever been picked up at an airport by boat.

Naturally it rained in Ketchikan. They get 162 inches a year. If they save stuff for rainy days, they must be all out of everything. The first thing I noticed pulling in was the traffic—float planes taking off all up and down the bay and flying about through the skies every which-way, big and little boats churning the waters far and near, and on shore, cars and trucks zooming along roads. We were back in the U.S.: more activity, cars, signs, roads, fancier store window displays. We didn't stay long because all this was just too much for those of us who had been traveling in quiet waters for so long, and for Daddy because it was the beginning of an adventure that he was eager to begin. I decided the rain was light enough to try my sheltered spot on the bridge with my journal while Daddy talked boats, charts, and weather with Fletch and Troy in the cabin below. But before long I brought my journal back down and returned to the bridge to just sit in the light rain. I thought contentedly of the friendship between my dad and Fletch, how they were alike in many ways, and my good fortune to be able to invite Daddy on this trip. After a while he came up the ladder to join me.

"Aren't you getting wet, Susie?"

"Not too bad. This is the best place to ride." I felt tempted to tell him how I could imagine I was flying, here on the flying bridge, but I sometimes felt my use of imagery was not easy for Daddy to respond to. "So, what do you think of the boat?"

"It's a beauty," Daddy said. "Must have cost him quite a lot."

"It's a big change in weather for you," I laughed, changing the subject in case I was about to hear again how I was getting duped. "So, what did you do yesterday in New Mexico?"

"Your mother and Kate Kalstead rode up to the Buffalo, said there was just a trickle in Tunnel Springs. I picked peaches. It hasn't rained for a month and a half."

"Do the McCoys still have Gallup?"

"Is that the tall brown one?"

"Sorrel."

"Yes, they've got Gallup and a new horse, a dark brown one, I think. Kate rode it yesterday because Tecaloté had a bad leg. Your horse is getting fat."

Petersburg, Alaska

We got in to Petersburg after twelve straight hours of traveling. I liked it more than Ketchikan. Petersburg had less traffic, and had wide sidewalks, welcoming pedestrians to stroll and relax. It was clean and pretty with artwork everywhere: bright Norwegian designs painted on doors and shutters, colorful flags on the light posts, brass inlays in the sidewalks. The quaint old homes were tidy with bright lawns and flowers. The town was arranged in a cluster, not in a long strip like Ketchikan. The harbor was well-run, and most important of all, it had the best showers of the whole trip, which cost only a dollar and never ran out of hot water.

In Petersburg we slept in, walked to breakfast at a small café, and even took a look around in the shops. We didn't leave until afternoon, and then we didn't go far because we stopped to fish for halibut at Thomas Bay. At first we only caught Irish Lords, but we fished on, in no particular hurry, enjoying the ambience of our surroundings. The expanse of sea lay calm in Steven's Passage all the way to the distant mountainous shorelines. Soft cotton-ball clouds nuzzled one another, filling the sky, reflecting pastel light. Miles and miles and miles of the longest sunbeams ever were cast from a departing mass of storm clouds to the northwest. We were in a wide-open area of water with land visible in the distance on all sides, sixty miles from Juneau.

Entering Gastineau Channel

As we traveled that evening, after finally catching a small halibut and placing it on ice for our supper later, a group of Dall's porpoise made a beeline for the boat to play in the bow wave. Dall's porpoise are black and white, fast, and very shiny, and look quite a bit like small killer whales. To get a close look at the porpoises, Troy, Daddy, and I got up on the bow and lay down on our stomachs with our heads out over the water, looking right down on the porpoises as they torpedoed back and forth. With my arm stretched out, I could

almost reach out and touch one that shot forward, just below me, turned on its side, and looked right at me. Its eye had startling whites on either side of a large iris. I had thought porpoise's eyes would be like seals' eyes, I guess, with none of the white showing. The eye that looked at me was more like a human eye. After several minutes the group of porpoise sped away, and not long after that Fletch, spotting some icebergs, slowed the boat and began looking for a place to anchor for the night.

A small glacier in a cirque valley nestled into shadowy purple mountains above us and glowed pale gold by the light of the low sun. Several sculptured blue icebergs floated near us, and the water rippled blue and gold as we made our way into the cove and dropped anchor for the night.

Troy would be leaving us in Juneau, and then it would be just Daddy, Fletcher, and me from there on to Fox Island, another 350 miles. After leaving Juneau it would take us two or three days to reach the edge of the open sea. There we would wait in the last protected spot for a favorable weather report for crossing the Gulf of Alaska. Once in the Gulf the farthest we would be from land would be about a hundred miles, and Fletch estimated crossing the Gulf would take us about four days, traveling both night and day. The southern coastline of Alaska forms a curve. From the place where we would enter the Gulf at Cross Sound, we could cut across this curve to Resurrection Bay. But rather than do that, which would take us very far from land indeed, Fletch planned for us to head first for Yakutat, and then from there to Prince William Sound, crossing the curve in two straight segments. After that we would hug the coastline another forty miles or so before entering Resurrection Bay.

At times Alaska can be threatening, like a man with dark moods, morose and unpredictable for days. Oh yes, it's still beautiful: I could see a cabin in the trees behind a driftwoody beach. I lifted my gaze to snow-clad granite peaks through breaks in the fog, back down to black forested islands. But on this day in Alaska, the sea and sky dominated: powerful, metallic, mysterious, dreary, ominous. I wanted to be in that cabin with a wood stove crackling, a contented cat on my lap, a good book to read, and a cup of something hot to drink at hand. I wanted to be on the beach, even, sitting on a log, a nice orange fire crackling away as it consumed salty driftwood.

I thought ahead, now that our crossing of the Gulf was drawing near and the safe part of our trip was over. Up on the bridge I opened my journal, deciding to plan and make lists for our homecoming. But fog enveloped me, frigid breezes blew down my neck and I shivered in spite of wearing one of Fletch's wool sweaters over one of my own. The only plan I came up with was to go to Seward when we got home, and see if a half-hour enveloped in heat in its new tanning bed was as pleasant an experience as I imagined it might be. I climbed down the ladder and entered the Main cabin where it was warm and noisy, and made a fresh pot of coffee.

We arrived in Juneau that evening, and had a send-off dinner for Troy at the Fiddlehead Café. Juneau is interesting because it is Alaska's capital, and yet it isn't connected by road to the rest of the world. To get there you have to take a boat or plane. It does have a short highway connecting parts of town, though, and this seemed to be as busy a highway as any town its size, which is about 30,000. It was also our first glimpse in a long time of real city life—men and women in suits and nice clean cars leaving parking areas for the commute home, like any ordinary place. Even so, as we walked to the café, I realized happily that one does not feel out of place looking unkempt anywhere in Alaska. A taxi came to the harbor to pick up Troy, and then he, too, was on his way south, back to New England.

I spent the next morning following Fletcher's orders to inventory, examine, remove, replace, and add items to the contents of our survival pack. The survival pack is a big orange sea-bag which will float, and in which the contents will stay dry no matter what. It contains food (hot cereal mix, canned sardines, canned bacon, etc.), fire items (waterproof matches, lighters, tinder, candles, etc.), pans, clothing, a tent, knives, emergency blankets, ropes and cords, flares, smoke bombs, distress signals, and a complete first-aid kit. While I did this, Daddy and Fletch borrowed a hand-cart from the harbormaster and walked into town. They returned a couple hours later with plenty of groceries and a few provisions, and it was time to go.

The Gulf of Alaska, First Leg

Our next stop was Elfin Cove, a tiny village about fifty miles out of Juneau. This was the last protected water on the very edge of the enormous crossing we faced. I intended to take a shower, find a good book, buy some chocolate bars with nuts and caramel, if possible, and walk around—on land, among green plants—all things I had been too busy to do in Juneau. I wanted to find a sturdy cottage and move into it, in Elfin Cove, build a nice fire and have a desk by a window, and sleep in a bed that didn't bounce unless I wanted it to. We tied up to the fuel dock, but when I walked out of the dock-side shower, it was time to depart. We entered the Gulf, traveling out from a shoreline of mountains that were nothing but granite and glaciers in a swirl of clouds.

I bundled up again and took my journal up on the bridge, but soon decided I wouldn't stay long. We had lost sight of land. It was lonesome. I wrote,

> The Gulf is nothing but ocean and sky. My voice travels nowhere in the fog. On damp paper my pencil marks show faint. I am insignificant.

> This place is indiscernible, fog touches water. In the bowels of our boat, combustion and machinery propel us forward, we skim along, churning up and down huge swells which are spaced far apart, and not too steep. Our smoke joins the fog and disappears.

I looked down. A living thing, a long-winged petrel, colored a deeper gray than the fog, skimmed over the water, just above it at a precise distance of about four inches. We traveled all afternoon, and then all night. For eighteen dreary hours, we slept, took turns manning the helm, and ate a little. We mostly ran out of things to say. Somewhere in the night we passed fairly close to Lituya Bay. I made instant soup as it was too rough to cook. At long last we rounded a headland and located a spot in Yakutat's small, scruffy, but safe harbor. We planned to stay the remainder of the day and one night and then leave early the following morning. We'd pull another all-nighter to reach Cape St. Elias on Kayak Island, near Prince William Sound.

Yakutat

We ended up waiting out the weather in Yakutat, staying that day and three more, getting to know the village and quite a few of its citizens and dogs, as well as our fellow travelers in the harbor. Yakutat has one main road, a café, a few bars, a grocery store, a general store, a hardware store, a post office, three churches, and two canneries on the waterfront. Our life there consisted of waiting and leisure.

I had always known that my parents hoped for a boy the third and final time my mother became pregnant, although I believed that once my father realized what he and I had in common he couldn't have wanted a more like-minded offspring. Our relationship consisted of my love for him, which I couldn't express without embarrassment on both our parts, and fishing. It was that which we shared in common. All my life we'd fished together, starting with lakes and streams in New Mexico, Colorado, and Montana. My avid desire was to be instructed in all the ways to catch a trout. Maybe it was hard for Daddy to get used to at first—a fishing daughter, a daughter who spurned all but running around the desert, mountains and woods on horseback or on foot. The boys and men of his Midwestern family hunted and fished and the women tended the home fires. But he had my mother, a Montana girl, to get him accustomed to the idea before I came along. Undoubtedly that was something that attracted him to her.

My father was a hunter and left with Mr. May and other friends each fall to kill a deer, elk, or turkey. That was his own world apart from his family, although we did accompany him when he hunted doves near Ambrosia Lake. I remember us all standing there with him on a cold, windy day covering our ears each time he shot into the sky, and Anne, about nine, curious about the preparations for and methods of bird hunting, asking earnestly, "When are you going to shoot one, Daddy?" He had laughed. Maybe his all-female family was a jinx on him that day. Hunting aside, I was a child after the heart of both my parents and I did not believe my father was disappointed I wasn't a boy, but of course that is not something that would ever come up between us.

Upon hearing from our harbor friends that dolly varden were in the bay, Daddy and I took the skiff and some poles and went fishing. We each caught two fat ones and I had one get away. As we cleaned them we watched curiously as an old wooden boat motored into the harbor, crunched up against the dock, and expelled a clan of seven boys and men all lurching on sea-legs, looking like they'd had a harrowing experience but game for more. Their boat looked like one we'd seen in the harbor in Juneau.

"Did you just get in?" Daddy asked.

"Yep, barely," the pirate-faced captain grunted. They began to unload seven bicycles that hung on all parts of the boat above the water line, along with various floats, pots, pans, poles, oars, and ropes.

"Where's your radar?" Fletch asked.

"We don't have radar," boasted the captain, mounting his bike. "That's why it took us so long."

"How in the world do you navigate?" I asked. He pointed to his ear with a wink that sent flakes of dirt and grime down his cheek.

"By the sound of breakers against the shoreline!" he said.

We watched them ride away and decided they'd be stopping by the café with stories to tell, so we walked into town. Any time we walked by, a crowd of friendly dogs joined us, tagging along happily, wagging their tails and frolicking together. The '64 earthquake hit Yakutat hard, uplifting parts of the inlet several feet so that now there was a picturesque scattering of rotting, yet still colorful wooden boats stranded in a reedy field between the harbor and town.

I was glad to be on land, or at least tied up in a harbor next to land. It rained most of the time, but I walked in the rain anyway, and if not, I was content to have a couple books to read that I got at the Senior Center for a quarter each. The weather on shore wasn't bad other than the rain, but out in the Gulf, winds twenty-five to forty knots blew over seventeen foot seas. Thirty-five knot winds or stronger are considered gales. Several other boats waited out the weather in the harbor with us.

I knew Yakutat was situated near the half-way point of the Fairweather Range. I'd heard the Fairweathers described as "one of the world's most stupendous chains of mountains." What I didn't know was the glory of that range, until the clouds finally blew away, revealing hundreds of miles of awesome sunlit peaks, diminishing in perspective up and down the Gulf Coast. Mount Fairweather: 15,300 feet. Hubbard: 15,015 feet. Alverstone: 14,565. Vancouver: 15,700. Augusta: 14,070. St. Elias: 18,008. And in between these, a hundred lesser peaks. The Northern Pacific gnaws at their feet, but the weather was clear, the ocean was not gnawing quite so hard on this day. I breathed deep, enjoying the brilliance of the sight before me. Our journey in sunshine could almost be pleasant, I thought. Except for the insecurity and basic fear.

Journal Entry:

> *Evening...*
> *Here we go. The weather reports are good so Fletcher up-and-decided we'd leave tonight. We're leaving Jim and Grady on the Lobster Yacht, the clan of pirates on the Ratter, the gregarious residents of Yakutat and all those happy, friendly dogs. I'm sorry to be leaving—I grew accustomed to living in the Yakutat harbor. The sky tonight is one color: infinite pretty blue. In it, serene clouds float about in puffy pastel colors. The Fairweather Range and Wrangell/St. Elias, 22 million acres of mountains, stands behind us and to starboard, as we travel west, lit as if from within. Malaspina Glacier, an amazing 35 miles wide, covering 1,500 square miles of earth, is just to our right. The ocean*

lies like silk, iridescent under a gentle breeze. From horizon
to horizon it reflects sky blue, silver-white, and pale gold.
We start a 24-hour run to Prince William Sound, which we
will hopefully reach by this time tomorrow night.

Prince William Sound, Thirty-two Hours Later

After thirty hours I began earnestly to conjure the reality of Cape St. Elias rising from out of the water, our Loran C reference point, our landmark, my hope. We'd long been out of sight of land. At last the Cape appeared, and it meant that within a few hours we would reach safety once more, in Prince William Sound. It took thirty-two hours of traveling, twenty-one of those over ten foot seas in twenty to twenty-five knot winds. For ten of those hours, from 6 p.m. to 4 a.m., we made only about fifty miles. I took helm duty from midnight to 2 a.m. That means sitting in the captain's seat, watching the Loran, watching the chart, making adjustments to the auto pilot if necessary, watching the radar, watching the compass, and watching out for logs. Fog enclosed us as we rode over twelve foot rollers, the line between sea and sky gone, a pure, featureless gray. I watched a pair of sooty petrels skimming inches over the water. At 2 a.m. as Fletch appeared to replace me, I crawled into bed, then awoke two hours later due to falling out of bed. I joined Fletch and Daddy. We were making only seven knots. We still had twenty-one hours to go.

The morning dawned clear and would have been pretty without the wind and challenging seas. *Fox Islander* fought through and over mountainous swells, steep-sided troughs, waves with vertical walls, turbulent white water. Over and over we took great slabs of green water over the bow which hit the deck with jarring force, flew onto the windows, obliterating the world, then washed away, leaving a view of another jade mountain or the bottom of another white-frothed trough. Fletcher was seasick most of the time. He had to lie on his stomach partway down in the bilge, swabbing water out of the battery compartment with a big sea sponge. I was just a little queasy. Daddy felt no ill effects at all. In fact, he was hungry. When it was mid-day again and he was on the helm he asked me to make him a sandwich, a chore that seemed so unlikely and out of place. As Fletcher ordered from his position on the floor, I tied a rope around myself, and lurched out the door onto the deck to where the cooler was tied down, and somehow made a sandwich for Daddy. He said it was good.

We traveled 223 miles from Yakutat to our anchorage in Port Etches on Hinchenbrook Island, Prince William Sound. As we pulled in behind the shelter of the island, the seas calmed. Three sea otters floated on their backs, watching us set the anchor, curious to see the new arrivals.

West of Prince William Sound

Here I am, on the bridge again, bundled up. (Not like at the beginning of the trip in Seattle when I wore shorts and a tank top.) It is the end of our voyage, and we have a nice day for it. Might even be warm, on land. It's around 6 a.m. We are traveling directly away from the rising sun, and I am facing backward, so the sun is shining on my face. I can view all the way we have come from here.

We should arrive Fox Island at around 5:00 this evening. After our long ordeal we slept in, then had a breakfast of pancakes, sausage and syrup. We each felt cheerful to have the 32-hour run behind us. Spent a leisurely day, traveling only about 20 miles, and going in on five or six beaches for beachcombing. Lots of stuff on those beaches on Montague Island. I found a glass float. We found an assortment of other floats, some dairy crates, a fancy boat hook, some rope, some lumber, and Fletcher found an enormous oblong black float about five feet long and covered with yellow netting, with some sort of light rigged on it.

When we get back, I plan to hug Tutka, then take a shower. I hope John has been taking good care of Tutka. I didn't like the way he called him an old fart bag.

End of a Voyage

When we at last rounded the point and entered our cove, happiness turned to dismay at the sight of a large Styrofoam and plywood dock floating in the quiet end of the cove. John met our skiff in front of our cabins. "Two old sourdoughs," he snorted. "Tough old fellow and his wife. Said they claimed their land around the time you did. They've got a cabin started. Friendly as hell!" Tutka ran to us, healthy, happy. I hugged and petted him, laughing at his joy, on the verge of tears from things I couldn't assimilate fast enough. Two white seagull feathers lay on the stones at my feet and I picked them up and stuck them in my braid. I looked toward the quiet end.

"You going to just stand there, Pocahontas, or help?" John said, throwing a duffel bag at me. I thought to whither him with a hateful look but I knew I was no match for him in this state. I hated it when he saw my emotions because that's when the insults started. I loaded myself up. *He* was to blame. He hadn't protected the place, obviously. I smiled and said loudly, standing there stupidly with a fifty-pound load of assorted bags, "Oh, it's good to be back."

"Shame about the neighbors, though," John said. "But you'll like 'em."

I turned and labored up the beach, my feet sinking into the stones under my load. They had every right to be there. But my cove, my beach! It wasn't exactly ownership I claimed, but rather I had been adopted by the silent trees, the mussel-covered boulders at the water's edge, the silver-gray tree roots that had torn free from somewhere and come to weather on our beach, making places for me to sit in their arms. The glades with slanting sunlight and wildflowers, shy maidens, trailing raspberry. All had spoken to me in voices that were inaudible but which held me, lovingly. My places said since I loved them so much, I was theirs and they were mine. Now someone had taken away some of my places. I felt too vulnerable. I returned for another load.

"I see you've got the shop finished," Fletch said approvingly. "Did we leave you with enough lumber?"

"Just right," said John.

"How'd it go with the Swansons?"

"They had a super time," John said. He laughed. "The whole

damn family got seasick as *hell*. Carl took them out to Johnstone Bay."

Fletch chuckled politely. "They had good fishing, though?"

"Oh yeah, did they ever. Made up for everything. Pocahontas here will be glad to know you're back just in time for the Pipe Fitters," he said, referring to the group of six men who had come out drunk one summer and returned the same way each summer since.

Oh, God, I thought. I need to run away, *right now*. I felt a short-circuit coming on. I *hated* John. He hadn't even given a proper greeting to Daddy, had just said, "Hello, grandpa! Welcome back to our island paradise! I thought you'd bring some hula girls!"

Once we'd hauled the skiff up he'd started unloading it like a fiend. A stupidly happy and insulting fiend. In no time we had all that was in the skiff stowed away and the three men went out to the *Fox Islander* for another load. I walked into the cabin with Tutka, stood by the sink looking out of the window at the new floating dock. Quiet inside, except for Tutka's claws clicking against the plank floor as he leapt in circles of joy. I let myself fall back onto the couch and gave him a proper scratching around the ears, talking to him to see his happy response. The blissful ignorance of dogs. After a while he lay down at my feet, flat on the floor, breathing a groan of contentment. I sat for a moment. Then I heard the scrape of the skiff on the beach again and thought of John's disapproval that I wasn't down there to meet them. Tutka jumped to his feet at my first movement and we went out the door.

Fletch and Daddy and I walked down to meet the new neighbors that evening. We learned that they also had a cabin on a lake somewhere north of Anchorage. I got the feeling their old place got too junked up and they'd been forced to move their whole summer-life to a brand new place. Their unfinished plywood cabin and the area around it was unbelievably cluttered. They'd tried to cover the various piles of equipment and furniture, lumber, and assorted items with clear plastic and a collection of ragged, rotting tarps.

Walking home from their place—they'd made us welcome with rickety lawn chairs pulled from piles, whiskey in Styrofoam cups— I made a quick adjustment. I liked Jack and Joan. I still felt bad. The Pipe Fitters were coming. We didn't have time to linger in

Seward the following morning, so the tanning bed was out. The best I could do was a long shower on the back deck of the sauna. And as soon as that group left, it was time for the next: my boss from Alaska Legal Services with his wife and the Chief Counsel with her husband.

Comings and Goings

I couldn't help but look up to my boss and my lawyer co-workers. They were educated and competent. Unlike me, they had real careers and made a living for themselves, dedicated to different things than beauty, places, and adventure, which were getting me nowhere. They made a difference for their clients, and worked on important cases. Made history, even. I felt I wasn't successful in my career at Legal Services, having quit, for one thing, and for having struggled with trying to fit myself into a life as a city-dwelling career woman. I worried that my partial success had to be evident to my boss and others. I was impressed by those around me whom I viewed as educated, accomplished, and socially competent *all* the time. It was a feeling very much like the envy I'd felt as a schoolgirl for "the popular kids," who thrived in a milieu beyond my ken.

Now my boss and co-workers would soon be visiting my realm on Fox Island. I worked around the place trying to ignore my nervousness, stomping around on the trails between the cabins, going about my work. Fletcher was in Seward and would be coming back with my *boss*. My attractive, competent boss, the Executive Director of Alaska Legal Services, and his assertive, competent lawyer wife. And the well-thought-of and beautiful Chief Council of Alaska Legal Services and her handsome, successful lawyer husband.

I did not say that I felt anxious, because I knew I was just as good as anybody and didn't need to feel nervous. So I wished it away and kept quiet. But the funny thing was, I noticed right away when they arrived that Fletcher seemed to be trying extra hard to impress them. *He* seemed nervous. *He must know how I feel*, I thought, *and he feels this on my behalf*. No, he didn't possess the obvious traits that demonstrated his feeling for me, but here he was, once again, proving my doubts wrong. We both wanted this to be an extra good trip.

The fact that it was a horrible trip wasn't because of the weather; the weather was fine: thin, high clouds, no wind, quite nice…but somehow lonely or indifferent, like the day held back and distanced itself from the hopes of the little people below. My boss and the rest of the group wanted to catch a few fish and see wildlife. Fletcher headed right over to one of the best fishing spots across the bay.

That day, there were no fish down there—not even one black bass. We usually could catch as many of those as we cared to tie hooks on the line. We went farther and farther, dropping anchor, pulling anchor, trying different spots, ranging farther yet. Of *course*, we had never, ever, ever *not* caught fish, and I knew that *of course* it was just a matter of time. At last we were far, far away, around Cape Aialik and into Aialik Bay, a four-hour ride from Fox Island, not something we usually did without planning for it, but such a trip was easier now with the new boat. Soon it was late afternoon on a hazy, glum, summer day and time to head back. My boss's wife had caught two palm-sized nearly-translucent flounders, delicate-looking, like something you'd get in a Japanese restaurant on a big white plate with a wobbly square of tofu, a little curl off a carrot and some green specks.

My boss caught an Irish Lord. Irish Lords are the ugliest, most hideous fish, prehistoric-looking, with bulging eyes, and even if they're only ten inches long, they have a mouth that can open up to the size of a large Florida grapefruit. They have a lot of teeth that point down their throat, and they're really, really ugly. They are packed full of bones, and they have stiff spines in their dorsal fin so that you have to carefully fold their fin down to get them off the hook, so the fin won't come back up and stab a row of holes in your hand. It's a good idea to don heavy rubber gloves before handling Irish Lords. I wondered who had something against Irish Lords when they named this fish.

As far as wildlife went that day, the residents of the fjords must have taken a day-long *siesta*, I guessed. The one bright spot was that we had been in front of the glacier when it groaned and calved off a huge berg, impressing our guests and creating a symphony of camera-clicks.

The trip back to the island seemed endless, as if we pushed through a bad dream. Riding beside Fletcher on the captain's seat, I stole a glance at our guests huddled on the red vinyl bench seat, gazing out the windows. They seemed happy enough, or was I just hoping? A couple hours ago, in front of the glacier, my boss's wife, her auburn hair wrapped in a red bandana and fire in her green eyes, had blurted out that she would be happy with a *waitressing* job if she could just do what I did during the summers. That made me feel good for myself but sad for my boss's wife. But then later, plowing through the heavy, jade-colored water of Resurrection Bay, I wondered if she still thought that way. What a disaster.

The end of this story is the beginning of many more. The Director and Chief Council of Alaska Legal Services and their spouses came out to Fox Island every summer after that, and always said they had a wonderful time that first visit. I had to wonder if my perception of the trip was affected by my anxiety and that maybe it hadn't been so bad. I only wondered this briefly, though, because truly, it was the only charter *ever* when we didn't catch one keepable fish or see some form of wildlife.

A week or so later, a family who called themselves "land-locked Norwegians" came from Wisconsin. We left Fox Island on a sunny and clear summer morning that made me want to sing real loud. The sea gurgled onto the beaches and against the cliff sides—a light, delicate lace that came and went, quiet and pretty. In the calmness, we were able to motor in close to Rugged Island and enjoy a long look at the sea lions which hauled out on the island's water-washed rock shelves. Fletch and I sat side-by-side on the flying bridge; Daddy and our guests stood on the spacious front deck.

"Did you say you're from Wisconsin?" Daddy said.

"Baraboo, up in the Wisconsin Dells area," said Chris Swanson.

"Sure I know where Baraboo is, I grew up in Madison!"

"You're kidding! My dad's from Madison!"

Fletch held the boat off the rocks. He occasionally moved it into reverse to keep the distance close but safe. I sat back, closed my eyes and listened to Wisconsin stories and our guests' delight at being so close to rambunctious wild creatures.

"He went to a one-room schoolhouse on the east side of town."

"Not the one out on Milwaukee street, is it?" asked Daddy.

"Don't tell me you went there? Did you know Einer Klepidall?"

"Well, sure I did!" Daddy said. "He was just a few years ahead of me. I knew all the Klepidalls!"

After watching the sea lions, we stopped to fish at a spot I hope Fletcher has kept secret. We put down halibut lines with a section of octopus tentacle on the hook. I watched from the bridge, ready to lend a hand or give advice if needed. "Fish on! Fish on!" shouted Mary Swanson, and as always, a pandemonium of excitement took place, enhanced—but also controlled masterfully—by Fletch, everyone happy and the boat rocking under the effort of the battle. When we could finally see the fish emerging into the lighter surface water after nearly half an hour, no one could believe how big it was. Fletch estimated it weighed close to 200 pounds.

This is how it goes with a big halibut: When someone gets one on, everyone else reels in their lines, because otherwise the big fish could tangle them up. When the fish was first sighted, Fletcher would go below and come back armed with a harpoon, sometimes two harpoons, and the .22 rifle. Whether this was as much for dramatic effect as it was out of necessity was never discussed between Fletch and me, but when I recall it, my memory winks back at me. To guests it was riveting. At last, when the fish was held on the surface, Fletcher, looking like Hemingway in his wool sweater, beard, and fisherman's cap, stepped onto the transom with one booted foot, reared back and then lunged forward expertly, thrusting the harpoon through the fish's head. A barb was released that prevented the point from coming back through. Then Fletch disengaged the harpoon pole from the line, handed off the pole, and depending on the capabilities of our guests, either handed the line to someone strong or tied it off on a cleat. The fish was usually thrashing, once again, but this would be its last powerful struggle. It would be bleeding into the green water. Fletch would then grab the .22 and shoot it in the head. The fish would be still. Fletch would throw a couple hitches of the harpoon line around the narrow spot where its body meets with its tail, bowing the fish to prevent any last thrashes once it had been hauled into the boat. The taut harpoon line is a handle used to haul the fish aboard.

Fletcher told a story about a man who was fishing alone in a skiff near Bear Glacier and had hooked into a big one. Though he'd thought he'd shot it dead, it thrashed violently when he brought it aboard, and as he tried to secure the harpoon rope around its tail, the harpoon tip gashed his leg, cutting an artery, and the man bled to death alone in his small skiff.

On the way back we found ourselves in the midst of three giant humpback whales. Fletch cut the engine and we bobbed and watched. A whale's breath startled us with a sudden, loud burst of vapor erupting just yards from us, like the sound, magnified many times, of someone pouring water from a bucket onto an overheated wood stove. Then its nearly black back rose slowly out of the sea, making an arc while at the same time traveling forward, and just as slowly slipped under, stunning everyone with this partial view's implication of the whale's full size. A moment later its tail, fifteen feet or so from tip to tip, black and dripping, rose out of the sea, first the part nearest the body, then finally the flukes lifting free of the water, dripping all along the edge, staying the longest in view, then slipping under without a sound.

Suddenly fifty feet away, a whale pirouetted straight up out of the water like a space shuttle, tipped sideways and landed full-length with a terrific splash. I'd witnessed this behavior before—humans call it "breaching." Fletch chuckled happily, letting the boat drift, and we were thrilled, as always, to see the giants and their antics, and delighted on behalf of our stunned guests. The whale did it again and then again as we watched. *It's the only time they experience gravity like we do*, I thought. All other times they're buoyed up. I wonder if it is as fun for them, experiencing above-the-surface gravity, as it is for us to snorkel? How far does he swim down in order to come straight up with that much force? I imagined him

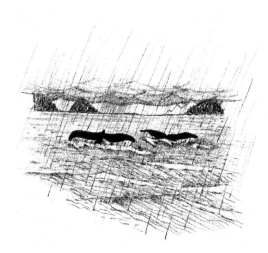

driving for the right depth, fifty fathoms, a hundred and fifty? And then turning nose-to-surface and fanning that tail hard enough to propel three-fourths of his fifty ton body free of the water and then tip, tip, tip, and KA-FLAM! He could just slip back more or less the way he came up, I thought. But no, he tips himself and goes crashing. Maybe he only does it to get rid of barnacles. But even if that is so, he still enjoys it, I was certain, like John leaning up against a spruce tree to scratch his back like a grizzly bear. Maybe they like to get a look around up here, too.

One final time, all together, the whales dove and several minutes later we heard their outbreathing quite a ways distant echoing down the bay.

We had *such* a dinner that night. Fletcher told story after story, and another about men halibut fishing. They were off Anchor Point, in Knik Arm. One had hooked into a big fish and it was just becoming visible under the water. "You got yourself a 'frigerator there, Frank!" That is fishermen's slang for a really big halibut because it's white, and heavy. Well, turns out he really *had* hooked a refrigerator! We got to laughing so hard, Fletcher had to get up and leave the table.

With Fletcher Away

Daddy had left to fish in other parts of Alaska, and Fletcher had gone to visit his mom and friends in Vermont. I missed him. It was the hottest day of the summer—seventy-five degrees. I worked at decking the shop walkway, wearing a baseball cap, shorts, a tee-shirt, boots, and a nail apron. In the evening, with the sun still high and hot, John, Carl Schuman, captain of the *Sea Chicken*, and I set off in the skiff to Bear Glacier to get some ice. We zipped along, flying over water flat and green as glass. We landed easily, and hauled the skiff above the high tide line. As we crested the beach, the area behind it was revealed to our eyes. It lay like a huge pasture of about fifty acres, in which herds of wild purple iris nodded their heads, and other wild flowers twinkled the colors of the rainbow in the tall grasses. Here and there a small group of young spruce and graceful white-bark birch trees, their leaves twirling in the breeze, sprang up out of the rich soil and seemed to be reaching for the heavens. All this was set against lofty, snow-veined mountains, dusky blue in color.

On an outcropping near the edge of the "pasture" a mother and baby mountain goat stepped out of the forest to watch us. Mountain goats are rectangular-looking animals. They have rectangular-shaped heads. Thick, wavy, long white hair hangs down from their straight backs to just a few inches above their black hooves, so that their shape, in general, is a rectangle. They have short curved black horns that go back from their head, their noses are a neat "V," and their teeth are very straight and even. I'm sure that since they are goats they have rectangular black pupils in their eyes.

The next day, another hot one, John and I left our lone guest, who had been brought out by *the Sea Chicken* the day before, happy with a book on a beach blanket, her baby and dog asleep beside her, and went off to explore. The other guests had gone fishing with Schuman. John and I hoped to climb the peninsula on the east side and look down into the neighboring fjord, Day Harbor, Schuman's destination for the day. John wanted to test his hand-held VHF by attempting to call Schuman. We cross-tied the skiff in a shallow cove and climbed upward, laboring over mossy boulders and through blueberry bushes and devil's club to what we hoped was the top of the ridge. Devil's club is a tall pithy plant with a straight stalk and huge leaves covered with innumerable fine spines. They stick in you by the thousands. The more furry animals can probably walk through them without problems, but I felt certain no creature could eat devils club. But then I thought of how rabbits and coyotes gnaw on prickly pear cactus in the desert, and I wasn't so sure.

The terrain was much too rugged—loose boulders under moss and fallen trees, all festooned with vigorous devils club—for us to get to a place where we could see into Day Harbor. John was still able to reach Schuman on the radio, so his mission was a success. I looked below into the deep green sea and saw a mysterious white cloud hovering in the water. We discovered when we returned to sea level that the "cloud" was a gathering of translucent white jellyfish, perhaps meeting in some mysterious annual event. We stared into the water amazed and mystified. It had been a lovely hike and it was good for John and me to do something together other than work. I had left old Tutka behind. He was fifteen years old now.

Fletcher called that night and was back from Vermont. He said he would pick up provisions and a hot water heater for the Woods cabin in Anchorage and drive John's truck down. But he called the next day to say he couldn't get John's truck going. I was disappointed and felt restless. I went down to visit Jack and Joan, our new neighbors, to get my mind off of it. Jack Marten was a bit paranoid, and sometimes when I went down to visit, I had to deal with something he suspected one of us of. But both were kind to me and always offered a lawn chair, coffee, whiskey, donuts, and whatever they had. Like most wilderness neighbors we helped each other out.

I had accepted their presence and come to like them, and though they had taken up residence in my world, it was distant enough. They weren't always on Fox Island. Still, when they were, I sadly missed being able to walk to the quiet end of the beach in solitude.

I came along the forest trail, which I had made when we built the Woods cabin, and which I liked to use sometimes instead of the beach to get to the quiet end of the cove. On the forest trail I was hidden. There were more boats plying the waters of Resurrection Bay now, and I valued being able to remain unseen. I entered the Martens' clearing and saw them sitting amidst all their junk. I said, "Jack, your propane tank is down by the tide line." He'd left it there and the tide was coming in. He barked, "That ain't your tank."

I said, "Well, yes, I know that, Jack, I just don't want to see it get washed away."

He grumbled and sat back. "I got plenty of time before it reaches the tank. Come and join us!" he demanded. "Git that chair from under the tree." Joan offered me a Styrofoam cup of whiskey, and we had an interesting conversation about porcupines and sharks and I listened as they told me the names of all the Steller's around their place. I named the jays at our place; probably the same ones, but the Martens had given them Spanish and French names—El Grande, Little Señorita, and Petit Cochon—that's French for waif-like pig. I tried and succeeded in not feeling possessive about the jays. The whole visit didn't take up enough waiting time, and it was now evening and Fletcher was still not back. Though it was late I went back to work on the shop walkway and deck, using treated two-by- sixes we had found on a beach. The small chainsaw didn't work so John had to cut some pieces for me with the big one. We worked together well into the night and got quite a bit of decking laid.

Fletcher still had not returned the following morning. Restless, I decided to work on the deck some more. John was asleep and as I needed his help with the chainsaw I stomped around on the rocks as loud as possible and finally began dragging two-by-sixes from under our cabin to the shop, making a racket on the rocks. Finally John woke and shouted his usual about what a great day it was, and was willing, as always, to get to work. He and I finished the deck and walkway by noon.

At last Fletcher returned and stepping out of the skiff gave me a quick hug and said, "It's time to go see if the reds are in!" This meant we had another adventure coming, and no guests for a while.

Red Salmon

On this trip we stayed at a public use cabin maintained by the National Park Service north of Coleman Bay, a sturdy cabin hidden in an alder grove. We awoke the next morning to see the fjord surfaced with small bergs. After loading our gear, we nudged our way through the three miles of tipping, clicking, sizzling bergs to Pedersen Glacier. Behind the boat we towed the aluminum skiff, and in the skiff we carried the red canoe, which in turn was full of fishing poles and gear for the day's expedition. Once we beached the skiff ashore, we hauled the canoe out of it. We dragged the canoe up over the beach. I never knew what I would see when we crested a beach. An abandoned camp? A mother and baby mountain goat? A lake full of driftwood? An ice-age pasture with woolly mammoths grazing in it? Behind this one was an eerie-looking lake, with one whole side right up against the glacier. With our two-horsepower outboard we motored slowly about in it for half the morning. The three of us and Tutka in the red canoe piled with gear and bristling with fishing poles would have made quite a sight if there had been anyone to see us. We had the world to ourselves. I would have pretended, had I been there alone, that I was in prehistory. And I would have been wary and watchful.

We fished and fished but caught nothing. When we got hungry, we beached the canoe on the lakeshore. After lunch, John lay back, wiggling himself a bed in the grass and fell asleep. Fletcher and I walked up the loveliest stream in a valley, its banks a bouquet of grasses, wildflowers, mosses, and lichens. The stream valley enchanted me but Fletch seemed hardly to notice it. In fact, he seemed distant since his return from Vermont. I tagged along after him like a happy little girl while he strode onward, looking to see if any salmon made their way up the stream. I wished he could be romantic—I had missed him so. I began feeling angry as I hurried to catch up.

Yes, I thought, he had said once or twice that he loved me; I knew this meant a lot coming from him. Still, I couldn't stop myself. I longed for more expression from him. Had he even said he'd missed me? I couldn't remember.

We walked long enough without talking that I had time to daydream a whole satisfying story of romance—with *someone*—on the moss-cushioned stream bank. Come to think of it, our lovemaking on the night of his return had been rather brief. And now, I felt myself to be on an adventure into the land of magic, and couldn't share the feeling. I complained silently, and without indulgence toward him, that he was there only for practical reasons. He had brought along tools to collect fish with, and planned to stay only the amount of time necessary, and do nothing other than what he had come to do. Not only that, this felt like a condensed version of my life with him. Was I just supposed to *infer* whatever he supposedly felt for me? Everything seemed rooted in practicality and business. It was maddening. A hug now and then, a word of praise, a public display of affection, was all I needed, or at least, would have gone far. I wasn't sure how long I could go on without the closeness I longed for.

This daydreaming to take my mind off the way things were with Fletch and me, or rather the way they weren't, now started to become a habit. I tried to ignore my desires, for with those thoughts I could sometimes feel ungrateful. On the other hand, I wondered whether I did myself a disservice feeling beholden to Fletcher. After all, I had given up my other life and now volunteered my labor, worrying at times over his dreams and the direction they would take. I knew my presence in his life enriched it, so why should I feel beholden? It was because of my gratefulness for being here, the pride I felt in the life I now led. I wouldn't have had any of that, if not for Fletch. I strove to be more acceptable to him and often felt I was failing. I began to fear that Fletch and I, in spite of all we had invested in each other, in spite of what we shared, were too different.

Finding no fish, we walked back to John and soon re-entered the silvery lake, and finally left by way of the lake's outlet stream through the beach at slack tide. Fletch then declared, to my delight and chagrin, that the next day would be a day of exploring for fun. I never thought that maybe he was in some kind of struggle to come back to the present from his trip to Vermont. I felt repentant for my anger. I remembered the way he had let me discover the new cove—with the black sand beach—in the new bay the time we'd walked across the peninsula at the narrow spot with Anne and Neal. I remembered how his eyes had twinkled then, and I wanted to hug him. But I didn't. In response he might only give me a pat or two on the back and loosen himself from the embrace. I just couldn't know.

We again threaded our way through bergs the next morning, this time to Aialik Glacier. Seals lay about on many of the larger bergs. When we approached, they looked up in big-eyed alarm and flipped over into the water. They watched us with just their heads out of the water, ready to slip back to their underworld. We came to a stop near the face of the glacier where Fletcher cut the motor. In the sudden quiet we heard the sound of millions of bergs dripping and popping. A huge slab of ice tilted out from the face of the glacier, sounds like rifle shots echoed off the mountains as it separated. The house-size chunk of ancient ice toppled with a great splash, but all the ice on the surface of the water dampened the waves so that our boat, the bergs, and the seals rose and fell gently, rose and fell, all together. We anchored near the side of the glacier, beached the skiff and walked like aliens from earth in a stark landscape among huge, blue bergs like sculptures slowly melting on the dark gray beach. Because the beach wasn't made of pebbles softened into

roundness by eons of surf, but of the sharp-angled gravel of ground-up mountains, it had a naked, savage look. A few feet away an animal, similar to a marmot, sat on a big berg. It had no fear of us.

Cormorant

I lay in bed asleep but was awakened by two ravens on a dead branch just beyond the window pane. One said, "WORK!" and the other nodded its whole body in agreement and said, "work, *work*." There *was* a lot to do that day. Fletcher had already left an hour earlier with a boatload of guests on a quest for big halibut. And though it was only six o'clock, it was already a sunny day with a slight breeze and sparkling water.

I was not fully awake as I walked down the path to John's cabin to see if he was ready to work. I'd had an unusual dream and was still pondering it. I had dreamt that I was confused and lost. A lot depended on my making good decisions, though I didn't know what the decisions concerned; I didn't even know which things needed decisions. I felt pressured and confounded, I didn't know which way to go, or who to talk to. Then the dream changed. I floated on my back in the silky waters of the cove, looking up into a soft, luminous, gray sky, serene and perceptive. I became aware that a black cormorant floated beside my head. I turned my head slightly and gazed at it. The graceful bird stayed near like this for a while, then it said, "*Always remember: there is a cormorant for everyone.*" And it flew away. I continued floating for a while longer until the raven said WORK.

I met John on the path between cabins. "I had the strangest dream," I said.

"Tell me all about it," he said, indulgent as he sometimes was.

Just as I finished, a jay flew out of a tree and landed on my head and stayed there. John and I looked into each other's eyes, delighted and amazed.

At last our final guests of the summer left, John went back to Oregon, and Fletcher was away in Seward. Schuman and his wife Sue stayed in the Woods cabin. In a few days we would ferry a group of kayakers to Holgate glacier, and then we wouldn't have any more charters until Labor Day, and after that we would close the place up for the winter.

Fletcher called and said he wouldn't be back until the following morning. I decided I had better get to work, getting Fox Island Lodge ready for winter.

Army Boats

With Fletcher away, and Schuman and the rest off on an adventure, I put Crosby, Stills and Nash in the battery-powered car stereo, and with a fire going and Tutka content on the floor in front of it, I sat down to do some bookkeeping. That's when things got weird. Two Army boats had entered the cove and as I did my paperwork, I kept track of them on and off. They were fishing.

The Army had a recreation facility in Seward and had begun renting out small boats to Army personnel from all over. When I went to get an envelope from the desk near the window, I saw one of the boats heading for the beach in front of our cabin. They came right up, so I went outside and down to the water's edge to help or whatever, but they pulled away from the beach and idled in the calm water a few yards from the beach. I said howdy and the guy said they were just looking. I waved an "okay" then headed up the beach back to the cabin, but on the way I heard the guy in the other boat over the P.A. say, "Is it a female? Is she alone? Did you see any others?" Wow, that was a weird thing to hear. My heart started pounding. I disconnected my music from the battery and connected the VHF and called them. Someone came on and said, "Fox Island Base, try channel 12, the Army channel," so I did. The guy said one of the boats was waiting to get a tow and he said, "You sure have a nice place there." I asked if anyone needed help but they didn't answer. I heard laughter coming from their boats—not over the radio. Then I called Fletcher but hadn't decided yet whether it was necessary to say anything, over the air, for all to hear. But then another Army boat showed up so I called for Fletcher again. We switched to another channel and I told him what happened, and he said to get the numbers of their boat. I looked with the binoculars, gave him the numbers, and he said he'd call me back. He called a few minutes later and said he had "taken care of the problem." I wasn't sure there was a problem but the more I thought about it the spookier it seemed. The way the guy asked if "It's a female" made me feel like a hunted animal.

The events that followed seemed strange. The Coast Guard came on and had a weird exchange with their mobile unit and then shifted to a secure channel. The *Salty 6* called me and I thought it was one of the Army boats but it was just Jamie, the pilot boat captain from Seward. Pilot boats help guide the big Japanese factory ships, which had become more common, and other big ships into the bay and harbor. Even Jamie's questions and conversation seemed to ask me to reveal a bit too much, about where Fletcher was, etc. Jamie's questions weren't related, but it seemed like they could be at the time, with my mind in the state it was. I handled everything calmly and logically, though. I never learned exactly what Fletcher had done to "solve the problem," but I figured he must have spoken with a few officers at the Army facility in Seward. Since he had been in the Army himself, he knew just who to talk to and how to put it. The Army boats had left and I was alone again. It was a weekend and I could see several boats farther out in the bay. My home on the beach felt exposed.

After I finished the bookkeeping, I got a harebrained idea to make a sail with spar and boom for the canoe, and sail around in the lake. I spent part of the afternoon on that. It didn't work but I ended up paddling all over the lake anyway, stopping to explore around the Marten's place now that they were gone. In the forest I picked a T-shirt full of plump blueberries and ate them all, also some salmon berries. I felt that end-of-the-summer feeling. One fat jay remained at the Marten's eating up a pile of cracked corn they had left. The jay followed me around for a while but then it had more important things to do and went back to the corn. I covered the Martens' canoe on the lakeshore with branches so it couldn't be seen, not that anyone would be there to see it, then paddled on home. I ate rice and smoked salmon for dinner, then read for a while and went to bed.

The next day, still alone, I repainted the seat in the outhouse, cut plywood to cover the unfinished interior walls in my studio, and caulked underneath to make it weather-proof for the winter. I neatened up the beach—it now looked like it should, as nature made it, with no clutter except for the lines out to our mooring buoy. We had a mooring for the skiff rigged up to a pulley on a float, which was anchored, so we could pull the skiff in when we needed it and pull it back out to its mooring from shore afterward. On the day the Martens left for good, Fletch and John had helped them pull their floating dock in. It was more or less hidden in the woods and now my cove looked like it used to look. It was a beautiful day. The sun set behind the mountain peak across the bay, and since it was now late in the season, I knew it wouldn't be coming back out on the other side again. It wouldn't be long until the first stars appeared again, and not long after that, the first snow would fall.

Last Days

I had a feeling the weather was changing, and it was a melancholy feeling. I could see haze at the end of the island, between the island and Calisto Point straight across Resurrection Bay. That's where we usually saw weather coming in. The wind was coming up. It would soon be time to pick up Mark Schultz after his kayak trip at Holgate Glacier. Then we would put the finishing touches on closing up the cabins. We would leave and go back to Seward, put the boat to rest for the winter, rouse the pickup truck from its slumber in the harbor parking lot, and return to Anchorage.

I had decided to return to New Mexico for a visit. I hadn't been home in over two years. I wanted to see my parents, my horse and dogs, and get together with old friends. I wanted to sleep in the desert where at night the Milky Way and constellations were a presence in the sky. I wanted to feel again the daytime and nighttime desert breezes on my skin.

Alaska Legal Services had agreed to hire me back. I felt good about that. I had to be back at work the day after returning from New Mexico.

I felt a flush of appreciation as I gazed out at the lake and

Mamanowatum, alive with new snow and the shadows of wind-blown clouds. There, in the cabin I'd helped to build, every window framed a scene of beauty. I was thankful for unspoiled wilderness, and thankful, too, that all the people would soon leave Resurrection Bay for the winter, leaving it to the animals. For the first time that summer I looked out and saw otters fishing in the lake. When people leave, the animals come around more.

I intended to accomplish a lot of work the next morning, but during my breakfast, a chorus of chirps interrupted my solitude. I thought, *Gee, that sounds like the land otters.* Leaving Tutka indoors, I tiptoed out the door and across the rocks, knelt behind a log, and watched as four otters, walking over the beach on their way to the lake slinked passed within a few feet of me. I stayed very quiet. In the lake the two adult otters dove for fish, brought their catch to the lakeshore, and shared it with the pups. Crunch, munch. I wondered when the pups would feed themselves. Soon, I figured, with winter coming on. After watching the otters until they click-clacked right past me again, I let Tutka out of the cabin and strolled down the beach with him, my thoughts of getting work done set aside for the moment. While I walked, I gazed at the pebbles that passed in a blur under my feet, all jumbled together, making patterns in the way they leaned up against each other. Lost in thought, I drifted to a stop, not really realizing it, and found that I was looking down at a small, flat rock that would take over my day. The upper length of it was curved exactly like an otter's back. I had just seen that curve on four otters, so I knew exactly how it was. I took that rock back to my studio, squeezed some paint onto my palette, and took up a small brush. After three hours I held my artwork in my palm. That morning I had spied on the otters, then I found this rock, and then I made it into a nearly perfect painting in my own studio by the lake. "The way a day otter be," I said to Tutka.

Too soon, it was the day to leave. We picked up the kayakers, returned with them to Seward, loaded the pickup truck and left Resurrection Bay behind. Before long the glorious fall colors in Turnagain Pass surrounded us, red and russet with slender, silver-white waterfalls cascading down narrow valleys still green, and a light dusting of snow on the mountain tips. We talked about the coming winter and plans for the next year. I tried to feel optimistic about Fletcher and me. Fletcher was glad I would be working at Alaska Legal Services again, and so was I. He made no mention of me teaching. We looked forward to dinner at a good restaurant once in a while, and cross-country skiing as soon as we got good snow.

7

Miles and Miles of Nothing But Miles and Miles

She was getting back to the earliest sources of gladness that she could remember. She had loved the sun, and the brilliant solitudes of sand and sun, long before these other things had come along to fasten themselves upon her and torment her.

–Willa Cather, *Song of the Lark*

Riding home from the Albuquerque airport with my mom and dad in their truck, the feeling of having come *Home* overwhelmed me, in a spiritual, inexplicable sense. It was more than recognition; it was being recognized. The vastness of land stretching to far horizons under a turquoise sky, the fall breezes, and the smell and taste of dust not only welcomed me, but claimed me with such joy, I never thought to resist. This reunion with a place: I'd felt it before, but not like this. *Perhaps, if I could tell Fletcher, and if he could understand!* But I feared he could never understand, and would not like it if I tried to tell him. He would feel threatened, as he seemed to be when I spoke of New Mexico. The conversation would go nowhere, and I could not share this with him. This being simultaneously claimed and set free was a private matter between me and a place.

"How does it feel to be home, Susie?" my mother asked.

"I can't even tell you. It feels so good."

"We're so glad you're here!" she said.

The McCoys let me borrow Gallup and Bo for a ride with Ned. It felt good to tug on my old riding boots again. Later, Katy and I took a hike from her parents' trailer in the Zuni Mountains. Over that week I decided to make some changes.

Katy had said, "Well if you're so worried what he'll do, why don't you just move back home?"

"I can't leave."

"You can't stay and you can't leave. And you come home to feel the same way about this," she said, encompassing the whole Zuni range with a gesture. "I'm glad *I* don't have that problem." She'd settled just seventy miles from her childhood home in the Zunis. I felt envy for her roots, her stability, her knowing she was where she wanted to be and would stay.

Ned had said, "Gosh, Susannah, it seems like you've put enough into his venture there, that you ought to just tell him he has to listen to you. Haven't you said anything?"

"He knows how I feel."

"Are you sure?"

"I'm not sure he knows everything, that I'm worried about our relationship, or how *much* I don't like the idea of expanding Fox Island Lodge. But he knows some. And I feel like a nag if I bring it up—an ungrateful nag."

"You're not, though! You have a right to a say! What's wrong with your relationship?"

"I'm too emotional. I'm too needy, basically. I guess," I said.

"What do you mean?"

"He doesn't always act like we're a couple. Like he pulls away if I try to hug him sometimes if there's other people around. And I've been unsatisfied a lot, if you know what I mean. Here's a weird thing. John's mom came out to visit this past summer. She's a little old lady with a bun. Like the kind that used to wear a bonnet, you know? She just stayed one day. We sat together on the beach couch. And you know what she said to me? I thought she's like this oracle that just appears and then leaves! Just out of the blue she said, 'How's your marital relations?' I said, 'Fine.' She said, 'That's good, because that's the cement in a marriage.' "

"Whoa. What did you think?"

"I thought, 'then we don't have much holding us together.' "

"Yeah, and were you thinking 'why is this marriage so *hard* if 'marital relations' are the *cement?*' "

"*Ha.* Well, we're not married, anyway, you know."

"Has he ever brought it up? Because I think by now I'd be worried if I was you if he's never brought it up."

My heart melted at the thought of Fletch. I thought of the times he had alluded to us getting married, the charming, uncertain ways he had approached it. I missed him, a lot.

"He sort of brings it up."

"But not really," said Ned. "He's always vague, or something."

"Well, I haven't exactly been sure about getting married anyway."

"To him?"

"To anyone."

"Oh, come *on*, Susannah."

"I like my freedom."

"So you're free? Do you like insecurity? What about a family someday?"

"Ned, you know me. I'm not domesticated, and I don't think ahead very well."

"You just worry ahead."

"Ha."

At dinner Daddy said, "You have to think of your future. What are you doing about security? You need savings! What about using your education?"

It was true. Although I contributed my own labor and income both on Fox Island and to our life in Anchorage, Fletch had the authority, and the life we had was his life. He owned the home, the land, the cabins, the business, the boats, the vehicles. Maybe it was time I began to feel I was due something. Maybe it was all right for me to have a say. I was tired of worrying about the direction he was taking Fox Island.

I said, "I've learned enough on Fox Island to be competent,"—and most important for me, I thought to myself, confident—"and I have a good winter job with a good salary, Daddy."

"Then you should be Fletch's *full partner*," he said. "In marriage, and in business. Both. You should be receiving an equal share in the business's assets and income in return, and it should be on paper."

Maybe Daddy was right. Fletch had been giving me a portion of the summer's income at his discretion more or less as though I were an employee. And here I had moved away from New Mexico. I had forgone a real career. I had given of my time and labor, and as much of my own income as I could spare over the past seven years. In other words, I had invested of myself. I loved our life in the wilderness as much as Fletch did, and it was a purer love. Daddy *was* right. I felt that now I could and should take equal part in the major decisions. I wasn't far from being able to run a lodge myself, except for not having a Captain's license. I had experience running both the big boat and the various skiffs, dories and dinghies, knew how to use the boat's equipment.

"I'm already planning that," I said, thinking on the spot, straightening my back. "I'm going to take the courses I need to get a Captain's license this fall. I'll be a more valuable partner."

I hoped that Fletch would see things my way and agree that my plan was good. If he didn't, then I would know I was at a milestone. I would have to make a decision about whether to go on participating at the same level as I had been, or give it up.

Mama and I were cleaning the dishes from the table when we heard a motorcycle pull up outside and then the sounds of footsteps. I answered the knock on the front door. Kevin stood there. "I heard you were home!" he said, with a huge smile. "And I want to know if you'll go for a ride!"

I stared at him. I looked past him at his bike. And then back to his eyes. "Do you have an extra helmet?" was the first thing I said directly to Kevin Martinez in years.

"I sure do!" he said.

I hadn't even thought much about Kevin in a long time, although occasionally I hadn't been able to help comparing him to Fletch. They couldn't have been more different. Kevin was a dreamer, a thinker, a lover, an adventurer, introspective and extroverted at the same time, and passionate. He read philosophy, the Bible, metaphysics. He brimmed with ideas and notions. And he was young. My role in his life had been as guide and protector.

Fletch, uncomplicated as they come, simply loved boats and the water, had business ambitions, told stories but never philosophized, cared about the issues affecting our world but never got worked up about them, read Tristan Jones and John D. McDonald novels, and was going to retire in a few years. On a winter's eve after work Kevin would be out volunteering at a homeless shelter or meeting with his intense friends at a coffee shop. Fletch would be meeting with his teacher buddies at the Long Branch Saloon and then coming home to watch a re-run on TV. My role in Fletch's life was as companion—he wanted someone with him on his sea adventures, and he needed my help to run the lodge. Kevin was more like me. But I didn't respect him like I did Fletch. I felt that in spite of everything that troubled me, in choosing Fletcher I had done well.

The pavement whizzed by below as sensations hit me: the smell of sage, a cold air pocket, the last rays of the sun on the mountain's crest, the warm leather of Kevin's jacket, a shift in his posture. With my arms around him, holding on, I became aware of my heart beat, a shortness of breath, mixed impulses for elation and caution. At last Kevin drove out onto the West Mesa, in time for twilight. Venus shone in the West where the sun had been, back when I'd sat at the dinner table with my parents. Birds roosted for the night in the cottonwoods along the river. Here on the mesa a few bats flew about. It was the magic hour, when you're not sure you're seeing everything that's there. Vapors rose from the earth, bringing forth sage-scent as I watched Kevin tearing dead limbs from living sagebrush for firewood. I sat on the Mexican blanket he'd dragged out of his saddlebags along with a bottle of wine and two clear plastic cups.

"Have you ever seen a scorpion?" I asked.

"I never have. I saw a tarantula once."

"What'd you do?"

"Nuthin. Why, would you have killed it?"

"I guess I wouldn't," I said.

"If I planned to be where it was I might kill it, if it was in the shed or around here, right now," he said. "But then again, I might not. I might just keep an eye out for it. I heard they're not as bad as people say."

On the blanket I rested back and watched the changes to the panorama before me, the Sandias turning dark pink before receding into the night. *This is just an outing. We'll enjoy catching up*, I said to myself, watching him scrape a bare spot for the fire with his beat-up boots. Turning, I could barely see Mt. Taylor's silhouette, sixty miles distant, and thought of my childhood home there. Near the horizon strands of cloud, like embers, glowed pink and gold. I watched Kevin strike a match to a handful of dry grass he'd stuffed into the gnarled sage, creating incense as the flame took hold. *I walk in beauty*, the Navajo song said. My eyes stung from pure gratefulness. I thought, *He belongs to this.* I watched the smoke rise into the sky. *I belong to this*, I said to myself.

As the fire grew bright and robust, we talked and watched the last colors fade from the Sandias. Sparks of fire flared orange, made tracks in the blue air, and died. Constellations appeared, the Scorpion, the Little Dipper. The steady light of the North Star reminded me of Fletch. I thought of Mt. Taylor and of my red sleeping bag on the green grass of our backyard. I thought of Qolus, wife of Thunderbird. I thought of my horse, who was getting old. Then, settling beside me, taking my hand in his, Kevin said, "Susannah, do you know something?"

I did not take my hand away from the heat of his, but I gazed off at the array of tower lights along the crest of the Sandias that now shone, from this distance, like a string of jewels suspended in the universe.

"Susannah, in the years we've been apart, I haven't formed one meaningful bond with a woman, do you know that? Not anything anywhere close to what you and I had. There's no one else like you." I stayed silent, looking away. His voice came low and gruff, like it was anger he felt, so intense it was almost threatening. "You're a standard no one can match."

His words left me with nothing to say. Even though he sounded angry, he hadn't let my hand go. He began telling me the things about myself that he valued, aspects of me he said he loved. I believed they were all qualities Fletch never noticed or appreciated.

Not just Kevin, not just his proximity and voice and words, not just my needs, but everything about being home seduced me at last into his arms. And afterward, still cradled there, his voice in my ear murmuring words of love, regret washed over me, like surf claiming a starving seal pup on a beach.

Love Hurts

The things that were really hers separated themselves from the rest. Her ideas were simplified, became sharper and clearer. She felt united and strong.

–Willa Cather, *Song of the Lark*

I flew back to Alaska the next day, having fashioned a determination. I looked out of the airplane window at the tops of thunderheads, bright and billowy, reached into my pack and took out my journal. A mish-mash of memories from the past seven years came, recalled incidents such as the bonfires Fletch and John built on Fox Island to burn garbage and extraneous stuff from blocks of old Styrofoam to empty plastic oil cans, and the poisonous smoke it caused. I had protested each time. Why did he persist? I thought of the time several of us, Fletch and Neal and a group of guests, stood on the beach drinking beer while the crab boiled. I had put my arm around Fletch's waist and he'd casually pulled away. Why? How, exactly, did he feel about me? I never could tell if he was just uncomfortable with public displays of affection or if somehow, I had disappointed him. I thought about the time we caught a strange creature in a crab pot that none of us had seen the likes of before. It was crab-like, but small, with a thick, leathery "cap" or carapace upon its back that held an odd pattern, like a hand print. Fletch had reached for his knife and dug into this leathery mass, probing, investigating, learning nothing, and tossed the creature back to live or die. What did he see as my role in his life? I needed to know where I stood with him. I wanted a say in our business. I didn't want it to go the direction he was taking it. I looked down on the barren landscape of northwestern New Mexico and thought about making Fox Island a haven for writers and artists, maybe a place for seminars and retreats. I didn't mind the idea of continuing to run charters as we did—the majority of the people we had out were regulars that came every summer and, with a few exceptions, I anticipated each visit with pleasure. We'd had some environmental education camps on Fox Island the past summer, which I had arranged through an organization in Anchorage. I wanted to do more of this, and more work with children. I would get directly involved in all aspects of this myself. I had already decided to study for my Captain's license that winter in Anchorage, so I could drive the boat sometimes, without Fletch on board. Give him a break, be more useful than ever. Then maybe he wouldn't have to hire another boat driver. I thought about getting college kids to come and help in the summer, in exchange for room and board, so we didn't have to work so hard. Fletch and I would have more time together. And little things. Sometimes whales don't mind if you come close. You can come almost close enough to reach down and touch them, and they go about their business. Other times, they move away when boats approach. They don't want you to be close. When we saw whales, I wanted Fletch to be aware of this, and stay at a respectable distance, and not participate in surrounding them along with the other boats. The practice had become for a boat captain to announce the presence of whales over the radio and then a whole flotilla would hone in on them. I was uncomfortable with this. I didn't want Fletch to allow guests to feed bait herring to the sea lions on Rugged Island. To me, this was asking for trouble, for the sea lions. I wanted Fox Island to be a beacon, and example for other tour companies, of which there were beginning to be many. I felt that I could accept one more guest cabin, and no more. And, I wanted to be a partner, not an employee.

If Fletch loved me, he would ask me to marry him. And, I said to myself, looking down on Utah, if he asks me, I will.

Further, he must recognize that we needed to be able to discuss important matters. I didn't think a marriage could work if the two partners didn't communicate, as difficult as it may be at times. And last, I would bring up the idea again that he had once proposed: that we spend part of the year in New Mexico.

I returned with an uncontainable passion for my ideas that overwhelmed Fletch and only served to unnerve him. I made an effort to rein myself in, sound reasonable.

"How about if I get a Captain's license this winter so you don't have to work so hard?" I said.

Fletch said he wanted things to stay as they were. He said John was at this moment in the process of getting his Captain's license in Astoria. He said he and John were going in on another boat, which John would captain next summer. He and John already had it all figured out. He just didn't know about my ideas. It was too much. What did I mean? He suggested that I try again to find a teaching job. He didn't want to talk about New Mexico.

"Don't stay if you don't want to," he said.

I felt miserable, guilty, and confused.

Kevin, meanwhile, wrote to say he thought we might get back together: that I might come back home. His letter had the same angry tone I had experienced from him in New Mexico. He asked, "Didn't you feel that way too?" I wrote back saying no, I hadn't. I had felt a lot, but no, I hadn't felt that. I said I was trying to save something here in the North. I tried to spare his feelings. But he turned vengeful. Furious with what he thought was rejection, he wrote a scathing letter. I came home from work one day to find Fletcher reading it. He knew everything. He said, "Sounds like your old boyfriend must still have a thing for you." I opened the wood stove, dropped the letter into the flames. Nothing more was said.

It was a time of endings and uncertain beginnings. In January, Anne and Neal divorced. There had been trouble, but I had thought they'd worked it out. I remembered Neal's belligerence when he drank, which apparently, especially in winter, was too often. Anne was the type of person who didn't take any nonsense from anyone, not like some women, I thought, who just hang in there spending most of their time wondering if they should or not. When it was all over, Neal had their house in Anchorage, and Anne, their cabin in Homer.

It had snowed all night and was still snowing. Fletch called me at work from school. "Let's go to the Park's Roadhouse tonight."

"Oh, good!" I said. "It'll be a nice break."

"Fine. I've got some skis here at school I think you'll like to try. Bring your skis too and pack our 'gaiters. The snow's pretty deep. Bring the camera. Get the other stuff together and we'll leave as soon as I get done with the ski meet, around 7:00."

"Okay."

"I sure do love you."

"Oh, Fletch, I love you too!"

Then, in February at Anne's cabin in Homer, with snow falling and another ski trip about to begin, Anne asked me if I thought I might like to own our parents' house in Placitas some day. I had lost all the confidence with which I had returned from New Mexico. That confidence now seemed altogether false, in retrospect. I couldn't conceive of owning a house, or of my parents *not* owning the house, but I said, "Well, yeah, I guess, why?"

"Mama called me last night," she said. Then, sparing no words, she continued, "Mama and Daddy are getting a divorce."

My bearings were slipping away: my parents separated, my home in New Mexico gone. They had been married, quite happily, everyone thought, including themselves, for thirty-two years. What would they do with my horse? Where did I belong? Who did I think I was, bombasting Fletch with complaints, anyway? What had I done?

Soon after, my mother called to say that Trinket, my horse, was on her last legs. My mother and father were in the process of moving away from the house and from each other, and she didn't know what to do. She wanted to have a veterinarian give Trinket a shot— "to put her away"—and then have the vet haul away Trinket's body. I was afraid Trinket would then end up as pet food and this about killed me. I reminded myself that Mama loved Trinket as much as I did, but that she had been raised on a hardscrabble farm in Montana, and could be awfully practical about death sometimes. I also knew my mother could be, at the same time, sentimental about the death of a dear animal, and would think she couldn't bear to do what I was about to ask, no, not ask, *tell* her she must do. I was afraid to say what I wanted, still reeling from the terrible results of my recent

256   *Susan D. Roebuck*

assertions to Fletch, but here the necessity to assert myself came again, so soon on the heels of a disaster. I said I wanted her and Daddy to find someone to dig a big hole with a backhoe, have the vet come out and put Trinket to sleep, and bury her there, in Placitas.

No one I knew in Alaska had any advice about what to do with a dead horse. I knew that I was asking my parents for a lot at this trying time, but I stuck to my guns.

It turned out that the man who dug Trinket's grave was a man Trinket and I had had an altercation with a few years before. I used to like to get on Trinket sometimes and explore all around Placitas, including other people's land and property. None of the land around there was fenced, and people's homes were few and far between, so if I was quiet and stealthy, I could see all kinds of interesting and thought-provoking sights. Once, I saw a big barn full of grow lights and marijuana plants. I saw wigwams, hogans, homes in the ground, grand, colonial *haciendas*, teepees. I saw the remnants of several communes from the '60s and '70s, including a valley of about fifty domes. One was made out of car hoods. I saw someone's yard full of rusted automobiles with cats slipping in and out and pens of plywood and wire for fighting roosters. I saw lots of dogs before they saw me, but this time I hadn't seen the dog—a big German Shepherd. My dog Sara had run right up to it, and it was furious. Fortunately, Sara made up in speed what she lacked in good sense and away they went. Next, just like the dog, the owner came dashing out of his house, which had clear plastic sheeting for windows. Instead of barking, the man was yelling. He said, "Get that goddamned horse off my property! Don't you know goddamn horses tear up the land!"

In response, Trinket began pawing the dirt. I was sort of speechless and didn't go anywhere, since he was walking toward me and it would seem rude or cowardly to ride off. As he strode toward me, shirtless, and I sat on Trinket while she pawed the ground, I thought to apologize, diffuse, disarm, charm, or *something*, but he was a very frightening man. He had blue eyes with the whites showing all the way around the iris. He was tall with a strong build and had brown curly hair and a mustache and was extremely good-looking.

"Look at the damn beast!" he roared as he got near me. "She's tearing up my land! What the hell are you doing here! Who are you? Where did you come from?"

All my unformed thoughts about what charming disarming things I would say remained unformed. I sat there stupidly for a moment and then I simply said, "I am very sorry sir, I won't come around again." And kicked Trinket into a gallop.

I later learned that his name was Morgan, and that he was a friend of some neighbors down the road. He had told them about the incident with me, and they had apparently said I was a very nice girl because he made a point later of apologizing to me. Later, when I found out he was a backhoe operator, I found it ironic that he had been so concerned about my horse "tearing up the land." Anyway, it was he whom my parents found to dig Trinket's grave, and he did so without asking for pay. About a year later he himself was killed in an accident with his backhoe.

At the same time that all this was going on, Tutka was nearing the end of his life, too. He still liked to go on walks as much as ever, we just couldn't go far. He lay around most of the time, his tail still thumped against the floor the instant I said anything to him and often if I just walked past. He still loved to lay his head on my lap or on Fletch's as we sat on the couch in the evenings watching television. Somehow Fletch and I had grown closer, as if we'd thrown up our hands at trying to work anything out and had just fallen back on pure comfort, in each other's company, in the exhilaration of skiing together through snowy woods. We never again discussed the episode with Kevin, or the ideas with which I'd returned from New Mexico. Tutka seemed a sad symbol to me now. Weakened, yet full of love for us both, he seemed vulnerable and dependant on us, and on our union. I wondered what else hinged on us.

As the days became longer in late winter, we planned our first spring trip to Fox Island in months. As always, Tutka came with us. That morning we made a comfortable bed for him in the back of the pickup for the drive to Seward. We opened the window between the cab and the camper shell and turned the heater up to keep him warm. But something happened to Tutka on the way to Seward. When we arrived, he could only raise his head and weakly wag his tail. After a while, he managed to stand up, but he could barely walk. Fletch lifted him out of the back of the pickup. We made our way down the ramp into the harbor and along the dock to the boat, with Tutka stumbling along with all his effort. Fletcher lifted him into the boat. Two mornings later, I turned to my journal:

> Morning.
> I am alone on Fox Island, alone with Tutka who is dying. He cannot get up or even move. He hasn't eaten in two days. He lies by the wood stove breathing heavily.
> Fletcher is in the cove now, pulling anchor to take some friends back to Seward. It is an early spring day of intermittent snow and weak sunlight, about 30 degrees. Tutka seems to want to move, but the life is going out of him. Fletcher and the rest are cruising away now, disappearing into the mist and snow. I feel profoundly sad here with dear, sick, Tutka.
>
> 2:00 p.m.
> Tutka died. As I sat beside him, stroking his fur, he breathed deeply several times, and then his heart stopped. For a while his reflexes told him to breathe, but no air was taken in. At last a faint tremor moved over his body, but by then I think he had died.
> To be honest, this is the way I had hoped it would be. On Fox Island, not in a vet's sterile room, and no pain. I hope I go like Tutka did, here, or another place I love so much. His body is so still now and so curiously heavy. It seems life makes us lighter.
> Weak sunlight reflects off the water, the waves gently break along the beach and two cormorants glide on the surface of the cove.

Fletcher returned. He knelt beside Tutka, stroking him. "Good dog, good dog," he said. I couldn't see.

"I'll take him out and bury him at sea," Fletch said. "I'll need to get a few things first. Then you can help me carry him down to the dory."

I had laid Tutka on a white sheet, and together we gathered it up and carried him to the dory, slipping on the icy rocks. The wind blew in gusts and lulls, snowflakes floated down. He was gone a long time. After a while I worried about him far away in the dory; he seemed to be gone so long, and he had gone out of sight. But then he made his way back. I met him at the water's edge. He got out of the dory, held me for a long moment, and said in a choked voice, "He sure was a good dog, wasn't he?"

"Yes." I had never seen Fletch cry.

"Let's get this boat pulled up," he said, and struggling together we hauled the dory up the icy beach and tied it to a tree.

It was hard to fathom that something living was now gone. Tutka with his handsome brown and navy blue eyes had always been a part of my life in Alaska. He had been with us since the first summer Fletcher and I met and headed down the Kenai Peninsula to run charters in Kachemak Bay. What happens with the pure and good energy of such a life when it no longer exists? Does it go into a puppy ready to give and receive love anew? Tutka was loyal, always ready to at least flick his tail a time or two. He was playful and smart and had no faults.

The next evening as Fletch lay napping on the couch, I sat at the table, writing in my journal.

> *I feel so sad without Tutka. I wish there could be a sign from him that he left knowing of my love and that he—well, that he is. I can't fathom that he isn't. I do hope to go as he did: after a long, happy, well-fed, and adventurous life. At last, then, two and a half days of utter weariness, in some way aware of getting to this place, Fox Island, once again, in the pick-up truck, then by boat, and then lying, as always, in front of the wood stove. Sure he was sick. It wasn't like he was feeling good. He felt about ready to die. That's how I guess one feels when one is about to die. But that's death. Life is long and death is only a short and instant part of life. Gosh, oh gosh, I miss him so.*

> *I will not cry and go off to bed to lie thinking sad thoughts. I will think about love, here on Fox Island. Even with this grief, it has meant so much to be out here with Fletcher.*

The wilderness way of life comes back to us so quickly and seems to make more sense than anything else. I love being in the midst of beauty. The fresh air and the work build my strength: hauling, sawing, hammering, lifting, laboring. I already feel stronger. My job in town seems remote, like a part I play.

Out here there is work, real work, to do. There are projects to start and birds to look up in the bird book. There are creative decisions of high significance, and there is sunlight through the fog over Bear Glacier, drumming the water gold. There's the consideration, planning, and carrying-out of a bath in front of the wood stove, and over by the Middle cabin, there's the red-stemmed rhubarb already coming up through the fallen foliage of last year's plants.

Death is a definition of life, and grief is the affirmation of love.

Alone on Fox Island, we came to each other for comfort. Nailing wainscoting to the wall of my studio, I looked over at him, and saw tears again, and felt our grief on us like a velvet cloak, so beautiful, but so heavy. Fletcher stood and enveloped me in his arms. We stood together, saying nothing. Outside in the cold, putting up a new fish-hanging pole between the dead trees, we laughed at ourselves, me perched high in the tree and him trying to balance the heavy cross pole vertically to hand it up.

"Should we tie a rope on it and hoist it up?" he said.

"No, I can grab it!" I said, clinging there, reaching and laughing. Then, "Wait," I said, "let's put a rope around one end and try hoisting it up."

"Susannah, sometimes you surprise me with your good ideas," he teased.

Mongrel

A puppy dog without a collar
Annexed me on my evening walk;
His coat suggested fleas and squalor,
His tail had never known a dock.
So humble, trusting, wistful was he,
I gave his head a cautious pat,
Then I regretted it because he
Accompanied me to my door-mat.

And there with morning milk I found him,
Where he had slumbered all the night;
I could not with displeasure hound him,
So wonderful was his delight.
And so with him I shared my porridge—
Oh! How voraciously he ate!
And then I had the woeful courage
To thrust him through the garden gate.

But there all morning long he waited;
I had to sneak out by the back.
To hurt his feelings how I hated,

Yet somehow he got on my track.
For down the road he sudden saw me
And though in trees I tried to hide,
How pantingly he sought to paw me,
And yelped with rapture by my side.

Poor dirty dog! I should have coshed him,
But after all 'twas not his fault;
And so I took him home and washed him,
—I'm that soft-hearted kind of dolt.
But then he looked so sadly thinner,
Though speckless clean and airy bright,
I had to buck him up with dinner
And keep him for another night.

And now he is a household fixture
And never wants to leave my side;
A doggy dog, a mongrel mixture,
I couldn't lose him if I tried.
His tail undocked is one wild wiggle,
His heaven is my happy nod;
His life is one ecstatic wriggle,
And I'm his God.

–Robert Service

Harbinger

Spring—or at least its whispered promise—suffused the air. On my walks along muddy roads I noticed little green plants coming up and watched geese flying overhead in exuberant migration. The snow began to melt, and the paved roads became bare and warm. Even our driveway melted, but the snow hill the snowplow made in our yard was still nine feet tall. I had been watching it. It was down from twelve feet just a week before. I took walks knowing that soon I could explore again many more places around the foothills near our house. Not soon enough, but soon. I would be quitting my job again, and I had less than a month of work left. I was weary of winter, of the gray snow lining the roadways pocked with road grime and debris. Weary of city life, of traffic, of the false world of television, of dressed-up women shopping in Nordstrom where I sometimes went for lunch on gray, dark days. I was weary of the frigid winds that blew off Cook Inlet into the downtown streets of Anchorage, blowing trash, of the panhandlers, misplaced Alaska Natives, so sad to me with their red eyes, dirty hair, and pitiful stories. I wanted nothing more than to labor again in the oxygen-rich wilderness.

A long and loud boat ride took us and our first group of 1988 to lonesome Johnstone Bay. Johnstone is a wide bay open and exposed to the Gulf of Alaska. I always found it to be a lonely, ominous location. It got tiresome riding on the swells and staring at the horizon trying to keep seasickness away. We anchored, and I brought out my favorite fishing pole, a strong, stubby old pole made of translucent green material. I stuck a herring on my hook and out it spun, down and down, to the bottom—*thunk*. Time to wait. I headed below to get the thermos and coffee cups. But as I turned away— BANG!—my pole flew out of the boat, taking with it the pole holder and six 2-1/2 inch marine-grade stainless steel screws. I ran to the side to see my fishing pole trailing white bubbles as it raced into the depths.

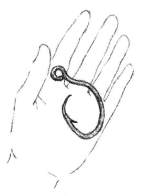

We all just stood there astonished. It was a disaster small in scale. In a big disaster, I'd hoped, upon hearing the news, that somehow the crew of the Challenger had ejected and would be found alive floating in the ocean. Now I had a similar thought—that maybe my pole would bob up somewhere—and I searched the water's surface. But no, that was the end of it. I had tightened the drag down the night before, as usual before stowing the poles, had tightened it down very hard, apparently, and just a moment ago I had forgotten to loosen it. It wasn't because it was my favorite pole that I was sad. It was the thought of what took the bait. It must have been a shark, or a porpoise, something powerful that could swim extremely fast. Something that now had a steel hook the size of my palm in its mouth, attached to hundreds of feet of unbreakable mono-filament line.

The incident weighed on me. On the remote beaches I was always careful to gather up fishing line and the netting that commercial fishermen lose at sea. I gathered up a few plastic bottles, although there were sometimes thousands in the beach-back lakes. I tried to educate people not to feed sea lions or close in on whales. I required guests not to throw cigarette butts or foam cups overboard and not to build fires on our beach except in the two fire pits, and to use driftwood and not the dead trees that eagles, ravens and jays perched in. I went to the trouble to save aluminum cans to be taken to Seward, the only items which at that time were collected for recycling.

But, as more people came to enjoy the fjords, the changes in Resurrection Bay had gradually become more noticeable. I had been there when I saw no other boats, no humans, for days on end. Now I made a habit of walking the beach a few times each summer to pick up Styrofoam cups, cigarette butts, plastic bottles and bags that floated onto it. I remembered the first summer when there were seals in the cove. Seals tend to be more shy of humans than sea lions, and I seldom saw them in Resurrection Bay now. I heard of a man getting pulled off his boat in the Kodiak harbor by a sea lion insisting on a hand out. It could happen in Seward, and then sea lions would be blamed for behavior that is only natural and for bad habits that could have been prevented but for the ignorance of humans. I constantly worried that people just didn't seem to know any better. Maybe they lacked experience or education, or maybe the fjords just seemed too vast, too grand, to be changed by human use. More likely, they simply didn't notice the changes, or possibly— but it was hard to believe—some of them didn't care. One of the great pleasures in my life on Fox Island was seeing the joy and wonder on people's faces, seeing their enjoyment of life during the time they were out there. It happened every time: the time off from work, the beauty, the fresh air, the adventure gave their eyes a spark, brought smiles, even rosy cheeks; they laughed and played. I tried in some way, with everyone, to help people understand and appreciate their part in it all.

The View from Here

Warm winds blew as I awoke on the longest day of the year. I came downstairs and looked out of the window that faced the lake, the window where I stood when I did the dishes. I could see the alders near the top of the island blowing; the whole peak covered in silver-green ripples, and above the blowing alders in the blue of the sky, three eagles soared in the current. I let my gaze drift down from the peak and into the forest just outside my window. In dappled sunlight and shade, wild geraniums bloomed blue, and the delicate white blossoms of dogwood, starflower, and shy maidens dotted the forest floor. Trailing raspberries glowed magenta, and chocolate lilies blossomed a deep purple-brown in the shadows. My prism in the window made rainbow sparks across the cabin wall in the morning sunlight, and I decided to take a hike. John had just completed roughing out the last length of the hiking trail I had started to the top of the island.

The trail was only a bit over a mile long, but rose 1,210 feet to Fox Island's middle peak. The first half, behind the lake, traversed over boulders overlain with moss and logs and forest decay through a dark spruce forest. Then it rose steeply under stately old spruce, whose boughs filtered out sunlight, and then through blueberry thickets, on up to the ridge. This spot was the low point in the U-shaped contour that framed Mamamowatum beyond. From the ridge I could gaze across to Mamamowatum, or look down onto Fox Island Spit, a bar that extended from Fox Island, covered with dead trees, and containing within its narrowness a tidal lagoon. Rockwell Kent had painted this very same view from this same spot. From this place, one turns right and follows the trail along the edge as it rises even more steeply over unstable rocky talus slopes covered over with alder and devil's club.

Even with the trail, the going was rough, but I was strong. I felt as vital and expectant and full of life as Robin Hood in the Sherwood Forest. I carried a bow saw and pruning clippers. At last, having worked on the new trail all the way, and having finally completed it so that anyone could now make their way without losing the trail, I topped out on the summit. I was on a grassy knoll, on the very tip-top of the peak, surrounded by alder forest just below eye-level. I turned slowly, taking in a 360-degree view of fjords, mountains, glaciers, and ocean. I breathed deep, laughed like a child. I wanted to bend my knees, push off the ground, spring up and be airborne. Like the eagles I would fly in big ascending circles while I decided where to go. I could go to Mamanowatum, land on her snowy summit, and if I wanted, I could go beyond Mamanowatum.

The view made me recall a horseback ride I'd taken when I was eleven. On a morning before school, in a place so different from where I found myself now, my mother surprised me. "Susie, would you like to stay home from school today?"

"But I'm not sick!"

"I know, you can take the day off from school if you want."

"Can I go riding?"

"Sure!"

Can you just imagine the joy I felt? Mama packed me a lunch and I walked the half mile to Trinket's corral. Since I had all day, I decided to take a long ride, to a place I'd never been. I decided to find my way to the top of Grants Mesa. Grants Mesa is a lava flow from Mt. Taylor, which is an old volcano that stands 10,020 feet. Mt. Taylor's Navajo name is "Blue Bead Mountain." It is one of four sacred boundary markers of the Navajo's ancient world. On that cold/warm spring day, Trinket and I had the whole wide world to ourselves as we made our way up the side of Grants Mesa. Everyone else was in school! But not me!

The most difficult part of the journey was finding a passage through the "cap rock," which is a formation on lava flows that forms cliffs along the top of the flow. But I had seen a place from below that had looked to me like a gap in the black cliffs, and this turned out to be right. I rode up through the gap, Trinket bounding upward, as she loved to do, and suddenly found myself on a straw-colored mesa-top prairie. The prairie was flat as a table, many miles long, and about a half mile wide, dropping off sheer on both sides. Lengthwise, on the distant far end, Old Highway 66 passed by on its way to Gallup. On my end the mesa rose to the flanks of Mt. Taylor. I turned Trinket around and looked down on Grants. I could see Mt. Taylor Elementary School, and boy did I feel great knowing I wasn't in school that day. I, alone out of all, was on top of the world! Under a brilliant sky, I galloped across the mesa with the wind blowing my long hair, and making amber waves in the prairie. On the other side I looked out over "miles and miles of nothing but miles and miles," as the old cowboys say, desert, distant escarpments, buttes, and mountains. At eleven years old, the only thing I could think of to do was place my hand over my heart and sing "America the Beautiful" at the top of my lungs.

Just like then, the view I now contemplated made me feel more privileged than any person I had ever met.

I could see No Name Island off the tip of Cape Aialik, Barwell Island with its swarms of sea birds off Cape Resurrection; I could see well into mysterious Aialik Bay to the west and into Day Harbor to the east. Farther east I could see the blue contours of the headlands and islands that make up Prince William Sound. I saw gravel streaked, massive glaciers flowing down from the highest regions of innumerable peaks. I saw along the shorelines numerous coves and bays with crescent beaches, tiny ones offering safety in embracing coves, and in the wide bays open to the wind, gray beaches several miles long, the white-ruffled swells combing in on them and breaking, silent, from where I stood. Far below, I saw a few boats, tiny white points trailing white Vs in the deep blue-green water.

Fall

The elderberries have ripened into red.
The salmon have spawned,
And now they're dead.
Fall is coming.

–Susannah Holmberg

Fox Island, September 7, 1988, Dawn
It is early morning—the sun is not yet up. But there is a
cloud by Mamamowatum, where the sun is going to rise,
that is edged in the brightest gold. Other little clouds turn
gold all around her peak.
At this moment, the sun rises off the very summit of
Mamamowatum. Ah, Sunlight! Steam plumes from the trees
along the beach like smoke.

Fox Island, September 8, 1988, Evening
It has rained hard since yesterday afternoon, all night, and
all day today. The lake is very high, with the shoreline grasses
submerged and water lapping at the trunks of trees. We are
worried that the lake will rise another foot and flood the
new room under the cabin where we have the new propane
freezer.

Last night I dreamt the tide was very high like it gets when
it's just a few feet from the cabins, and the lake rose, until
the ocean met the lake, and looking out the upstairs window
all I could see was turbulent water with a few trees sticking
up here and there. I thought, We are going to lose
everything.
I finally got out of the warm bed and came down here,
checked the level of the lake, made some coffee and built a
fire. Fletch sleeps on upstairs.

Fox Island, September 9, 1988
It's a lovely, fall day. No rain—though in the night it rained
almost as hard as it sometimes does in New Mexico—a
genuine cloudburst. It's still cloudy, but they are warm
clouds, and at times there is enough sunshine to cast a
shadow.

I hate to leave. The four jays are here, hopping from branch
to branch. A while ago I fed one almonds from my hand
while standing on our deck. He sat on my finger, digging his
little claws into it, and jabbed at the almonds and glucked

them into his throat. Once he took four and there was one left, so he flew down to ground and glucked the four out, flew again to my hand to grab the last one, back to the ground again, and then spent several minutes trying every combination of nuts and maneuvers trying to get all five in. Finally he did. I never saw a bird's throat stretched out like that.

Anyway it's a lovely morning, so soft and quiet. The bay is empty now—no one but us here. Far away a small plane flies over Harding Ice Field. The drone of the small airplane engine this time of year has reminded me of my childhood home. I was a very small girl outside in the front yard mixing up all the snippings from Mama's garden into a big salad bowl. Of course it was sunny and the sky was big. Little like that, maybe age four, I could look up from my salad-making and see great distances—and no other kids out, me all alone, the last street on the edge of town, all the mothers indoors tending to things inside their homes. And then, too, there was that drone of a small airplane far away going somewhere, the harmony to my happy humming song. I love it here. I sometimes think I own Fox Island. I know Fox Island owns me.

Epilogue

Fox Island will soon become in our memories like a dream or a vision, a remote experience too wonderful, for the full liberty we knew there and the deep peace, to be remembered or believed in as a real experience in life.

–Rockwell Kent, *Wilderness*

I didn't know, at the end of that summer, that I would never see many of the friends who had become so much a part of my life again, would never climb to Fox Island's summit again, clack along the beaches to look for painting rocks, or gaze upon snowy Mamamowatum framed in the U-shaped valley from the vantage point of my kitchen window. I didn't know that I would never again "belong" on Fox Island.

Fletch returned from another visit to Vermont that fall to tell me that he had been with someone there and had had "an awfully good time" with her. We soon parted, and that's making a short story of a painful ordeal for both of us.

Within a year my life changed course entirely so that now I am married nearly fourteen years to a good man whom I love. I am the mother of a fine young son, and live in as unlikely a place for me as I ever could have imagined—the heart of Dixie in the lower 48 states. I am a teacher and a writer, a keeper of a vegetable garden, an old house, and three dogs. I have learned to play the fiddle; I love the old time mountain music that still thrives here, if you know where to look.

I visit my mother in New Mexico each year, and she and I have completed many week-long backpacking trips into New Mexico's remote southern mountains. There, I fish again in streams so small and clear that I must sneak up on the fishing holes, approaching behind the cover of trees or boulders, or crawling to them through tall grass. If I remain unseen I am sure to catch a fish as soon as my fly drops onto the surface. I get a heck of a thrill when a fish takes the fly; I'm out there alone jumping up and down and laughing. When I come back to camp, my mother looks to see if I have fish, and I do, and we enjoy a fresh-caught trout dinner cooked over our campfire. For a pole I use a willow branch I cut each year when she and I arrive at our secret stream, about six or seven feet of spider web-weight line, and a fly tied by my father. My father still spends his summers in Alaska. He spends his winters here in the South with us, with stops to fish and visit in many of the places in between.

Fletch also went on to marry, though not the woman he met in Vermont. He sold his land on Fox Island to one of Alaska's largest tour companies, which was the only tour company in Seward—getting its start with just one boat—when we arrived to build our cabins on Fox Island. The tour company now has many boats and runs twelve tours each day, out from Seward, around Cape Resurrection, and into Aialik Bay. On Fox Island they built a massive log lodge between the Main cabin and the Woods cabin. Each day during the summer they bring hundreds of people to enjoy a salmon dinner. They also offer a tour of the fjords with an overnight stay on Fox Island. Our cabins are used for staff housing. My father tells me the old A-frame, where John lived, has burnt down.

Fletch now owns a lovely and successful lodge just beyond the town of Seward, accessible by way of a road "with a few potholes." He continues to do both sightseeing and fishing charters, and also does good business ferrying kayakers to remote starting points.

John still has a house in Astoria and owns a boat very similar to

Fox Islander. He retired from teaching and spends each summer in the Inside Passage, living off the ocean and visiting friends along the way. He spends his winters in Fiji. He has not returned as far north as the Gulf of Alaska. He and Fletch are not on speaking terms.

My sister Anne lives in Homer, on the same bluff as Fletch's cabin—in fact just across the road from it—the one he and I and Tutka lived in the first half of our first summer together, before we moved to Fox Island. Neal returned to Oregon, his home state, and I have lost touch with him.

My friend Natasha and her husband moved to Eagle River, north of Anchorage. They have two children. She is still a teacher and she and her husband are Scout leaders. My friends Katy and Ned still live in Albuquerque. Katy is a veterinarian—her long-held dream, and Ned is a doctor.

I have been back to Alaska twice, once to research and market my book, *The Alaska Wolf*, and once to attend a trade show, but really both times to just be there again and to see my friends and family. I do not regret that I don't live in Alaska anymore. I gained so much from my life on Fox Island with Fletch. It was sad to lose that life, and I can't suggest that I switched lives painlessly.

In March of 1989, the *Exxon Valdez* oil spill happened. Fletch called to tell me he was working on the spill. He had cancelled the summer's charters, but asked if I would stay on Fox Island with a couple who had begged him to let them come, as they had planned. We rode out to the island with a man who took advantage of an opportunity and had taken up the job of water taxi for the armies of bird and wildlife rescuers. His boat was a Boston Whaler with two 200 horsepower engines. It took fifteen minutes to reach Fox Island—a trip that used to take us over an hour. My last stay there, during the first days after the spill, with guests who had been out every summer, and had become friends, was very sad.

The sudden change from my existence in a beautiful and mysterious setting, a place and life always complete to me, always vivid, haunted me and made me feel out of place in city life. Soon after moving to the lower 48 I became reluctant to speak of my Alaska. I became impatient with the haunting's interference in my new life.

For many years I dreamt almost nightly of Fox Island. Over and over, I dreamt of large, unfamiliar buildings. I dreamt of the sense that I didn't belong there, that someone else had taken my place. That has happened. In other dreams I dreamt of roads on Fox Island, condominiums, telephones, laws, streetlights, trailer courts, the flickering of television in people's windows, garbage trucks. These things all together will never happen. Once, I dreamt of horses on a Fox Island returned to complete wilderness, and me on a horse. There were many trails, and I could go places that I'd never been able to go before (for although Fox Island is a small island, its steepness and dense forests make it hard to move upon).

When I woke from the horse dream—a good one—I lay in bed and recalled a time when Fletch and I and Tutka had journeyed out in late winter. Deep snow lay on the island, and it had melted and re-frozen and hardened to a glaze, so that we could walk anywhere we chose. We walked in unfamiliar places, borne up by snow as hard as the floor of a dry stock pond in the desert. On the way back to our cabin, I remember we crossed the frozen lake. It was snowing very hard. Snowflakes covered Fletch's dark hair and made Tutka look like a snow bear. Tutka's legs splayed out at comical angles as he frolicked, trying to get a purchase on the ice, and Fletcher and I stood there and laughed, my mittened hand in his gloved one.

I dreamt of horses on Fox Island. I don't think that will ever happen. I rarely dream of Fox Island now. My life goes on with beauty, new goodnesses, intertwined lives, and an abiding curiosity and sense of wonder—along with the same old unquenchable love for unpopulated country. A feeling of gratitude comes to me more often as I age. I read recently that gratitude is when memories are stored in the heart, and not in the mind. The writing of this book has completed that transformation for me.

I see that so much of what we have is good. And there it was, all along.

Acknowledgements

Many, many people helped make this book. I thank Victor Holmberg of Montana, Lare and Kate Aschenbrenner, my sisters Anne Marie Holen and Betsy Arehart in Alaska, Emelie Powell of Chattanooga, and my mother Dora Mae Holen in New Mexico for reading early drafts.

Tom Keyes, Katy Harvey, and my mother (again) in New Mexico, and Chris Noel of Boston read and commented on the next revision. Chris, especially, made me face those passages that I had blithely skimmed over that he said were "pivotal."

My neighbors Linda Ellis and Jeff Cole provided hours of technical support, printing expertise, design work, and Irish Coffees. How lucky I am to have such neighbors!

Parthenia Hicks, of Tribewriter Editorial Services in Los Gatos, California, has been a terrific editor. She, too, zeroed in on places that I didn't want to talk about much and suggested that I should. She provided moral support and encouragement every step of the way.

Anne Marie spent a beautiful Homer spring weekend proofreading this manuscript. Next time we'll try for a dreary week-end. Thank you, Annie!

My mother painted the cover illustration, in oil on masonite. Betsy Arehart took the back cover photograph. She and I were traveling through the Matanuska Valley in Alaska that day.

John Little, who is in this book, read the boat journey section and gave valuable help. That was the final section for which I needed an expert's help, and then John up and wrote to me out of the blue. Since he spends his summers plying the waters of the Inside Passage, he was just the expert I needed. I thank John for this and much more.

My husband, Michael, has seen this whole thing through from the beginning—seven years ago. He never gave any sign that he doubted me. He gave encouragement, not with obligatory support, but by actively listening. And by making me laugh!

If not for my sister, Anne Marie Holen, I may never have published a book. In 1987 she started her own desktop publishing business—when desktop publishing was brand-new—and suggested to Betsy and I that we illustrate and write a book, and she would publish it. We had a meeting at her cabin in Homer and decided to make *Alaska Wildlife*. It's success has launched me with confidence into the world of writing and publishing.

My sister Betsy Arehart has been a steadfast business partner for many years now. She is my good friend and graces me with her gentle sensibilities.

Thank you to all the characters in this book. What a wonderful life it is, how lucky I have been to spend time with you.